Spinning a Dream

A Sailor's Ultimate Journey
Around the World Alone

by

Dave Rearick

SEAWORTHY PUBLICATIONS, INC. • MELBOURNE, FLORIDA

Spirit of a Dream
A Sailor's Ultimate Journey Around the World Alone
Copyright ©2018 by Dave Rearick

Published in the USA by:
Seaworthy Publications, Inc.
6300 N Wickham Rd.
#130-416
Melbourne, FL 32940
Phone 321-610-3634
email orders@seaworthy.com
www.seaworthy.com - Your Bahamas and Caribbean Cruising Advisory

Cover images inspired by photographs from Billy Black.

Library of Congress Cataloging-in-Publication Data

Names: Rearick, Dave, 1958- author.
Title: Spirit of a dream : a sailor's ultimate journey around the world alone / by Dave Rearick.
Description: Melbourne, Florida : Seaworthy Publications, Inc., [2018]
Identifiers: LCCN 2018027687 (print) | LCCN 2018043891 (ebook) | ISBN 9781948494106 (E-book) | ISBN 1948494108 (E-book) | ISBN 9781948494090 | ISBN 9781948494090¬(paperback :¬alk. paper) | ISBN 1948494094¬(paperback :¬alk. paper)
Subjects: LCSH: Rearick, Dave, 1958---Travel. | Voyages around the world. | Single-handed sailing.
Classification: LCC G419 (ebook) | LCC G419 .R43 2018 (print) | DDC 910.4/1092 [B] --dc23
LC record available at https://lccn.loc.gov/2018027687

Table of Contents

Acknowledgments

It seems simple; sailing alone around the world. But simplicity is a very complicated process. While I sailed alone on Bodacious Dream, many, many people took part in making the adventure a success. And many more helped make telling the story a straightforward experience.

There are hundreds of people, both men, and women who shaped my sailing ambitions. From early days on the beach boats to attending complicated electronic issues on technical race boats. I could never list all of you, but you know you were there, and I Thank You.

I do need to mention a few members of the band: Jonathon Pond on the computers, Tim Eades onshore support, Alan Veenstra on night watch, John Hoskins on weather analysis, Lynn Duttlinger on the paper shuffle, Mattie, Andrew and everyone at the Hinckley Yard in Portsmouth on preparations, Lapo, Gordy, Mattie, Stetchy, Bickey, Magnus, Ridley and the whole gang in New Zealand, David Minors on Electronics, the Bodacious Racing Team/Family, and so many others around home and around the world who helped or like Suzie, made minutia go away.

The whole crew at Commanders Weather, led by Ken Campbell were invaluable at routing me through weather systems and around the world, not to mention being a human voice in the middle of nowhere. Mark Petrakis tirelessly brought the entire experience alive by managing my blog and posts. Tegan Mortimer distilled the magic of science and nature bringing it to a comprehensible level. And my dear friends Bob Cuddeback and George (Freckles) Gosnell, both lifelong sailing friends and mentors.

Turning sailing around the world into a book has been eerily similar; taking many people to bring Spirit of a Dream to fruition under the singular name of one author. There are the many who inspired me, continuously asking, "when will the book be done?" and those who read chapters and encouraged me with their feedback. Thanks, Lynn, Sue, Jean, Tim, Alan, Craig, Laurie, Mark, Tom and the others. I hope you found the final edits acceptable!

A big thanks to Seaworthy Publications for taking an interest in publishing the book and with patience, educating me on the process.

I can't thank Sam Bari enough for his endless patience, mentoring me as he edited the manuscript. His tireless efforts went beyond the call of duty, always taking the time to present a solid reason for the changes he recommended.

Without the support of my sister Nancy and her husband Rick Usrey, who have worn many hats over the years, from support and encouragement to proofreading and graphics, I'd still be talking about writing a book one day. My sailing friend Tom McDermott also fits in here somewhere, actually everywhere. Forever in my court, on land or at sea, I still owe him a beer at the Schooner Wharf while we listen to the song Southern Cross. And to Mary who allows the spirit in me to be.

And in simple, modest terms, none of this would be without the support and encouragement from Gaye Hill and Jeff Urbina. Two great friends and Bodacious Dreamers. Thank You, Jeff and Gaye!

If
by
Rudyard Kipling

If you can keep your head when all about you
Are losing theirs and blaming it on you;
If you can trust yourself when all men doubt you,
But make allowance for their doubting too;
If you can wait and not be tired by waiting,
Or being lied about, don't deal in lies,
Or being hated, don't give way to hating,
And yet don't look too good, nor talk too wise;

If you can dream—and not make dreams your master;
If you can think—and not make thoughts your aim;
If you can meet with triumph and disaster
And treat those two imposters just the same;
If you can bear to hear the truth you've spoken
Twisted by knaves to make a trap for fools,
Or watch the things you gave your life to, broken,
And stoop and build 'em up with worn-out tools;

If you can make one heap of all your winnings
And risk it on one turn of pitch-and-toss,
And lose, and start again at your beginnings
And never breath a word about your loss;
If you can force your heart and nerve and sinew
To serve your turn long after they are gone,
And so hold on when there is nothing in you
Except the Will which says to them: "Hold on";

If you can talk with crowds and keep your virtue,
Or walk with Kings—nor lose the common touch;
If neither foes nor loving friends can hurt you;
If all men count with you, but none too much;
If you can fill the unforgiving minute
With sixty seconds' worth of distance run,
Yours is the Earth and everything that's in it,
And—which is more—you'll be a Man my son!

Sailing Singlehanded
is Raw and Honest

Two days ago, crossing the desolate South Atlantic Ocean, the autopilot on Bodacious Dream, my sailboat, failed. After scrambling for control, I fixed it by switching to the backup autopilot. This morning, while sipping a juice box below decks, 1,200 miles west of Cape Town, the backup failed.

"NO-----!"

I flew through a maze of scattered obstacles to jump on deck, grab the tiller, and take *Bo* back through the messy jibe and steer her back on course. Now I have a serious problem—I have no autopilot and no backup. My electronic helmsman, whom I named Otto, has packed up, leaving me hand-cuffed to the tiller for the six or seven days it will take to reach Cape Town. This twitchy, fast, racing boat's helm cannot be left unattended for more than seven or eight seconds without veering off course and careening out of control. Making the situation worse, the weather forecast for the last few hundred miles to Cape Town predicts 35 to 40-kt winds. The hard, southeast wind means awful, upwind sailing—brutal conditions with a crew of four, riotous when alone, and alone without an autopilot—ludicrous.

I hope the problem is just a glitch, but when I touch Otto's *on* button, the failure alarm screams again. I shut it off and wait a moment. I look around coyly as if someone were watching before trying again. Without compassion, the alarm instantly screams, supporting the adage that repeatedly applying the same solution to a problem while expecting a different result is a sure sign of insanity.

All that I love about sailing alone now haunts me. Sailing singlehanded is raw and honest. When I'm at sea, I'm alone with right and wrong. Nobody lies to me; no one promises a check is in the mail, and nobody fixes my problems. If I don't fix this problem right now, I will pay the proverbial piper. My dream has taken a nightmarish twist.

* * *

While I hand steer *Bo* to keep her on course and at one with the sea, Otto stands by, incapacitated. I know what I have to do to fix him, but performing the complex task while maneuvering through the wild, blue waters of the Atlantic will take meticulous planning, with no room for error. Taking a few deep breaths, *Bo* and I find a rhythm as I come to grips with the severity of the situation.

Though I claim my dream has taken a nightmarish turn, this is far from the truth. This is not a dream or a nightmare; those generally conclude in a comfortable bed between crisp, clean sheets and warm blankets. This is reality; a frightening situation that could end badly.

Driving *Bo* is comforting; her response to my slightest adjustment in course makes me confident she will keep us safe. As I calm down, I allow my mind to wander before tackling the monumental task of repairing Otto under extreme conditions.

I've dreamed about a boat like *Bo* since I was 12 years old. She came to be nearly four decades later in an email from my good friend Jeff, a fellow Great Lakes solo sailor and the owner of *Bodacious 3*, a racing boat I captained for him and his wife Gaye. The email was simple and that simplicity supported its improbability. It read, "I've been thinking, if you really want to do this solo thing around the world, we need to get you the boat you'll be doing it in."

I read the email repeatedly, gauging it against previous false starts over the past 40 years and then shared it with a close friend, asking him what he thought. Tom's sage reply was, "I think you found your sponsor."

Racing a boat around the world is an expensive endeavor for a regular guy like me. I'm a carpenter and homebuilder. Teaming with a sponsor who can market the excitement to promote his business is a standard arrangement in this sport.

* * *

A new racing boat begins with a design brief, an outline of the intended use and accomplishments. A naval architect takes the dreamer's desires and finesses them into a formal design, a process similar to that of an architect designing a home to fit a client's needs.

The Kiwi Class 40, of which *Bo* is Hull No. 3, was briefed to be a grand prix, Class 40 racing sailboat with an all-around performance plan intended to win major offshore and trans-oceanic races including the Global Ocean Race, a singlehanded race around the world. The race I intended to enter.

After looking at a number of designs and builders, I sailed hull number one of the Kiwi Class 40 production. Within minutes of taking her helm, I knew she was our boat. She felt intuitively perfect. This is a knowing; it's the feeling a writer gets when finding the perfect word to complete a sentence; a photographer, the shutter speed and light for a photograph; the runner, a cool day; or for an artist, the exact color of a shadow. For me, that moment told me the Kiwi Class 40 would be my boat for the Global Ocean Race. A phone call confirmed our intentions and set construction of Hull No. 3 in motion under the watchful eye of Lapo Ancillotti and Paul Hakes. Hull No. 3 would become *Bodacious Dream*.

In September of 2011, with construction already in progress, I flew to Auckland, New Zealand to connect with those involved in building *Bodacious Dream*. It was important for me to meet the craftsmen who had begun the construction, to introduce myself and earn their respect. I wanted to be a person to them, not the name of someone half a world away. I wanted to know them and for them to know that I would care as deeply for *Bodacious Dream* on the oceans of the world as they would while building her in their shop. I wanted them to have a share in this dream.

Lapo stood in the Auckland Airport arrival area, conspicuously displaying a *Yachting Magazine* to make it obvious who he was. We had never met in person; we had only talked on the phone or communicated by email.

Over the following days in Auckland, we met David Minors who would procure and install the electronics; David Ridley at Hall Spars, builders of the mast; and Richard Bicknell and Magnus O'Doole from North Sails who had begun to design and would make the sails. Flying south to Wellington, we met Paul Hakes, Will Otton, Mattie G., and the crew building hull number three. I was like a young boy at Christmas. Every meeting seemed exciting, as much for them as for me, and the project felt special.

When we arrived at the build shop of Hakes Marine, Lapo and I walked through the large open doors. There, serene and comfortable, sat hull number three with her deck hanging in the air above, waiting for the moment the two would formally meet. By the end of that week, her hull and deck were permanently joined and she allowed me to gently caress her curves. I stood in reverence of the skilled craftsmanship of these men and the birth of *Bodacious Dream*. As a collection of people, we had become acquainted by a purpose and united by a dream.

Bo's inception brought my life-long dream to reality and began the adventure. *Adventure* is a powerful word, defined as an unusual and exciting, typically hazardous experience. Sailing around the world alone on a 40-foot racing sailboat is every bit that and then some.

As *Bo* was being built, I vowed to write a book and share the tale of this once-in-a-lifetime experience with the many others who harbor similar dreams—fulfilled or not. I am honored to recreate the adventure as I lived it, complete with the accountings of the many emotional and spiritual rewards, frustrations, and minute-by-minute anxieties born of the imaginings of what lies beyond the next wave or may come with tomorrow's wind.

Outward Bound

Day 1—October 2, 2013

*U*ntethered from the dock in Jamestown, Rhode Island, Bodacious Dream glides through the water while I stumble through the motions of setting up sails. Otto aims recklessly at the area of moored boats, exacerbating my dry mouth. I'm acting like a rookie besieged by nerves, choking as I pull ropes, turn winches, and occasionally look up to confirm the rising mainsail is unencumbered by the tangle of lines that control it. I push the buttons to adjust Otto's course to the left, then continue hoisting the mainsail. Billy Black, the preeminent yachting photographer, circles erratically on a small powerboat, documenting our departure.

Extending his arm, he points out another tangle of lines at the end of the boom. Embarrassed, I stop and unravel the tangle. I hope no one is left onshore as witness to the amateurish gaff; but I know a few friends are still watching through tear-wrinkled vision and will remain until I am out of sight.

The stumble, like most in life, is quickly put in order, and *Bo* sails past the harbor at Newport, Rhode Island, historic Fort Adams, the Dumplings, and Castle Point.

My friend, Joe Harris, sails alongside in his Class 40 racing boat, *Gryphon Solo II*, kin to *Bodacious Dream*.

Tacking back and forth on the fresh, cool sea breeze, pulled shoreward to fill in under the rising air warmed by the sun on the dark land a few miles inland, we make our way out Narragansett Bay to open water. Class 40 boats are quick and responsive, and sailing at eight knots is easy for *Bo* and *Gryphon Solo II*. As we clear the Brenton Reef and Beavertail guiding lights, the radio kicks up.

"*Bodacious Dream, Bodacious Dream*, this is *Gryphon Solo II*."

"Go ahead *Gryphon Solo*, this is *Bodacious Dream*." (Standard radio communication between radio operators.)

"How you doing over there, Dave?"

"Going along pretty well Joe, how about you?"

"Doing great. What a beautiful day to depart on huh?"

"Yup."

"You should be able to bear off now and head for Bermuda." Joe offers.

"Uh . . . OK . . . So, what's the course for Bermuda?" I respond, embarrassed to not know this. The past few days hadn't allowed me the time to look up this simple, but important fact—the compass heading for the first course of this long journey. In a frantic, last minute fight with electronics and communications systems, I decided to stop in Bermuda, 600 miles away, to give me time to fully exorcise the gremlins from the electronics and be certain all systems work properly.

"165° there, Admiral!" A nickname Joe occasionally calls me.

I adjust Otto's course 20° farther off the wind, and ease the sheets to trim the sails. *Bo* was sailing tight on the wind and *heeling* more than necessary. Now, she levels out, picks up speed, and sails for Bermuda with the grace and nonchalance of a beautiful, confident woman walking the Champs-Élysées in Paris. Joe sails alongside for a while longer, then, with a personal, silent wave of respect bears off and tacks back toward the bay. My only human companion left is Billy Black. While taking a few final photos, he nods respectfully, then extends his wishes for a safe passage and turns for home. As I sail toward the empty horizon it occurs to me that Billy has photographed many solo sailors heading out and not all of them have made it back.

* * *

Every journey begins with a first step, and I have just taken mine. I ease down, sit in the cockpit, and allow the erratic energies in my body, stirred by the toxic mix of adrenalin and anxiety, to pass. As the horizon recedes farther and farther away, my pulse slows and my breathing relaxes.

I've held fast to this dream as changes in life came and went, as flows of finances stalled, or inspirations faded. Year after year, I battled, often alone, to keep the dream from wearing out like an untended hull in an old wooden boatyard. Joe Harris holds the same dream, and now I wonder how he feels as he watches me sail away. I've been in his shoes, watching friends start world-girdling races while I was left behind, tethered to shore.

Completing final items on the list this morning, I hid tears and emotions beneath layers of callus gathered during the years of chasing my dream. Now, I'm finally on my way, alone, and I ask myself quietly . . . "Will I be able to do this—will I finish this dream? Will I check it from the list and come closer to being the man I or my father envisioned?"

An answer will not come easily or quickly, and it's fair to speculate, it might not come at all. Many a solo sailor has been lost at sea, some of them my close friends—vanished, their whereabouts unknown to anyone but themselves—out here, alone, forever.

* * *

The horizon is empty now with just one lone sailboat on a distant tack. I'm outward bound, sailing away from the young dreamer I was, and starkly realizing my new heading is toward the old dreamer that I am.

Standing in the cockpit, I look forward, my forearms resting on the hard dodger designed to protect me from the wind and spray. Blue skies thin to a pale hue at the horizon and the sun lights every wrinkle on the surface of the ocean. The spray is tart and the wind crisp and sweet. A sense of relief drains through me as my legs tingle and I release a deep sigh—I am on my way, free to succeed or fail by my own doing, no longer influenced by the intent of others, be it good or bad. *Bo*, Otto, and I are sailing around the world. A desire to celebrate is halted by a strong reservation to exhibit hubris. There is no place for that out here.

Adjusting to Being Offshore

The beauty of sailing offshore begins when the harbor blends in with the horizon. Gradually, almost unnoticeably, the horizon becomes indistinct in all directions as we enfold with the waves and head for a place defined by a set of coordinates on this enormous, round planet.

As the sun falls below the horizon, I'm alone and no longer attached to the harbor behind me, but to a course set by mysterious, magnetic forces below the surface of the earth. Without land in sight, a grid of latitude and longitude defines my existence.

As the last of the evening light disperses across the sky, *Bo* and I follow this course, slipping back and forth from conscious to subconscious. The sea and wind have control of my destiny, leaving me with the simple task of existing in harmony with them, respecting the things I cannot see or control, and honoring my desire and dreams. *Bodacious Dream* and I sail as trusting friends across the ocean as I drift through sleep and memories.

* * *

Sailing toward Bermuda, the days come and go like tidal rips, flooding with the rising sun and ebbing with the set—defining the ageless rhythm of a day at sea. A rhythm I've come to feel and experience near the root of my soul. Waves rise and fall, winds build and ease, tides come and go, and I, reintroduced to solitude and the lack of land-borne intrusions, find a rhythm. Energies ebb and flow, my fatigue rises, and sleep prevails.

I force my preconceived notions of life onboard to match the rhythms of the sea, but I am reminded I am not in control here. I am the one who asked to be in this eons old, established environment. Of the yet-to-be discovered things I expect to change, the ones that will change are inside me and will only change as the sea finds fit. The sooner I accept this, the sooner I'll stop wasting time fighting it, and the more I'll learn by flowing with it.

* * *

Adjusting to life on board takes a couple of days. Ashore, there's a pattern to life. Meals come at certain times, work shifts at specific hours, sleep falls at night, and the weekends are simpler, coming with subtle changes. At sea, one day doesn't distinguish the beginning or end of anything. It's merely a moment in the continual, ever-present, slowly flowing circulation of rhythms.

On shore, we define time with man-made devices. At sea, time's only necessity is to mark the passing of longitude. Left alone on deck under starry heavens, amid the silky flow of wind and water; I realize time is happening, as it always has, in its own way, unchanged and unamused by our attempts to define it by mechanical genius.

I eat, sleep, rest, and read. I watch sunrises follow sunsets and sunsets follow sunrises. I don't keep count of the days but of the miles declining between Bermuda and us. As Bermuda comes within 100 miles, I'm only aware of the end of day four by reading the words I write in my log: *End of Day 4 . . . beginning of Day 5. We should be in Bermuda about midnight, winds forecast to switch to the south and build—messy night coming on.*

As we beat upwind in the messy night to the waypoint marking the entrance to the port of St. George's, I listen to the Radio Bermuda signal as it becomes stronger. Finally, within solid range, I call and communicate my intentions with the operator monitoring the coast for ship traffic.

Reefs and coral heads, the remnants of a volcano 600 miles off the East Coast of North America, guard the island from wayward sailors like me. Every so often, these reefs claim a sailor's vessel, their dream, and their life. Modern electronics allow Bermuda to follow us using radio, radar, and Automatic Identification Systems (AIS), tracking our comings and goings and keeping us safe from the perils of the reefs.

In the dark, wind-whipped night, Radio Bermuda sings out joyfully from my VHF.

"Captain, I copy your information and have you on radar. Are you familiar with Bermuda? Do you have proper charts?"

"Yes, I am familiar," I answer, and acknowledge I have both paper and electronic charts. My mind races through the incident of an experienced sailing friend who returned to Bermuda to avoid a hurricane, but without the proper charts, lost his boat on a reef.

"Okay *Bodacious Dream*, proceed at your will. Check in with customs upon arrival in St. George's. Please contact us if you need further assistance."

Bodacious Dream and I continue pushing against the wind, clicking off a series of waypoints as we slowly invade St. George's harbor. Clear of the broken cliff entrance, we sail into the large harbor while still harassed and buffeted by stiff, 20-kt winds. Moving along in both real life and electronically on the chart plotter, I compare the two to make sense of the location of the customs dock, camouflaged by the lights behind it onshore. *Bo* is pushed around by the strong winds as we circle slowly, taking time to gain a perspective on the depth of field flattened by the contrast between darkness and shore lights.

Checking the charts thoroughly, we approach the side of the customs house when my nerves flare. Intuition grabs at my gut and my mouth goes dry. Something is wrong . . . I back down hard and reverse out of there, stepping back to distance us from the issue and gain a better perspective and more nerve. Circling, I consider the options. Should I anchor, circle until dawn, or look elsewhere for docking? Where is the channel? Where is protected deep water? Am I too tired for this? What time is it? I ask again, "What time is it?" I realize I'm back in the grasp of shore, no longer in the soothing rhythm of the open sea.

A sweeping light diverts my attention—a flashlight on shore signals me back to where we just departed. I study the motion and question the intent. Motoring closer, I yell, laboring to project my voice over the wind. "Is there deep enough water there?" A faint "yes" comes back, carried by the hiss of the wind. I circle again to steady my nerves and begin another approach. *Bo* turns the corner of the stone pier of the Customs House, opposed and pushed sideways by the stiff wind and tidal current. A dock line catches the piling as the keel sucks into the muddy bottom and stops the boat . . . "Ahhgh!". . . I pull the line, back *Bo* until she floats free, and tie her to the pier.

The customs officer greets me and asks, "You're alone?" I answer, "Yes," apologizing for my un-seaman-like maneuver and the sailor's language while I cross spring lines to secure the bow and stern. He motions me to the office when I'm ready. It's 2:00 a.m. and I'm tired, unnerved, and again filled with a toxic mix of adrenalin, fatigue, and anxiety. Yet, I am relieved. I've secured *Bo* to the pier without incident.

I grab the important papers and walk the few steps to the office. The officer is pleasant and pleased for the distraction in the otherwise empty hours of the lonely night. While chatting, he sympathizes with my solitude and allows *Bo* to stay tied to his pier until morning. Pointing to the harbormaster's office down the dock, he explains they'll help us find proper dockage at daylight.

Back on the boat, I remove my foul weather gear like a young kid shedding layers of a snowsuit, and let them pile up on the cockpit floor. I grab my last can of Coke and drink it, flushing the erratic energies from my body and reflect on my first small, but distinctive victory as the journey begins.

I stretch out on the cockpit sole and fall asleep, waking to the sun and life of Bermuda.

Bermuda

Bermuda's close proximity to North America and its connection to the UK have allowed it to build an economy based on tourism, offshore economics, and hosting sailors crisscrossing the Atlantic Ocean from North America, Europe, and around the world—to stop, rest, and enjoy the beauty ashore. I am one of those—heading south across the ocean to Cape Town, South Africa, drawn by Bermuda's beauty and the need to rest.

* * *

Awake, I walk the short distance to the harbormaster's office for advice on dockage—a place for *Bo* to lie alongside a pier and for me to rest my mind. I know of the St. George's Dingy and Sports Club facilities, and after considering different options with the harbormaster, she calls a man named Bernie, a Dingy Club member, to inquire if I might dock there. Bernie is close-by and drives over to pick me up. Standing tall, thin, and older than I expected, he's a delight to a tired sailor. We drive the short distance to the club and survey the docking options.

In many parts of the world, the standard arrangement for docking is stern-to or Med Style—perpendicular to the dock. This requires setting an anchor off the bow as the boat backs into the dock to secure the stern to the pier. The bow, attached to the anchor is kept from swinging to either side while the crew accesses shore by stepping off the stern of the boat. Sailing alone, it's difficult for me to consider docking in this stern-to arrangement. Bernie assures me business in October is minimal and I am welcome to dock in the simpler, parallel arrangement alongside the pier.

A couple of hours later, *Bo* and I are tethered to the hard, concrete pier and my edginess subsides. I let go of the subconscious worries vaulting through my mind as I rinse *Bo* with fresh water and wait for the club to open at 4 o'clock so I can purchase a cold beer and a shower token for my own rinse.

I chose to stop in Bermuda to confirm the electronic communication links and clean up unfinished business before completely severing ties to my day-to-day world. With the electronic and business issues resolved as the first days pass, a check of the weather lowers my expectation of a quick departure.

A high-pressure system dominates the weather pattern, leaving little wind for sailing. Studying the nautical charts and proven sailing routes for this leg reveals the need to sail far to the east toward Europe before turning south to cross the trade winds and currents pushing west.

Unless a globe is examined up close, it is difficult to see how the landmasses actually wrap around the earth. For the convenience of printing on paper, the round earth is flattened, distorting the vertical longitudes of the extreme northern and southern latitudes and moving continents, sometimes out of the way.

The globe shows a heading due south from Bermuda will land us on the northern shore of Brazil and force a long, upwind struggle against the prevailing southeast trade winds to clear its eastern, bulging tip before heading further south. Sailing east from Bermuda, north of the adversely flowing trade winds, will position us to make a turn south for a favorable crossing of the trade winds to clear the bulge of Brazil.

The days in Bermuda pass in a steady routine as I wait for favorable weather. Once awake from *Bo's* rustic comfort, I walk downtown with my computer stuffed in my pack and stop at the harbormaster's office to log into the Internet and check weather routes, emails and peruse the proverbial list of details before returning to *Bo* for an afternoon of work. The days end with a shower at the Dingy Club, more emails, more computer time, and always, another check of the weather. This routine wears on me. An uneasiness seeps into my subconscious, rising to my consciousness as an adverse wind builds. The short, choppy waves in the harbor play a staccato percussion on *Bo's* side as the rising tide pushes us hard against the concrete pier. Squeaky complaints from the fenders reinforce my edginess. I'm unable to sleep as an intense worry brews inside me.

I am so vulnerable tethered to this concrete pier. My dream, my boat, even my physical being is at risk. My nerves wear thin as the dock lines chafe. I scour the weather for a window to leave Bermuda, but I am left with only one, to wait another day . . . then another . . . and another. The knot inside me tightens with each unfavorable weather forecast and the realization that I can't alter these things. Finally, Thursday's afternoon forecast looks promising. I study it intently and promise *Bo* we will leave Bermuda on Thursday, regardless.

Thursday arrives and *Bo* is ready for departure. With everything in place, I step onto the concrete pier and pace to and from the clubhouse, wearing away the excess hours while my mind climbs up and down my work list. At noon, I can't wait any longer and head back to *Bo*. On the way, I stop by the other transoceanic sailing vessel tied at the dock to say goodbye to Kurt, the first mate, and ask if he'll help with the lines.

"You leaving now?" he replies inquisitively. My reply is simply, "Yes."

As we walk over to *Bo*, I give Kurt the book *Unbroken*, which I had just finished reading and recommend highly. As we move about untying the mooring lines, I notice his voice seems quiet in contrast to the upbeat, lyrical United Kingdom accent I've come to know over the past days.

As I release the last line, I step aboard *Bo*, push away from the pier and motor forward into the deep water of the bay. I look back at Kurt, still on the pier, and wonder what he's thinking, watching another sailor head out to sea. Is he worried for my safety or intrigued by the adventure awaiting me?

Bo turns about and heads toward the narrow opening between the sharp cliffs at the harbor entrance. I'm sure my feelings are different from Kurt's. I sense he worries about my safety and the storms I'll meet, while I feel we are heading to safety. Hours later it occurs to me how quickly I used up the last moments of human contact I'll get for a very long time.

Freeing *Bo* from the pier untied the knot plaguing my gut. With my dream moored to the concrete pier, I was agitated. One missed step could break an ankle; one storm could crush *Bo* against the pier and leave me in an emotional collapse with years of effort lost. Three miles beyond the cliff-protected entrance, *Bo* and I are safely on the open sea again as we pass the buoy marking safe water.

The low hills of Bermuda slip over the edge of the earth as the late afternoon sun eases below the horizon. Twilight drains from the sky, and without fanfare, darkness takes over and surrounds us. It's the simple cycle of the eons—the sun rising, setting, light and darkness, over, and over, and over again. It's just another night among billions of nights. I tally up the distance to Cape Town, South Africa, our next harbor, 7,000 miles plus or minus, and reduce it to weeks, instead of days . . . six or seven of them—nearly two months.

Bo sails easily in the darkness under the command of the autopilot nicknamed *Otto*. A box of electronic magic, controlling an electric motor connected to a hydraulic ram, pushing and pulling the rudder as needed to keep us on a straight course. Otto tends to the day-to-day function of steering while I eat, sleep, or like now, gaze off across the dark waters to ponder the complex simplicities of life, desperate to comprehend the enormous distance defining my dream.

There's peace in this darkness, but competing inside me, an anxiety of the unknowns brews . . . I've been to sea before. I've stopped in Bermuda before. I've sailed alone across the Atlantic before—but this time it's different. I'm headed out, out beyond my known horizons to unknown seas, to unknown weather, to problems and timeframes I haven't experienced before. I think of the list of failed equipment on a ten-day passage and interpolate the math out forty or fifty days. What-ifs jump in and out of my mind in this distraction-free dark night. I reach for my kitchen timer and look for sleep to relieve me from these worries.

Soft cushions and warmth are minimal as the damp dew collects on my body while I drift through sleep, awakened every 15 minutes by the kitchen timer to check on *Bo* and the navigation. The night passes slowly. Eventually, dawn coincides with the time on my watch and I witness the sun rising, opening the depths of my world to the horizon, and setting another cycle of daylight experiences into play.

The Struggle for Momentum

Except for an occasional diversion around an island or reef, navigating a straight line to sail from one place to another in the open expanse of the oceans would seem logical. However, years of collective experience have defined the best sailing routes around the world—and none of them are straight. Trade winds blow consistently from east to west across the middle of the Atlantic and Pacific while the westerlies circle endlessly below the magnificent capes of South Africa, Australia, and South America. Wind flows like rivers in the sky and currents flow like rivers in the ocean, sometimes with and sometimes against the sailor.

The Gulf Stream current in the Atlantic exemplifies this. The warm river of current flows north along the eastern seaboard of North America before it bends eastward across the north Atlantic to cool and sink off the European continent. Currents flow in all the oceans and scientists study five main gyres that circulate endlessly. A sailor lives in harmony with this flow of wind and water, because like life, it's quicker and easier. To us, our route is direct, though it often meanders and weaves among these variables.

On this leg, *Bo* must first sail across the Atlantic before turning south. We must find patience and wind to work eastward and stay north of the opposing, free flowing trade winds blowing from the coasts of southern Europe and northern Africa. Once far enough east, we'll turn south to cross the trades and the westward current they create. The distance gained sailing east will allow us to slip west with the current and still clear the bulge of Brazil.

The ocean is calm and serene east of Bermuda. The weather is beautiful for basking in the sun, reading books, or playing tennis on land, but not for sailing. Unexpected, the calm tests the limits of my patience.

Over the past 40 years, I've often considered what it would take to float alone in the sea, or remain stranded on a mountain waiting for rescue, but I haven't contemplated the endurance necessary to wait for wind on a calm ocean with 7,000 miles left to my destination.

As days pass, the mileage adds up slowly. I begin every weather briefing with, "Can I head south now?" and Ken Campbell from Commanders' Weather Service, a noted weather router in New Hampshire, struggles to find a different, negative, yet calming, answer each time I ask. His mantra remains, "You must get further east before heading south or you'll be forced to beat upwind into the trades to get around the bulge of Brazil." In 55 years, I had never even thought of the bulge of Brazil. Now this place consumes the entire focus of my life.

Beating upwind against the trades is more than undesirable; it's the equivalent of hell on water, especially in the fast, flat design of a Class 40 racing boat. The persistent trade winds and inherent currents accompanying them have been flowing west for as long as the earth has revolved on its axis. They are completely unaffected by the mental energy I focus on them, suggesting they change. I hope they're amused. I've always believed, *if you can make them laugh, they won't kill you.*

Day in and day out we edge eastward, hoping for an 8-kt speed average—200-mile days, but settle for little more than a hundred. Today's tally is only 67—an average of less than three knots. I dig deep through the stores onboard to find patience packed among the bins of repair parts, spare lines, batteries, sail ties, foul weather gear, flashlights, oil and engine spares, fuses, electrical connectors and full duffel bags of freeze dried food. There isn't any. I am challenged by impatience and exasperated by the rate of cookie burn.

With not much to do but read books, contemplate weather options, and be angry that I was too busy on land to load more music and movies; though I did load Charlie Brown's Christmas, Rick Braun, Richard Elliot, and Jimmy Hendrix, my impatience eats away at the cookie and chocolate supply. *Bo*, as my conscience, scolds me for eating more than the day's ration and I resign, I must endure this.

I remember a younger self, 36 years ago, when Captain Ed at the Hurricane Island Outward Bound School spoke as they dropped me off on a small island for four days . . . alone . . . with no food and only my foul weather gear and a piece of plastic as armor against the rugged Maine Coast. "Anyone can survive without eating—that's easy. The real challenge is finding food and keeping fed." I heard the echo of those words and manipulated them to inspire me. "Anyone can eat all the cookies in a hurry— the challenge is to make them last." I set a limit of two cookies per day with a plan to celebrate with four when I get the okay to begin our turn south.

The days and nights add up, but the miles don't. Six days have passed since leaving Bermuda, and we've made less than 700 miles in the heat and humidity. The nights are better, a bit cooler with a little more wind, but in my impatience, Cape Town has become unobtainable, a world too far away. I search for a closer goal, a suitable substitute for this stupid dream of mine, but supporting such a reason for departure from the plan would challenge the great minds. I convince myself I'm up to the task and the least I can do is consider an alternative.

I look at the islands of the Caribbean and contemplate Antigua, recalling *Bo* and I triumphantly arriving after crossing the Atlantic alone from Portugal last season. Antigua would be nice, but I find my commitment too tenacious. I can't make the decision to divert from my dream—certainly not without a reason beyond my control.

At night, in the dark depths, I explore the endless heavens using Star Walk, an application on the iPad that displays the stars and satellites. This deepens my feeling of aloneness in the middle of nowhere. I calm myself with the soft music of Rick Braun and Richard Elliot, and offer the exotic melodies of their horns playing *Sao Paulo* to the gentle breeze wandering off into the dark vastness of the empty ocean. I accept my impatient, anxious mind and the similarities to my life on land—pushing one limit or another until finding peace in the fatigue and solitude of an accomplishment.

* * *

Before my planned October departure from Jamestown, a group of family and friends gathered to wish me goodbye. My sister Nancy and her husband Rick orchestrated the visit, bringing my mother, sister Margie, and brother Tim. Other friends attending the boat show in Newport appeared along with my close friends and sponsors, Jeff and Gaye. We gathered for a couple of days, culminating in a dinner on Saturday night at the FISH Restaurant in Jamestown. Retiring to the outside deck after dinner, the gathering morphed into a roasting of the honored guest—me. Respectful jabs at mental instability, jokes of past exploits and other musings worked to obscure the tension, worry, and fright my close family had for my future. With much flair, John Hoskins, the navigator for Bodacious Racing crewed vessels, spoke for the crew and family of Bodacious and pulled interesting gifts from a bag, each with a unique story or a pointed jab. First was a book about Mike Plant that John suggested I might not read until returning. Mike was a solo sailor from Wisconsin lost at sea a number of years ago. Next, a Cape Horn rounding kit—a needle, earring, and shot of whiskey to deaden the pain. Tradition has it that a *Cape Horner*, a sailor who rounded Cape Horn, is allowed to wear a gold earring in the ear facing Cape

Horn—left for rounding to the East, right for rounding to the West. This earring provides shipmates, upon the sailor's death, enough revenue to allow for a proper burial and celebration.

A few more books, and then last, from the depths of John's bag came a surprise, a soccer ball, complete with magic marker eyes and a one tooth smile. My new companion around the world; his name already branded on the side—*Franklin*. A cousin to *Wilson* from the movie *Castaway*, John found Franklin loitering at the small hardware store in Jamestown, Rhode Island. Franklin found a comfortable spot in the upper bunk on *Bo's* port side where he could withstand the pitching and rolling by bracing himself between a box of spares and a bundle of foul weather gear. This perch allows him a keen view of my daily antics— quietly commenting every time he feels I'm less than diligent in my efforts. With each passing day, Franklin becomes more endearing to me. We are now a crew of four: *Bo*, Otto, Franklin, and less significant—me.

* * *

Day seven turns to eight, nine, and quickly enough to ten. We sail slowly east, catching wind from bits and pieces of weak weather fronts to make distance. Help from Hurricane Lorenzo passing a safe distance away gives us one of the only shots of real, favorable wind.

Finally, the time comes for *Bodacious Dream* to gradually alter her course. Though still heading east, we edge our point a bit south, aiming for the narrowest band of doldrums on the other side of the trade winds. This area of little wind exists because of a convergence of weather variables canceling each other out and leaving a vast area of the ocean windless except for quickly moving squalls of stiff 30 and 40-kt breezes with heavy rain lasting half an hour or more. This area is the bane of all sailors, testing spirits and breaking hearts, even more than the horrific storms in the desolate southern oceans of the world, where sailing alone is an exercise of mental control beyond explanation. In the doldrums, the lack of wind can drive a sailor mad.

As Otto turns slightly south, though still pointing well east of the bulge of Brazil thousands of miles away, I am excited yet tempered by the impact of this miniscule change. The turn of a few degrees reduces the distance to the bulge to a couple of weeks. I group it into days, four days to cross the trade winds, four to cross the doldrums and another four, plus—maybe a few more. I still struggle with the parameters of time, but then, time shouldn't exist out here. Routines continue day in and day out, a change in course is only a change in course, and water flows by as miles add up, making time seem nonsensical.

Fluffy clouds cover the sky as evening nears. In my log, I pen the details of the day—latitudes and longitudes, wind and speed, distances to and from Bermuda and attitudes of both *Bo* and me. *"We're moving along nicely, anxiously awaiting squalls. The first appears to the east and behind us. It won't be long before we are hit."*

I was right. In the early dark of night, I feel a change in the wind brushing my neck. Tingling with enhanced sensitivity, I smile. I've become a sensitive mariner, able to pick up the slightest change in the wind, the sound of wavelets or smells in the air.

There is dampness to the cool air, familiar to me from years of dealing with powerful squalls on the Great Lakes, a trademark of the rush of wet wind from the center of a collapsing storm cell. At a distance, the feeling is subtle; a couple of degrees drop in temperature and a change in humidity gives a heavier, meatier feeling to the air. Up close, the change is *in your face* with heavy winds and driving rains.

I scramble to prepare *Bo* for the squall hidden in the darkness. Using the extra sensitivity of peripheral vision, I look away from where I think the squall is to pick up the slightest differences in the shade and darkness of the clouds. The winds increase and the rains begin. It is no longer important where the squall is or where it's going— it's here. I quickly grab the helm, ease the main sheet, and focus my attention on the compass course and wind angle. I taste the trickle of brackish rainwater as it rinses away the remnants of hot days from my cheeks, then rub my face and beard to hasten the cleansing so I can enjoy the sweet taste of fresh water on my tongue.

Bo's large sails are feathered slightly into the wind, just inside the proper angle for power. They wiggle, shaking off the rain as we drive through the 30-kt squall. The speedo ratchets up and the hiss of the wake sounds just like the rain on the water. The sounds are instinctive to me, soothing—like a baby's giggle to her mother.

Bo takes off, climbing past 12 knots and making comparatively huge miles in the 30 minutes of squall before the wind eases back down to the high teens when we adjust course and return her sails to their proper trim. We gain five or six miles in the quick squall, but after it passes, we slow down to a snail's pace again. Under control, I drop below and turn on the radar to check for more squalls. They show up as white blobs speckled with red dots highlighting their intense centers. Six of them are within the 12-mile diameter of the radar's sweep. We're surrounded. I study the locations and plan our moves, calculating the time until the next squall hits. It's early; early in a long night of constant attention to the weather.

The squalls come incessantly, all night, all day, and all night again, each slightly different, but all heavy with rain and wind. I amuse myself consulting with Otto and *Bo* on the projected arrival times, where we'll intercept them, how long they'll last, and whether Otto or I should drive. Otto gains my respect and drives through most of them. I drive occasionally for fun and the rinse of fresh water.

As the squalls continue, we use them to work south. As the seas increase, *Bo* begins to skip over the tops of waves, landing in the trough ahead; flexing and pounding like a drum, allowing the air to rush in and out of the companionway. One, two, three, pound, pound, pound . . . one, two, three, pound, pound, pound. I store this rhythm in the data bank of my cranium. With each fall into a trough, *Bo* shudders and I remember.

The tightly tuned rigging holds the mast vertical and strong, allowing the sails to capture the energy and lift of the wind and infuse it into the framework of the hull. Counteracting this energy, the long, thin keel holds a 4,000-pound bulb of lead three-and-a-half meters below the water, forcing the energy to escape by moving the boat forward.

Slamming a 10,000-pound boat through ocean waves thousands of miles offshore takes a commitment of faith, a faith as significant as any. Faith in the shape of the design, the intelligence of the engineers, the integrity of the components and in each human hand along the way as they assemble the complex, interwoven network of those components, ultimately creating a sum of the whole stronger than any individual piece.

The fate of a sailor on the open ocean is as fragile as one miscalculation in an engineer's equation, a nick in a steel shroud or an oily finger on the hand carefully crafting an epoxy joint. One failure can compound the loading, increase the pressure on the equipment absorbing it, and cause a succession of failures. A lucky sailor's succession of failures stops at some strong point—a bulkhead, a deck fitting, or some other significant point in the equation of fate. An unlucky sailor's calamity ends, ultimately.

On the Fine Edge of Life

Bo and I pound through the squalls peppering the steady trade winds blowing from Europe. The seas continue, the pounding becomes regular and the shuddering takes on a predictable, fathomable rhythm. Tired, I lay down on the cabin sole, spooned to the curve of my lover's hull and backbone, and set my timer for a 15-minute nap near the end of the night. I drink in the relaxed feeling, stretching out my muscles to oppose the past days of tense, hunched over, cat-like moves. As my eyes close, Bo sails along, rising and leaping over waves, progressing steadily toward Brazil. She rises up the side of a wave, surges into the air and as the wave moves out from under her, lands in the trough, shuddering, shaking, and then rising again.

The timing and progression of the tremors don't match my bank of stored data. My eyes open as I lay still. *Bo* rises over a few small waves, and then surges into the air again and lands. Shudder—twitch, twitch, twitch. My mind quickly logs the feeling—the odd twisting, shuddering, and bouncing. I sense it—the keel is loose.

I roll over, scramble to my knees, and open the access port to the keel bolts. I put my hand on one of the two large nuts holding the nine-foot-long, 4,000-pound keel to *Bo's* heart . . . she rises again, then falls, the bolt moves and the boat shutters . . . I scream emotion with the full capacity of my lungs. The energy is wasted, the cry for attention is pointless over the thousands of miles of open ocean.

My mind races . . . there is no prolonged process of problem solving. There's no committee work. I grab a light, inspect, and clamber over the center console to the storage area, throwing containers and bags out of my way to put my hand on the large, industrial-size ratchet. Though an unusual tool to have on board, there was no question in my mind that I would carry it. Circumstances and superstitions drove me to that decision.

I return to the keel, then pull, then ratchet, click, click, pull, click, click, pull . . . Still I pull more, an alarming number of turns for the large nut on the inch-and-a-quarter bolt. I'm not sure how much I pull, but I grunt the two nuts to tongue biting tightness and then stop to sense everything—the boat, the rhythm of the waves, the shaking of the mast, the rise and fall of Bo. The boat is pounding; my heart is pounding; everything is pounding in a cacophony of sounds and rhythms. I search my senses intently to determine if any of them are out of tune, out of rhythm or overstressed.

I go back to the cockpit and grab the helm, steering *Bo* to feel her soul. She talks to me as I hold her hand. She's smooth. I'm frazzled. I stare into the dark vastness of the ocean and contemplate ultimate failure—how far I am from everywhere, how far I am from the conclusion of my dream. I touch the *on* button to put Otto back to work and dive below to hold the bolts one more time, grasping them while on my knees as if in prayer.

I am awake all night, aware of every twitch, even my own. I think hard on the situation at hand. Who should I call? Who can I discuss this with? I need someone to talk to, but the world is asleep and I am alone. I remind myself, this is what I came for. This is what I wanted to know and experience . . . the edge of life. When it hangs, am I man enough to hang with it? I check the bolts regularly. Each hour they require tightening.

In my memory, I review the engineering drawings and with each turn, I wonder if I am pulling apart the welded framework inside the keel structure. I too shudder, thinking about the consequences.

I will call Alan and Tim, both in Chicago, time zones away and soundly asleep. Alan can help me work through the thought process. Tim will stand by to deal with disaster. Damn, this can't be happening . . . "Why not?" I ask myself aloud. "What makes you any different? Why can't this happen to you?"

Four hours pass in my log. Each hourly check requires turns on the bolts. It's still early, but it's time to call. I can't wait any longer and call Tim Eades first.

"Hi Dave, what's up?" Tim, the captain of *Bodacious IV* the crewed racing boat, is aware of the unusual timing of the call. I explain the situation and finish with: "I'm okay for now, but not sure what's ahead for me. I'm going to call Alan to talk with him. I don't want to call Jeff and Gaye; I know what their reaction will be. I'm sure they'll insist I head for the coast and end the dream. I can't do that. I can't." I give Tim my lat and longs . . . my speed and course and promise I'll call or text on schedule to keep him up to date. He agrees, and solid as ever, supports me.

"Alan . . . Dave here."

"Hey what's up?" Alan too is aware of the unusual call. I explain what's going on and Alan's years of experience sailing and handling boats comforts me. Calmly, he asks questions about the boat, about the configuration of the keel, about the number of turns.

"Have you marked and checked? How tight are you going?"

"Tongue biting tight," I tell him. We chuckle . . . laughter is good right now. I explain that I don't want to call Jeff and he agrees. We both know the directive the news will bring. I can contemplate ultimate failure, but I can't contemplate the lesser—a course change to shore and a safe harbor—ending the dream. We agree on a course of action and to call him back in an hour. He tells me to hang tight and I thank him for making it sound so simple. He humors me with his remark, "I've got the easy job sitting at the kitchen table—warm and dry, with a cup of hot coffee in my hand."

I head back below to investigate further, pulling everything away from the structure of the boat to look for the slightest crack or opaque area indicating delamination in the fiberglass work—anything unusual. Everything looks okay. I grab the ratchet and tighten once more. Secure in my belief they are tight, I mark the nut, the washer, the deck, and the bolt. I count the number of threads above the nut and take dimensions. I scribble these notes on the fiberglass like a kid writing on the bedroom wall, not caring if I mark it up.

I look at the Atlantic Ocean chart and my stomach turns. I force myself to consider the option and make a plan to head to the East Coast. I convince myself this is only for insurance. If I don't plan for it, it will happen. If I plan, it won't. Either way, it's a gut wrenching, painful thought.

I head back on deck, take *Bo's* hand and we sail together. She feels tight and good, soothing my nerves as we sail up and over the waves through the gray of the day. She seems aware of my worries and tells me things are okay. She's at home and happy out here at sea. I settle down and feel fatigue rise to the surface. Time has vanished again, and I haven't slept for who knows how long.

Time is up. I check the bolts. The marks indicate the nuts are backing off a quarter turn per hour. I tighten them again, mark the wall, and return to sailing. I'm relieved, but cautious. Another hour slowly passes and I check. The indication is the same—the bolts back off a quarter turn per hour. I tighten and mark the wall. After four or five cycles, I call Alan and talk it through. I'm confident I'm not pulling the bolts from the welded steel framework and tearing the boat apart. We discuss more options and end the call with me asking him to call Tim to update him and relieve me of that job. I want to avoid any discussion of alerting Jeff and Gaye—something I respect as Tim's loyal priority.

The cycles of tightening continue consistently as I ponder the options. Cape Town is 6,000 miles away. The weather won't improve and the storms will increase. Will the issue get worse? Should a good seaman make for harbor? Am I a good seaman or a foolish, stubbornly proud seaman? As I look at the chart, stare at Cape Town, stare at the east coast, and stare out the companionway, I hear my dad's voice quietly reciting a line from Rudyard Kipling's poem.

"If"

If you can make one heap of all your winnings

And risk it on one turn of pitch-and-toss,

And lose, and start again at your beginnings

And never breath a word about your loss

It's time for me to bet the farm. I need to tighten the bolts with all the force I can muster, hoping to lock them in position. I'll put the ratchet on the bolts, brace my back to the bulkhead, put my feet on the handle, and exert all the force my legs can generate. This will either lock the nuts or tear the bolts loose and the keel will fall off, resulting in ultimate failure. If the keel falls off, there's no better time than now for that to happen. If not, I might fix the problem.

I set up the ratchet . . . put myself in position . . . and think—are you sure? What if this? What if that? I pause and go back on deck to grab *Bo's* hand and sail, so I can feel and hear her intuition. I consider the keel falling off while I am jammed in position below. *Bo* will flip. What will happen? An awful scene from the movie *White Squall* runs through my head . . . only I am alone.

I place the ditch bag in the cockpit and tether it to the boat with a slipknot I can untie as I scramble past in a hurry. I place the VHF radio on the ready and clear a path out the companionway. If *Bo* capsizes, I might have 15 seconds to get out . . . out to the open ocean—to float alone.

I sit down in position again and consider even more "*Ifs.*" Then stop, drop my head, and take a deep breath. I look inward and say, "Come on Dave, let's get on with it." Words from astronaut Alan Shepard run through my head . . . "Let's light this candle." I back up against the bulkhead to test one more limit in my life. Grunting, I push and pass through it, tightening the nut.

I anticipate the snap and the slack in the ratchet, indicating a broken bolt or weld . . . it doesn't come. I move to the other bolt and repeat, pushing through my limit again. There is no snap, and no instant slack in the ratchet. I take a deep breath, mark the nuts in their new position, and go back on deck, driving *Bo* for an hour until nightfall. Drained, I've done all I can. I've gathered my winnings and bet them all on one turn of pitch-and-toss. I hope I have won. An hour slowly passes before I check the bolts—they haven't moved. An hour later, another check shows no movement either, it all seems so simple and behind me now. My faith slowly returns.

With the tension easing, I drift back to a memory of an important, pivotal day in my life. I was 21 when something caught my eye as I walked toward the opening garage door to start another day. A box, discarded by my father sat on top the garbage cans. It seemed strange and out of place. In the mix of unfamiliar items sat an old, leather-bound book, the front cover missing, and one corner nibbled away by mice. I lifted it from the box and looked at the author's name on the spine—Rudyard Kipling. I thumbed through the first couple of pages and found an inscription to my father in my mother's handwriting dated in the early days of their life together, near the beginning of their young, ambitious dream.

Mom and Dad had separated five years earlier. I had never seen this book before, but I knew Rudyard Kipling was one of my father's favorite authors, and in particular his poem, *If*. I found *If* listed in the table of contents, and opened to that page. In the strange gray light of the garage, I read the verse.

I had heard the words of this poem uttered from my dad's memory many times over those first 21 years, often to punctuate distinct issues troubling my restless, agitated soul.

I read the last line . . . *and which is more,— you will be a man my son.*

Discarding the book was symbolic of this point in my father's life. Taking it from the trash and asking him if I could keep it would have disrespected his honor as he tried to wipe clean a slate of broken dreams and start anew. Without mentioning it to him, I tucked the book under a pile of old wood and tools in the corner of the garage, pulled the garbage cans to the curb, and began my day. My father died later that year.

Reading the poem as a restless, unknowingly inexperienced 21-year-old, I thought, as a simple course of life, I could check off the items and in a few years, be a man. The next 40 years would teach me, in the same way I learned to prepare a boat for an extended ocean passage, that as I accomplished a goal or crossed an item off the list of preparations, like the points to becoming a man in Kipling's poem "*If,*" the list would morph, and like fractal geometry, continually reveal another layer of details beneath the first. I would learn that the process of becoming a man, preparing a boat, or living a dream is endless.

Inky Dark Nights,
Similarly Deep Thoughts

The four of us continue sailing. Each check of the keel bolts reveals no further slippage, and with each check, my attention becomes more focused on our destination and less on the abandonment of my dream. With Cape Town still more than 5,000 miles away; we sail from squall to squall, catching our breath in between. Otto does the bulk of the driving, Franklin watches carefully from his bunk, and Bo seems happy while I contemplate and study. I pore over charts and weather, think and do math, and calculate the distance to Cape Town, divide it into days, adjust it up and down, and consider the elation of arriving to a good meal and a cold beer. I focus on the charts and struggle to establish Internet connections for weather maps. I get information from Commanders' and sketch the missing weather in pencil over my path, educating myself about trade winds and doldrums. Which is where, and where is which?

Sometimes the trade winds are there, and other times they aren't. I'm even dumber than I think. I calculate a thousand miles to Recife, a harbor on the Brazilian coast 4,700 miles from Cape Town. Precise calculations seem evasive, time seems insignificant, and speculation seems just plain wasteful. While I look for finite math answers, I am perplexed by the constant, uncontrollable variables. I shut my mind off, grab one of the books I've brought and begin reading about Steven Jobs and Steve Wozniak and how they navigated unknown territory to bring the world to where it is today. I compare my own frustrations. Jobs and Wozniak moved the world. Here, the world moves me.

* * *

The degrees of latitude, the parallel lines of navigation marked incrementally north and south beginning with zero at the equator drop away slowly. We sail south through 10°N into single digits and I ponder my journey into unknown territory, continuously stretching the boundaries of my life's experience.

Ten months ago, those bounds were stretched to 15° N while crossing the Atlantic from Portugal to Antigua. Now, I push them farther. The equator looms 600 miles south of here.

Over the many years of sailing, I've studied and read about the southern oceans. Now I'm headed there. With each mile sailed south or southeast, my limits stretch, and my imagination converts to experience. Each day, each moment, each wave is new for me.

* * *

Reading and light sleep take place in short increments to relax my mind and refresh my spirit. Sometimes the reading comes first and other times it's the sleep. Sleep, though routine, is seldom the same. Sometimes I wake only to check and reset the timers; other times I wake and sail for hours. It's all subject to interruption from time to time by a miscalculation or unforeseen event, most often a squall where my books get wet, my clothes get wet, and my hair gets wet. But the rain is warm and we're closing in on the equator. Each breath of wind results in a new mile, and like life, each breath marks another moment.

I do most of my sleeping during the day, so if I am abruptly awakened, it's daylight and I can make quick sense of any disorder onboard. The days are warm. The nights are more pleasant with the temperature of the breeze feeling nearly the same as my body. *Bo* glides over waves, sailing through the night as if she's slipping along on flowing silk.

Lying on the deck in my t-shirt, shorts, and harness, I look up through the fluffy, broken clouds, and search the stars for another sailor on a distant planet, wondering who they might be and if they might be searching for me. It amuses me to think people believe there is no life out there. I can't believe it, lying here in the secure womb of the warm earth.

I have the ability to fall deep asleep in a moment and wake just as quickly. Short naps are no problem. The diversion of a long, deep sleep is like a drug, one I know would be addictive if I weren't careful with its use. I've studied sleep, dreams, and brain works through books and conversations with experts and found there is such a thin level of understanding in the complex world of sleep. The warm air, stars, and sailing at night are sedatives. My eyelids become heavy and fall closed.

I find myself struggling with two mates on an island in Maine as we drag ourselves to high ground, away from the tidal zone as a storm surge comes ashore. The reality is intense, the smells, the hard granite shore, the spruce, pines, and the hues of blue seen only in Maine. Even the conversations are realistically animated when I am startled awake, and find myself soaking wet. Rain is falling hard and *Bo* is skipping along like a kid running through a mud puddle—a squall has overtaken us. I scramble for cover under the dodger as my eyes dart from one instrument to another to check wind direction, course over the ground, boat speed and trim. In the long instant, I assess the situation and take *Bo's* hand, driving through the squall as it intensifies before quickly passing.

With Otto back in command, I stand up in the cockpit, in my favorite posture with my arms resting on the coach roof and scan the horizon for another problem. In this moment, I ponder the existence of humans on boats in this intense, multidimensional mix of dreams, reality, and thoughts, and conjure up contemplations enough to scare those without similar experiences. The squall moves away, the dream passes and the night clears. We put down miles toward the equator as Brazil edges closer. This will continue for days and months, as it always has—sailing for miles through inky deep nights among similarly deep thoughts.

Crossing the Equator

Crossing the trades with their blue skies and azure ocean, the winds are warm and steady though still carrying an occasional squall. While miles flow out behind us, somewhere ahead lies the equator and a waypoint at Recife, the Brazilian harbor just under the bulge of Brazil where the coast bends back to the southwest. A week away seems close, but once there, we can afford to sail west of south, down the South American coast to the favorable westerly winds a couple thousand miles south. Another couple thousand miles . . . the horizon is like Kipling's poem—forever unfolding in front of me, and never obtainable. I now believe the world is round, and life is a circle. I'm not sure where it began, but the end seems nowhere in front of us.

During a contemplative gaze across endless miles of empty water, I am not surprised to see something floating. I am excited for the diversion and study it—the log bobbing in the water morphs into a sea turtle. I grab the binoculars and watch him pass. I look around, expecting to see another, but there's nothing out here. Realizing there is no hurry, we tack around and sail back and forth until we find him. I watch as he bobs up and down, attempting to hide by diving, though his back flipper feet are still visible, flailing in the air. It takes a while for me to comprehend his size in the vast, open ocean, but this guy is large. His head is the size of Franklin's—a soccer ball. His flippers are as big as my hands, probably larger. I laugh, thinking he'd take up the entire cockpit, flailing, flipping, and thrashing about. In the days of yore, he would be a meal for a crew of sailors—fresh meat, fresh fluids, and soup, but not for me. I don't fish on board. I'm keenly aware that whatever I would catch, I could only eat a small portion, and the rest would be waste. This isn't fair for the ocean or life in general. I think of abundance as having enough, not more than I need. A philosophy I adopted from reading Yvon Chouinard, the founder of the clothing company Patagonia.

Instead of fishing him out of his life, I sail around him and wonder. Why is he here, so far from anywhere? Thousands of miles from shore, thousands of miles from the nourishing currents of the world. What's out here? The answer is obvious—his life is out here. This is his home. Then strangely, I realize I am the traveler, journeying through his region of the world, and I should be open to learning the peculiarities of his life.

Circling again, I see myself as the voyeur, a peeping Tom in his territory, and I know I should show more respect. I tack away, back onto my course, and over my shoulder, wave a gesture of admiration and thanks for allowing me to pass through his world. I wonder what the turtle thinks of me.

* * *

Two days later, Friday, November 5, 2013, Otto steers *Bo*, Franklin, and me across the equator. We cross 00 degrees latitude at 22:27 hours. Seafaring tradition dictates a tribute to Neptune and a hazing of those onboard crossing the equator for the first time.

Bo and Otto made their first crossing when shipped from New Zealand to the U.S., but for Franklin and myself, it's our first, and a celebration is in order. If additional experienced crew were onboard, they'd strip me to my skivvies and cover me with a sticky, gooey mixture of slop left over from the galley's stores. Alone, I'm not so inclined and in lieu of the mess, reserve a package of freeze-dried lasagna for dinner. To celebrate the moment, we will share a toast of the whiskey and Irish Cream that Joe Harris gave us on departure from Jamestown. I pour a splash on the deck for *Bo* and a touch for Franklin. Otto is busy driving and will have to take his later. Before taking my own, I stand at the rail and offer thanks to the ocean, to Neptune, to the stars and the universe, and share a generous portion overboard with the sparkling, phosphorescent waves flowing along the starboard rail. We cross the equator into the southern hemisphere and continue sailing toward the Southern Ocean.

* * *

Recife is still 600 miles farther—three more days of concentrated sailing to clear the Bulge. We're sailing as close to the wind as comfortable, pounding out the distance as we parallel the coast, a few hundred miles to our west. I think of the pink dolphins of the Amazon River, their fabled spirits sacred to the local Indians.

I wanted to sail there and find them, to see their pink color, their famed twinkling eyes and swiveling heads. They are the only dolphins that can swivel their heads like a human. I wanted to experience their spirit and magic so respected by the local Indians, but sailing for the Amazon is more difficult than I expected. I laugh at my naiveté, thinking it would be as simple as stopping along the interstate to see the world's largest chair or biggest ball of yarn. It's not. It won't happen this trip. For now, the Amazon remains on my someday list.

In exchange, a pod of bottlenose dolphins swims by to visit. These uplifting creatures seem to always arrive when my vibe is low. They swim alongside, cavorting in the bow wake, laughing and jumping, elevating the drab mood brought on by the drudgery of pounding across the wind. I talk to them as if they are friends. My loneliness evaporates when they respond with their clicking, giggling voices. I wonder what they are thinking. What do they feel? What are they saying? I sense they want to tell me something, and worry they are warning me of a pending problem.

We sail along together for an hour when they quickly depart; slipping over the horizon, bound somewhere else . . . maybe home . . . maybe Europe. I imagine the fun of having a world and playground so large to play in, and then laugh . . . I do—on *Bo*, the world is our playground.

We sail through sunrise and sunset, the days of November passing page by page in my logbook. Armistice Day comes and goes, and we pass Recife a few hundred miles to starboard. Thanksgiving isn't far away. I project beyond Racife to the next waypoint—my impatient, land-borne traits still evident.

The Great Races

Sailing the great racecourse around the world, clearing each of the magnificent capes, is a pinnacle event for any sailor, the equivalent of an alpinist climbing the highest peak on each continent.

Beginning in the North Atlantic, starting from North America or Europe; the great racecourse heads south across the trade winds toward the coast of Brazil. It then continues further south, along South America, to reach the westerlies before turning east to the southern tip of Africa—the Cape of Good Hope.

From Cape Town, South Africa, the route heads east to the continent of Oceana, considered Australia and New Zealand. Sailing to clear Cape Leeuwin, the southwestern most point of Australia, the elegant tall ships from Europe would make port to empty their holds of European ballast before reloading with Australian grain to race east around the southern tip of South America, known as Cape Horn, to their home in Europe where the supply of wheat and grain had run low in the winter months. Known as the *Great Grain Race*, the first ships returning to hungry Europeans would garner the best prices for their grain.

Before reaching the Atlantic Ocean and the leg home to Europe, the ships had to round Cape Horn. Cabo de Hornos is a small island off the tip of South America lying at 56° S latitude, just 400 miles north of Antarctica. There is no end to the legendary stories of battles between mere mortal mariners and the relentless storms and weather, incessantly circulating the unbroken ocean, south of 50° latitude. The sheer thought of *HMS Bounty* enduring 39 days of constant storm to only make 65 miles is enough to turn a sailor's eyes away from considering the route around Cape Horn on the charts. The waters of the Cape teem with the spirits of terrified sailors lost to the sweeping hand of a fateful wave.

Looking at the geography of the southern tip of South America, it appears like a childhood dam built by snickering young boys in a sandbox and then washed out by a stormy bucket of water. No doubt, on a grander scale, the isthmus between Antarctica and South America has given way to these incessant storms over the eons. And yet, men and women, made of only flesh and blood, bones and sinew, continue to pit themselves against the powers of the oceans, compelled by some mystic influence to round the Cape and earn a personal respect for themselves.

In early 2012, *Bo* and I entered the Global Oceans Race, our chance to singlehand around the world below the major capes. Later that year, the race was canceled, leaving us two options; quit or continue, and sail around the world alone.

Joshua Slocum was the first to sail solo around the world in 1895, taking three years. In 1969, Robin Knox-Johnson was the first to circumnavigate non-stop in 312 days. These accomplishments sowed the seeds of spirited dreams, stirring restless sailors to pursue their limits and respectfully test themselves against the sea.

Joshua Slocum was first. Now, 120 years later, the tally of sailors sailing the world alone is less than 300. Wet, worn, tired and hungry, these amazing men and women, mesmerized by the sea, try desperately to satiate a hunger.

I came to this around 1970; sailing off a Lake Michigan beach with Pam Tittle on her Sunfish, a small, 12-foot beach boat owned by her family. Quickly, I too became corrupted and found myself captivated by the stories of Joshua Slocum and Robin Knox-Johnson and set my sights on achieving such an accomplishment. Though my home waters of the Great Lakes can throw out a tempest as severe as any encountered at sea, its distance from ocean harbors and major sailing venues imprisoned my passion, forcing perseverance to become my confidant and friend and displace my youthful impatience.

Endless Miles to the Turn

1,800 miles south, down the coast of South America, lays the next waypoint. There, we'll look for a reason to begin our bend toward Cape Town, turning slowly southeast and then east. Bo will dance along the northern edge of the strong westerlies, using the cold fronts coming north from Antarctica to drive across the South Atlantic Ocean before turning back north to Cape Town on the southern tip of the continent of Africa. There is a fine line between too far south and too far north. Too far north and the winds are light, too far south, the winds are heavy, and ice broken free from Antarctica, speckles the ocean.

The miles to Cape Town still total 3,500. They don't seem to change; they've remained at 3,500 for weeks. I struggle to understand this, but realize it's my own inexperience surfacing. Each time we reach a waypoint, I find another layer of unknown variables, adding miles and time to the equation.

* * *

Exuberance, more than reality defines my sailing. I expect favors from the weather and sea, acting entitled by some royal bloodline of which I am not. I am a self-taught sailor from the North American Midwest—the nearest ocean from my home is a thousand miles away. I was not born into a family of sailors, nor do I have any idea where this part of my DNA comes from. If some connection linked my aptitude to a past generation of seamen, it would make sense, but there isn't one. Instead, an underlying tide drives my soul to seek its peace at sea. I sail, watch, and try to understand these oceanic rhythms. Something is out here, something I'm not sure I'll ever know well enough to explain, but I hope I'll learn to accept it and live by its rhythm.

In the meantime, while I continue to learn, I find it hard to extinguish my disrespectful hubris. I still want favorable weather and course to shorten my journey by miles and days.

* * *

I continue calculating using contrived units of measurement, but begin to give reverence to the thought that they really don't exist at sea. I don't think we sail miles, but through points of change. We don't count days, but note the passing of sunlight and darkness. Our less than significant existence here is recorded on an eons old timepiece having no hands, no beginning, and no end.

I return to more pedestrian thoughts and calculate the miles into days before sending the expectations home through a satellite transmission. Loved ones make plans, friends plot progress, and others wonder aloud: "Why is he doing this?" But the four of us—*Bo*, Otto, Franklin, and I continue sailing south, toward the next waypoint on our journey.

Sunrises roll into sunsets and circle back again. With each rotation of the earth, I try to gain another 200 miles toward the next waypoint and eventual turn toward Cape Town. The sailing is steady, the winds rise and fall, squalls come and go, and we sail. Fresh rain-water rinses away dried salt and old thoughts, allowing for the new accumulation of both.

* * *

I read books when I'm settled, and when I am not I grab *Bo's* hand and sail. Waves pass by endlessly, each slightly different from the one before. My mind logs wave data, as it has for 40 years, categorizing wavelets, waves, swells, wind waves, rogue waves, waves from shore and waves from somewhere else. There always seems to be one set driven by the wind, another driven by the pulsation of the weather system and a third set comes irregularly, from nowhere in particular. Occasionally, these odd waves catch me off guard and slap me in the face with a shovel of water. I laugh and shout some crap back at them, often calling them *idiots*, affectionately of course, as if they were close friends in a jabbing duel. Sometimes I'm lucky and zoned in. Sensing their arrival, I dodge their rudeness and confidently taunt them as they pass. But in the end, I always back down and apologize for being in their way. I know my insignificance and realize I'm only here by their grace. I shrink inward and carry on, hoping to create little awareness of my passing while gaining the respect of the sea. With my hubris nearly gone, I've become conditioned to *Bo's* movements. She rises up over a few waves and lurches before slamming into a trough. She seems to laugh and be more playful now . . . either that or I'm more relaxed and able to appreciate her motions and trust their meanings—progress towards the waypoint. It's hard to understand which it is, and less important to know.

* * *

Books are read, miles pass, days pass, weather passes. Another wind shift, another sail change, another squall line. What used to be significant worries are now regular and routine events. No options are left. Cape Town is our goal—turning back is unviable, so we continue sailing and call it routine. Highlights are meals, sleep, chocolate, and daily functions. Yes, even at sea, our bodies have necessary, daily functions.

It's simpler than you might expect. My body becomes regular with the consistent routine. I eat a meal in the middle of the night, snacks throughout the day, and a juice box at sunrise, an orange thereafter, and a can of tuna or salmon just after the sun relaxes, having ascended all morning. My body, tuned to the regular intake becomes ready about mid-morning and seldom is anything important enough to push this off until later. On shore, there's always something else going on, but at sea, while alone, though from time to time a squall or storm might arrive at the same inopportune moment, there is nothing to delay the event. I simply place the bucket in my preferred corner, block myself in by the cabin sides, and take care of business. I take a moment longer to perform personal hygiene, cautious about cross contamination and the resulting illness it can wreak on an otherwise enjoyable passage.

When *Bo* is surfing along at high speeds, it's a bit more sporting and requires a leap of faith to relax and perform the function. Sitting patiently, I watch the speed rise into the teens on the knot meter at the nav station, and hope nothing goes pear shape (a British reference to turning upside down), resulting in a real life example of *crap hitting the fan*.

Destination Cape Town

November 20th, a Wednesday, more than a month since leaving Bermuda. Bo and I have become accustomed to being at sea and I move around as if I am in my living room, occasionally taking walks out in my backyard. The turn toward Cape Town has happened gradually over the past few days, actually, a week. I expected a turn more like rounding a mark on a racecourse, specific, precise, and documentable. Instead, I have to rewire my thoughts, and adjust to the size of my world. We are rounding a high-pressure system—the St. Helena High, which covers most of the South Atlantic. I look at the course penciled on the paper chart, and see I am rounding in a precise manner, only the radius is 1,000 miles, not the tightly choreographed, two boat lengths around an orange, inflatable, tetrahedron racing mark in a confined harbor. Cautiously, I calculate something near 2,000 miles left to Cape Town. My perspective has changed immensely in the past month. This now seems close, maybe a couple of weeks away. In comparison, I remember my first offshore race many years ago. It took an entire day to sail the 30-mile course. An accomplishment I still remember fondly.

I project my desire to the universe to arrive on Saturday at noon, November 30th. Then I shy back, realizing I am again showing my hubris.

* * *

The next weather update becomes a lesson from Ken explaining the weather systems of the Southern Ocean. Bubbles of cold air push up from Antarctica as cold fronts, changing the comfortable sailing on the north wind to the abrupt and sporting conditions of a frontal passage. The systems come regularly, two or three over the course of 10 to 15 days. In the days before the front passes, the wind comes comfortably from the north, working its way to the northwest, and the sailing is good. The miles pass easily in the stable weather. As the front nears, the winds increase, pushing through the 20s and into the 30s before switching abruptly to the southwest and gybing the sails as the front passes, though still allowing *Bo* to sail on the same course.

Preceding the front, the waves, winds and squalls increase, and the unstable, messy weather wreaks havoc. Once the front passes, the weather begins to stabilize, taking a couple of days for the wind to move forward to the southeast, then through the east to the north where the cycle continues.

Entirely backwards from my ingrained northern hemisphere life, I am cautious with the first front, watching the weather and preparing for the worst. The cycle progresses over 48 hours. The winds circle the compass and *Bo* jibes as the front passes, and the winds shift forward across the southern quadrant. *Bo* clears her first frontal passage just fine. We struggle with the wind forward of the *beam* from the southeast and east and pound into new seas. As the winds shift, the waves follow and leave an old wave mixing with a new one, making the sailing rough and miserable.

A few good days pass, and we set up for the next front. This time, the winds are much heavier, the squalls stronger, and the edge a bit nearer. I wonder aloud if these first passages are practice and how much worse future ones, in the deep Southern Ocean will be. Ken rates this one as *"particularly"* strong. I keep quiet, but wonder how *"particularly"* rates on a scale of one to ten. In time, I'll become accustomed to his rating system. Strong, fairly strong, not so bad, *kinda* bad, fast moving and strong—*particularly* is in there somewhere, I'm just not sure where. I'll learn to interpret the strength of weather by reading between the lines.

* * *

The Southern Ocean looms monotonous, like staring across a desert. In the desert, I see nothing but brown at first. Out here, I see nothing but gray. In time, all the colors of the spectrum, in infinite variations, reveal themselves. Towering gray seas become hills of slate blue and black purple or deep aqua before blooming with brilliant white as they topple from the unstable crest. Dull grey skies streaked with odd layers of clouds take on faint greens and silver with creamy whites and pink-toned lavender toward the end of the day as the light refracts through the long angle of the sweeping clouds.

We sail ahead of the next front, intently watching for the telling signs of change. There are infinite changes, yet, when I check my log, my notes reflect monotony. I've logged the same wind from the same direction for more than a day. The change will be more obvious in the next few hours as the front arrives, but the contrast could go unnoticed unless compared to the log of the preceding, patient march of stable weather.

* * *

We've steered a course around the South Atlantic high and head easterly toward Cape Town, South Africa, 1,800 miles away. For the first time in a month, my boat is aimed, more or less, at our destination. Though strange, circuitously and difficult to comprehend, I've been aiming at this destination since day one—40 years ago.

Thinking back through those 40 years of dreaming, I note the interesting similarities to my life. To many, my course and direction belied my intent, but these were the paths I had to walk and crisscross to get to this place in time. Pride fills my thoughts as I sit quietly, enjoying a rehydrated dinner of rice and chicken. I am beyond the point of beginning, beyond the point of return, and regardless of what might impede my progress, I feel indigenous to the sea, embedded in the wind and currents with Cape Town my only obtainable destination. However, I might hypothesize my demise, the goal remains in front of me, and my destiny is defined. If nothing more comes of my life, I will have sailed solo to Cape Town, South Africa—an accomplishment in itself.

Thanksgiving at Sea

I *try to push the last of my hubris off the stern and into the wake flowing behind me. This poor wake, polluted with my errant, immature thoughts connects me to the beginning of my journey, thousands of miles ago. But after folding over and blending into itself, it's severed somewhere behind me, and the waters have returned to their ways, as if I had never been there. I hope my insensitive thoughts of arrogance and doubt dissolve on their way to the bottom of the sea.*

Without much fanfare, I've come and gone, past starts and stops, past false horizons and around islands, navigating emotionally filled days and quietly serene nights. I made good use of the wind and water, and perfected physics to reach this point in life where my destiny can only be denied by harm.

The days pass steadily. *Bo*, Franklin, Otto, and I enjoy the sailing—day in and day out. Conditions considered less than ideal back home have become our everyday standard. Winds in the mid-20s circle the compass and allow us to work eastward toward Cape Town.

* * *

The winds ease off in the afternoon and the seas follow, no longer pushed ahead of the wind. The western skies open slightly as the sun sets, and the evening takes on a relaxed feeling, as if I had finished a long work project or a hard run. It seems sensible to take a moment and relax, to not push for more sail, not push for more miles, but to breathe easy, walk slowly, and enjoy the moment, the evening, and the night.

In the darkness on deck, the weathered clouds move quickly to clear the sky, opening the roof above us to unveil one segment of stars at a time. Phosphorescence flows off the folding wake as a quarter moon backlights the clouds to the east, eventually rising above them to give the illusion of a mountainous coast off to port as Otto drives and makes gentle cooing sounds, like those of a haunting owl. This beauty reminds me of canoeing in the Canadian lakes north of Minnesota when I was 17, where we listened to the mournful, wiggling cry of the loons sounding out their sorrows. Memories continue to wash over me as I log, 00:00, Thursday, November 28th—Thanksgiving.

A contrast hits me deeply. My father passed away on Thanksgiving night at age 49, leaving an accumulation of shattered dreams and unfulfilled promises. And here I am, at 56, living my dream, alone in the vast Southern Atlantic Ocean on a Thanksgiving many years beyond his last.

* * *

Back home, on the shores of Lake Michigan, I imagine my house is quiet, awaiting the day's festivities. In my absence, my sister Nancy is hosting Thanksgiving. The aroma of roasted turkey will fill the house as friends and family arrive. Laughter, music, and stories will marry with the delicious fragrances from the kitchen. The stone fireplace will radiate warmth, and the wood smoke will linger in the crisp air outside.

My closest friends will look out the windows, across the empty horizon of Lake Michigan and imagine a speck; a man and a small boat on the open ocean. Our scenes will be nearly the same. Lake Michigan, though extending only 300 miles to the north, can appear as empty and forever as the miles of this ocean. Though different, the emotions they evoke are the same. Since Jamestown, my perspective has changed, and while I might have the right to be lonely, today, I am not.

I've sailed thousands of miles to be here and I'm thankful for the grace the sea has afforded me. I've weathered storms and squalls, secured the keel, absorbed beauty, and dealt with the human weakness hiding behind my false bravado. My body has adapted to life onboard and I am as fit as ever. Although a few pounds lighter, they were pounds I had no need to own. I'm everywhere I've ever wanted to be, and I am thankful for the day.

On the bulkhead is a note, in the familiar thick, black line of a Sharpie pen. "Call home at 2200 hrs." Nancy and my dear friend and longtime companion, Mary, along with my technologically savvy nephews, arranged for my appearance at Thanksgiving—though in voice only by satellite phone. I work through the chores of the day and add additional ones to help burn up the time.

Focusing on the weather conditions and compass course, I take *Bo's* hand and drive. Otto enjoys the time off, and *Bo* and I relish the time together. We sail up and over waves and down through the valley of troughs. When I close my eyes, I feel we are waltzing on the floor of a grand European ballroom in the late 1800s. Each wave lifts and settles as I steer to the firmness of the rudder and lead my dance partner by the persuasion of my hand. I surf away into a trance, filled with memories of past Thanksgivings, Thanksgivings when grandparents and great grandparents sat at the head of a table longer than a young man's imagination. I recalled the changes we made to tradition when my sisters' boyfriends filled a slot in the day's schedule, and of my own changes, wanting to connect with friends for soccer or football before the large afternoon dinner with the family.

I remember the house full of people, with a card table set in the spare room for us kids, and the inevitable decreasing number of family as we grew to young adults and set off on our own courses, each of our compasses pointing in different directions.

Drifting back onboard, I see the compass has wandered off the proper heading. In irony, I make a correction to put us back on course. The sun finally sets, and a dark infinity takes over from horizon to horizon—2150 hours turns ever so slowly, minute by minute, to 2200 hours. I pull the iridium phone from its docking station and punch the numbers to call home. The phone rings.

I imagine the scramble of people in the kitchen looking for the source of the alarm and see Nancy let go of a wooden spoon in an effort to grab the phone before the limit sends it off to the automated answering service.

"Hello!" We exchange Happy Thanksgiving's as Nancy links the phone with the computer so we can talk on speakerphone across the room and across thousands of miles. I hear the familiar voices of friends shouting greetings. What they say isn't important, but hearing their voices is.

Nancy offers a toast with an odd twist on tradition. *Bodacious Dream* is always abundantly stocked with Hershey's Dark Chocolate Kisses. At home, everyone grabs one while I scramble to find one for myself. In unison, we unwrap the foil across the open miles of universe and take in this symbolic sharing of the dream. As the chocolate melts away in my mouth, we limit our tears and protect our emotions by ending the call— "Goodbye everyone!"

"Goodbye Dave. . . be safe!" The phone goes quiet. The laughter, the music, the aromas, slowly, like the taste of chocolate—all disappear.

I was wrong. I am lonely.

Electronic Wizardry

A modern boat is filled with electronics. Navigation is handled by GPS-enabled chart plotters and iPads providing a constant stream of location information. Computers link with satellite phones or dome antennas to the vast ocean of information available on the Internet—weather, emails, and detailed product manuals. Satellite phones work as simply as cell phones and include automatic location software, keeping those ashore constantly up-to-date with the boat's location and progress. Instrumentation collects signals from sensors at the top of the mast, in the hull, and from electronic compasses before calculating at lightning speed, things I used to calculate in my mind. Wind speed, angle, compass bearing, distance, ETA and so on—an endless collection of information, much of it useless, though we amuse ourselves flicking through electronic pages and marveling at the available data.

Monitors display electrical power, both generated and stored, and a hydro-generator hangs over *Bodacious Dream's* stern, constantly generating electrical energy and passing it through a box of blinking lights on its way to recharging the batteries. When I'm sailing at eight knots, the batteries are perpetually full of electricity. Even when the KVH satellite dome is turned on to make communications via satellites, the generation of electricity seems adequate to keep the batteries charged. Though in the deep Southern Ocean, the KVH only provides distraction and humor. No longer in the northern hemisphere, it laughs, telling me I'm out of range . . . I think it's probably suggesting I am out of my mind.

Deep below the decks in the cramped stern lazarette are two electric-driven hydraulic rams—the core of Otto's equipment—

and each one is attached to a separate rudder, and the two rudders are linked together, operating as one. The hydraulic rams are connected to the ACPs (advanced control processors)—the electronic brains making sense of information from either of the electronic compasses and marrying their input with boat speed and wind direction, as well as pitch and roll, before sending a signal to the rams to push or pull as necessary to adjust the helm and keep *Bo* sailing in proper trim to the wind angle or compass course.

Lots of black voodoo happens inside these pieces of electronic equipment, making decisions in the blink of an eye, maybe even faster, but to a human at sea, the blink of an eye is a sufficient unit of time.

Otto drives the boat 90 percent of the time and communicates his good nature with a series of continuously mumbled sounds. Describing his language does no service, but it ranges from a squeaking door, to a clicking squirrel, sometimes pulling, and sometimes resisting the rudder. Sometimes pushing and retracting at lightning speed as *Bo* twists, pushed by a wave on one side and wind on the other. Regardless, Otto's constant chatter keeps us on course—Bo physically, and me mentally, comforted that everything is working well.

To a solo sailor, the autopilot is the most important piece of equipment on board. Without some system to help steer the boat, sailing long distances is not possible; hence, the need for redundant equipment, not to mention the granting of a persona, in our case, affectionately—Otto.

* * *

We've sailed 6,000 miles since leaving Jamestown with a set of fresh autopilot rams. Subconsciously, I monitor the chatter of the clicking squirrels and cooing birds in the stern lazarette. Occasionally, a change in the sounds occurs and I dismiss it to my expertise as a worrywart. Other times, I change from the port ram to the starboard ram to give proper rest and reassurance the system of redundancy is working. Making this change is often an intensely fun exercise, peppered with needle-like adrenalin spikes.

I consider intuition a subconscious driver and when nagged by worry, change Otto's drive rams. Though it sounds as simple as turning a switch—it's not. My first step in the procedure is to remove excess clothing and belly crawl to the stern of the boat. Poking my head and shoulders through the marginally large enough access hole into the lazarette, I listen closely to Otto's hydraulic drives. When other crewmembers are around, I am not so inclined to engage in audible, verbal communication with Otto. But when alone, and unburdened by the opinions of others, I can spend minutes talking with Otto about life in general and his state of being. This confined space is unnerving at best, but oddly, in some ways, it's relaxing. I can see the wake extending out behind us through the clear escape hatch at water level in the transom, and listen to Otto drive back and forth while stretching out horizontally, convincing myself I am doing something important.

By doing a maneuver similar to a competitive swimmer's turn at the end of a pool, I reverse course and pop back up in the main cabin. I redress in my foul weather gear, harness, and tether and return to deck where I settle into the driving position. The digital display in front of me allows me to adjust Otto's course left and right in one-degree or ten-degree increments as well as turn Otto on or off. With the push of a button, I can command him to tack or jibe and ask him to steer to a wind angle or compass direction.

Switching smoothly from one ram to the other is an important skill to acquire. To do this, I turn Otto off and take over the driving to find the groove in the wind and waves that will allow me to let go of *Bo's* tiller for a count of seven—the time I need to get below, change the switches on the ACPs and get back on deck to grab the helm before *Bo* slips wildly off course into a messy jibe or a roundup. In those seven seconds, I need to swing down the companionway, twist around, turn the three switches, reverse, and get back out to the helm to control the boat.

Convinced I've mapped out the rhythm of the wind and waves, I prepare to make my move. I let go of the helm and begin counting, at the same time I grab the upper edge of the companionway, and do a feet first submarine dive forward into *Bo's* belly. When I land, I sense everything is wrong and reverse, climbing back out on deck to grab the helm and prevent a jibe. I miss-judged the rhythm of that particular wave set. Patiently, I start the process again and when comfortable, count 1 . . . 2 . . . inside . . . 3 . . . turn around . . . 4 . . . hit the switches . . . scoot back . . . 5 . . . 6 . . . back outside . . . grab the helm, and steady *Bo* on course before hitting the *on* button to give Otto command. Minutes later, with Otto sailing well, I drop below, crawl back to the lazarette and listen intently to the nuances of language from the new ram. Crawling back into the cabin, I clutch a few Hershey's dark chocolate kisses and take a deep breath before penning in my log, "Changed auto rams, now on starboard."

Losing Otto

The winds press and sailing is work crossing the southern Atlantic Ocean. Damp, cold, and abrupt, the job is being done and we're consuming miles. Wind speed hangs in the 20s and Bo skips over waves, falling into troughs and laughing as she sprays me with salt water. She seems content, but she's like an annoying kid, and I am weary of it.

The brightening of the gray skies slowly sets morning into play. A small orange, a juice box, my look across the horizon extending in wider circles, shows nothing but gray hills and shadowy skies. *Blah* seems to describe it best. My only bright spot—the miles to Cape Town have dropped below 1,200.

As each day passes and miles disappear, the odds of failure seem to decrease—failure of the boat, failure of equipment, failure of me. The odds are down. Checking the scorecard, I convince myself I'm still ahead. I am sound, sort of dry (life at sea on a sailboat is always damp), and I have enough food and plenty of water. Fuel is on pace for the last 1,200 miles, but chocolate is thin, and the cookie count is nil. The batteries are good, though the hydro generator mount failed a week ago. The windex (wind indicator) is gone from the top of the mast and so is the wind speed and direction wand. I have a spare, but it's working sporadically.

I ate my last lasagna dinner a few nights ago and shortly thereafter, Otto failed, sending *Bo* into a Chinese jibe—on her wrong side, the boom improperly pressed against the rigging and water ballast pinning us down in one nasty mess.

It came by surprise. We were sailing fast. I was below decks and let my attention slip to something other than *Bo* when the movement of the boat suddenly seemed weird. After all this time at sea, I've become accustomed to the direction of the force of gravity, the heel, the forward momentum, and normal pitch and roll. These motions, repetitive and consistent are embedded in my subconscious. But in that strange instant, these motions were no longer comfortable, and instead they felt strange and unusual. Instantly, alarms went off—the instinctive one inside me, and the failed autopilot alarm.

Leaping through the companionway to the cockpit, I grabbed the helm and with only an instant to assess the compass course, wind direction, and comfort zone, I swung the helm, spinning *Bo* through another jibe to steady her back on course. On my knees in the cockpit, keeping my head low, I surveyed the boat, the rigging, the sails, and at the same time, adjusted my mind to the waves and wind. I didn't have time to put on a PFD (personal floatation device) or tether, increasing my anxiety in the cockpit.

With *Bo* stabilized and settled on course, I ran through the options and pushed the on button to see if Otto could steer—an error message came up instantly with a code number and alarm. I dropped my head and uttered an irresistible adjective. My instincts know the error codes, telling me the hydraulic ram had failed. The fix is simple, switch rams.

I held *Bo's* tiller and drove. While steadying her, I steadied myself, and logged data for the path of control and took count of the seconds. One . . . two . . . three . . . four . . . A half hour later, I was calm and ready to switch the changeover box to the port ram. "Ready . . . Set . . . Go!" In a slinky, quick move I was below decks, tripped the switches, and back on deck. *Bo* held her course and I grabbed the tiller. I punched the *on* button and Otto's staccato bumping and grunting assured me he was okay. Untrusting of things, I took a short, deep breath and waited. A half hour passed before I settled down, but the fact remained, I had lost an autopilot ram. I now had only one autopilot. *"Two is one and one is none"* reverberated through my mind. "Two is one and one is none" . . . "Two is one and one is none." I rationalized the starboard pilot had driven five of the six or seven thousand miles, so the port one should last the remaining thousand miles to Cape Town. The hair inside my ears tickled with every sound from the lazarette. My muscles tensed every time *Bo* lurched. My eyes searched for any nuance of a problem onboard while questions of *what ifs* pounded my patience. As the hours passed without further incident, my worries began to ease and I turned back to the routine of sailing.

That was two days ago. Today, while enjoying my morning juice box, the port autopilot failed, tossing *Bo* into an unexpected jibe and me into a frantic state to regain control.

"*Damn!*" Why didn't I fix the starboard ram when I could have?

With *Bo* stabilized, there's nothing to do at this moment but sail. I take a deep breath and settle in with the means I've used all my life—I stare out to sea. Steadying my mind, I seek answers. Calming down my dear friend, *Bo* calms me down too.

I take a few stabs at tying lines around the tiller to keep *Bo* on track longer than seven seconds. She holds course long enough for me to jump below and grab my jacket, PFD, and tether— not because they are necessary, but because they put me in my comfort zone. I feel naked sitting in a car without a seat belt; without my jacket, PFD, and tether, I feel the same way.

Subconsciously, I do what one always does first—stabilize the patient; the patient being a combination of *Bo* and me. If I don't take care of me, I can't take care of *Bo*, if I don't take care of *Bo*, *Bo* can't take care of me. In a circle, we are one. From here, we move toward a solution. A line from a Dave Mallett song runs through my head . . . "*Don't cry, baby, we ain't beat yet.*"

Over the next couple of hours, I assess the port pilot issue is unsolvable. I already reasoned the starboard pilot has lost its hydraulic pump. I can replace the starboard ram with a spare onboard, but it's an unfriendly job on shore, let alone when bouncing through seas. I should have fixed it when things were calm. Now I have to fix it.

While steering *Bo* faithfully through the waves, I make a mental list of the procedure to replace the starboard ram and walk through it in my mind. I need to gather the tools—hex head wrenches, socket, ratchet, wire cutters, small Phillips-Head screwdriver. Next, I'll crawl back and break loose all four mounting screws, one at a time, to make sure they'll all come out. I'll continue around the horn loosening the four screws so the unit drops evenly. When it's down, I'll disconnect the information wire and cut the power leads. I'll have to remove the heat shrink from the wire connectors. I revise the procedure to do this first, before dismounting the unit. I run through the procedure a few times, practicing it in my mind.

After the unit is down and disconnected, I'll crawl back to the main cabin and copy the wire lead connections to the new unit. On purpose, I put a male connector on one lead and a female on the other. This will be easier to do in the cabin than in the crawl space of the lazarette with *Bo* lurching through the waves. Once the new unit is ready, I'll reverse my course of action, adding additional tools—wire ties, heat shrink tubing, a heat torch, and a bit more nerve and patience.

My mind stumbles over the complications I'll inherit if *Bo* loses track of her course and trips over a wave, broaching into another Chinese jibe or tacking into irons. If it happens, everything will have to remain in disorder until I can climb out of the lazarette and get on deck to sort it out. It won't be easy for me to climb out of the laz with *Bo* pinned on her ear after a Chinese jibe.

I now know what I have to do below decks, but before I can do it, I have to figure out how to steady *Bo's* helm. First choice is heaving to, a process of tacking through the wind, leaving the jib back winded, and tying off the helm. When accomplished successfully, the boat will act as if she is parked, balanced perfectly between the forces of wind and helm allowing me to concentrate on the job all day if necessary.

I tack *Bo* over, keep the jib sheet in place, and tie off the helm to leeward. *Bo* is unstable and runs off quickly, turning into the wind as expected, but with too much speed and nimbleness she turns through the wind and tacks over, sailing off, careening weirdly out of control. I try various adjustments to the jib trim, main trim, and helm position. After a frustrating hour of trials, I put *Bo* back on course and calm us both down. *"Damn,"* I think. I have to reef the mainsail and set the storm jib for this to work. To do that, I'll have to tie off the helm long enough for me to go forward and make the sail changes. She'll have to stay on course for 30 minutes or more.

Balancing Act

Sailing a boat is about balance—balancing the loads and pressures so they all work in harmony with no one force overwhelming another. I grab a sail tie from my pocket and secure the helm to a pad eye in the middle of the cockpit. With another line, I tie the helm to the outer rail. These two points prevent the helm from moving back and forth, allowing Bo to sail along nicely, but only for 30 to 45 seconds at a time before I need to adjust her course.

I add more slack in the line so the helm can wander back and forth, and ease the main sheet to reduce pressure and improve the balance. She responds better now, steering for a couple of minutes at a time before needing adjustment. With this arrangement showing promise, I drop below to grab an elastic bungee to spring the helm and provide a constant pressure, the travel limited in the opposite direction by the sail tie—balance at play. *Bo* responds favorably to the refinements and sails for fifteen or twenty minutes without the need for correction.

I contemplate the repair to the auto ram and estimate I need two, 30-minute sessions to execute it. I wonder if this arrangement can be relied upon to balance the helm instead of making the sail change. As *Bo* sails along, tended by this haphazard arrangement of lines and bungees, I gather the needed tools and place them in a pouch, all the time keeping my eye on the helm.

Mentally, I run through the procedure, grabbing each tool as I do each job. Believing I have it fully worked out, I step on deck to monitor *Bo's* sailing. She sails balanced as I gaze on the horizon and think of the *"what ifs."* If she crash-jibes or tacks, I should stay on task until I am done. I have to prioritize, worry about only one thing at a time and allow the consequences to be as they may.

I decide this has to work. I swing below, remove my PFD, tether, and jacket, and place them in simple order for an emergency trip on deck. I grab the tools, do one last mental run-through, and then stare aft, out the companionway doors at the wake flowing behind us. A few minutes and deep breaths seem to pass. *Bo* and I are now one. We must be together on this.

I slip into a mental state I rarely visit anymore—totally focused. I turn thoughts of fear and claustrophobia into feelings of comfort and concentrated confidence. I am comfortable here. I'll be comfortable there. I drop to my knees, crawl back to the lazarette access port, place my tool pouch inside the small, cramped zone, and push them to the center. I pull myself inward, over the edge of the access and twist to the left to proceed over the center drainpipe, my fleece snagging on the cutoff bolts above. My chest has the hardest time clearing through the narrow passage, but I make it and feel the pipe on my gut, then my hips, and now on my thighs. I am through and *Bo* seems to be staying on course. I shimmy further in and roll over onto my side and back, feet toward the centerline of the hull and my head jammed into the space between the hull and deck at the outer rail. With a maneuver of my foot and leg, I pull the tool pouch up to my hands, remove the hex head wrench, and proceed to break loose each of the four bolts. One, two, three and last, four—each one breaks loose. I move back to the heat shrink tubing, dissect it, and unplug the unit. Unwinding the bolts, the unit, supported by my arm leveraged by compromised shoulder muscles, slowly drops to the hull—it's free. I unscrew the control wire and slide the unit and tools back to center and shimmy over the pipe to exit out the access hole in the reverse direction of my entry. I crawl back to the cabin with tools and unit in hand.

All is going well. I give a glance out the companionway at *Bo* and with no more difference than trusted comrades, continue my work setting up the new unit with the proper wire connectors. *Bo* is doing her job. I am doing mine. Our teamwork so far, is flawless.

Now ready to install the new unit, I reverse the entire procedure, crawl back through the access, over the pipe and lodge myself into position. I pull the unit to me, place all four bolts into their respective holes, and lift the heavy unit into position—upside down on the underside of the cockpit deck. It takes both hands and arms to lift the heavy, unbalanced unit into place, and, in a planned, orchestrated move, I grab the wrench from my clenched teeth and turn the first bolt, catching a thread. I move to the second bolt, kitty-corner from the first and with my shoulder screaming in pain from holding the heavy unit up against the ceiling, I catch a thread of the bolt so the unit can hang on its own. I release my grasp and adjust my arm to quiet my shoulder while putting in bolts three and four. Turn-by-turn, the unit lifts into place before I finally torque each bolt tightly. I screw the control wire block back on and scoot inward to make the electrical connections while *Bo* continues to drive without hesitation. While attempting to make the electrical connections, I find I screwed up. The male tries to mate with the male, the female with the female. *Damn.* I was near perfect in my procedure. Fortunately, in some subconscious recognition, I put the box of connectors in my pouch so I can cut off the wrong pieces and install the correct ones. I slip the heat shrink tube onto the wires, make the connections, and heat the tubing, shrinking it tightly around the wires to waterproof them. With the wires tied up, ends clipped off, scraps of plastic and junk picked up, I survey my work and it all looks good. I walk through the procedure again and check for mistakes. It's simple, but simple mistakes are still mistakes. I shimmy backwards out the lazarette and into the cabin, drop the tool pouch, and jump on deck. I hit *on* and nothing happens. "Damn!" *Bo's* arrangement of ties and bungies is still steering but I am broken—crushed. The new unit doesn't work.

In a flash, I remember I had turned off the power to the rams before starting the procedure. I drop below, hit the power switch, tape it on in perpetuity, and confidently return to deck and touch the *on* button. Otto grunts to life. I watch and test . . . up ten . . . down ten . . . left one . . . right one . . . I remove the Chinese string game controlling the helm and with a deep breath, look out across the ocean, relieved. It's never looked so beautiful. Each wave is friendly, each cloud seems just right. There is no sunshine or bright colors of Disneyland, just a seascape, a boat, and a solid seaman sailing again—alone.

We celebrate with a reward of food, reading and the jazz of Rick Braun. I now plan, after dawn tomorrow to fix the port ram, reminding myself that I have only one ram, and recite the mantra— *"Two is one, and one is none."*

After my morning juice box ritual, I climb back into the lazarette to inspect the port ram and see the problem instantly. A simple fitting linking the ram with the rudderstock has unscrewed itself. A simple turn of a wrench corrects this. I am chagrinned, but thankful. We are back at full strength. Two is one.

Hard on the Nose
to Cape Town

With Otto at full strength, Bo sailing well and making miles, I turn my focus to Cape Town, now less than a thousand miles away. A thousand miles is still a week of sailing. I play math with the calendar, plotting the end of this leg as if I am in control of the weather and vagaries of the sea. I plan our arrival for Saturday about noon, figuring this will be enough time to check in, shower, shave, and head out on the town for a well-deserved dinner and cold beer.

Weather is the barricade between Cape Town and us, and like a good politician, I have a backup consultant if I don't get the weather I want from Ken at Commanders'. John Hoskins, a good friend, fellow solo competitor on the great lakes, and the navigator/weatherman on Bodacious Racing's crewed boat follows me, and we communicate regularly.

Between Ken and John, one of them will have the answer I want—the other will probably have the truth. My hubris is brewing again, defiantly believing I have a choice in the weather, as if it were an item on a dinner menu.

I plot, figure, and calculate two more cold fronts coming, but if we're lucky, only one will reach us before we arrive. If all goes well, we'll arrive on the backside of the first front in beautiful weather.

Ken burst my bubble during our phone conference. The good news is, there is just one minor cold front coming; the bad news, there will be a very strong 35–50 knot wind from the southeast enhanced by the funneling effect of the mountains and coastline. This is quite typical, Ken explains, telling me a story of people being blown off the docks during the last Volvo

Ocean Race stopover. I'm not amused, and begin to pout as Ken insists the strategy must be to sail to the southeast, and bank against the strong, prevailing wind.

"Do not point towards Cape Town," he insists. Resisting the temptation is hard as the miles decrease, at less than 1,000 miles of a 7,000-mile leg, I feel like a runner wanting to coast downhill to the finish.

Flat-bottomed boats like *Bodacious Dream* are built for speed, with a long, narrow keel extending over nine feet below the water to a heavy bulb leveraging them upright. The length of the keel's cord (the distance from the front to the back) is short on purpose to decrease drag. When these boats are sailing fast, this short cord provides plenty of resistance to slipping sideways, but when the boat slows down to a knot or two for docking, the resistance is nonexistent. *Bo* will slide all over the harbor, bouncing around like a bumper car. Sailing in 35 knots of wind is one thing; slow docking maneuvers in 35 knots of wind, alone and fatigued is foolish. I don't want to sail into Cape Town in 50-kt winds, let alone try to dock.

With some days before Cape Town to ponder this, I call John and ask him what he thinks the weather will do—a second opinion of sorts. John responds: "There's a thermal low developing which will cancel out the strong SE winds. It will be beautiful if you can arrive there in six days."

"Hell yeah Baby, that's what I'm talking about!" My spirits rise. Cape Town is nearing. Otto is working flawlessly and regardless of how the event is scored; I remind myself, if I make it no further than Cape Town, I've gone beyond the limits of most people's dreams and desires.

To fill my time and satiate the encroaching anxiety, I plot, calculate, and consider more options. I know Ken is right, but I'm hoping John is too. Ken's retort when I approach him about the thermal low is short and to the point. "It's hard to predict this phenomenon, Dave. It might develop as forecast, but it's more likely, it won't. You have to prepare for the odds-on favorite—the prevailing winds." Reluctantly, I turn *Bo* away from Cape Town and sail to the southeast as best I can.

The strategy is simple. Over the next three or four days, the cold front will pass, allowing us to sail southeast with ease. When the winds start moving forward, we'll sail as comfortably as possible, curving around to the east and northeast like a hooked golf shot. Once the big southeast winds hit, we'll sail however *Bo* sails best and as close to the course to Cape Town as possible.

"Don't worry about ending up north of Cape Town," Ken explains. "If this happens, we'll figure it out later, if the thermal low sets up, you'll have favorable winds to come back south, or in from the west." I know Ken's right. I respect his experience.

The weather sets up as Ken forecast, and following his strategy to a T, we sail to the southeast on southwesterly winds. As the winds build, the miles to Cape Town abate, and the sailing is wet and wild with just whites up—an old sailor's term for sailing under main and jib. Acutely tuned to the slightest noise or twitch, I am startled by a loud bang. Pins and needles of adrenalin shoot instantly into my muscles. I jump from my skin, landing in seven places at once, madly looking for the source of the noise when I notice the Solent is loose. The halyard has broken.

In short order, I clip onto the jacklines, slide forward to the bow and pull the jib down. I know exactly what to do having solved this problem in pre-sailing practice sessions.

Grabbing the halyard for the A5 fractional spinnaker, I attach it to the Solent, and swiftly re-hoist the sail. We are back underway, as nonchalant as anything I've ever done on a boat. In the cockpit, I unclip, shake off the water, and fly on the adrenalin. It will be a while before it subsides. Sailing through the day and night, Cape Town gets closer with each entry in my logbook.

The wind, as Ken predicted, is slowly *backing*, and moving counterclockwise around the compass. Each shift puts the wind more on the nose, and pushes *Bo's* course to the left to compensate. By night, we are pointing at Cape Town and the winds are increasing. The bands of 35-50 knot winds have arrived. I reef the sails and hunker down, sailing the best course in the general direction of Cape Town. The winds continue to build, reaching 35 knots with the gusts pushing higher. As the winds continue to back, I continue to adjust Otto, now pointing north of Cape Town.

Fully *reefed*, I hunker down and listen intently to Otto and the wind sizzling in the rigging. *Bo* rises up, over, and pounds through the waves, leaving an air of uncertainty in every moment.

Pointing north of Cape Town, 400 miles away, is misleading in a time and distance calculation. We now use VMC (Velocity Made Good on Course) to calculate, which takes into account the actual vector of positive direction toward a determined waypoint, in this case, Cape Town. The math is complicated, but it considers the fact that we aren't sailing toward Cape Town, and calculates our actual gain in angle, presuming we'll tack or jibe to the *other board* and ultimately reach our waypoint. Our actual VMC, given the amount of zigzagging necessary, is near four knots. At this rate, 400 miles will take 100 hours—four days. My emotions slump thinking we'll end up somewhere north of Cape Town pinned on the African coast and have to beat back south once the winds subside. I could be out here another week. I hate roller coasters, especially emotional ones.

* * *

Night pounds at my anxiety, but near daybreak the winds slack off to the low 20s. They continue decreasing to the high teens and I wonder, with cautious hope, if the thermal low is setting up, canceling out the strong southeast winds. Have I sailed through the outer band of high winds into the low? Throughout the morning, the winds continue decreasing and shift abruptly to the northwest—all favorable things. Cape Town is now directly on the bow and less than 300 miles away. The reefs are out and *Bo* is sailing at good speed, heading directly toward our destination. The sun breaks through the clouds, doubling my emotions on the happy side. "Cape Town is obtainable," I whisper quietly, aware that the slightest hint of arrogance will be considered irreverent by the sea. I am filled with distrust and stay alert, not napping, or allowing distraction. I concentrate on getting as much from this favorable wind as possible, afraid the gods will notice my good fortune, slap me in the face, and strip me of this pleasure.

As the end of the day nears, the winds decrease even more and the sailing becomes quite pleasant. The mile count declines and my projections for arrival become less prone to error. I chuckle, thinking about the time I've spent calculating arrival dates, and yet I recognize the importance of the exercise; not only today or last month, but twenty years ago when I thought of ways to get here.

* * *

The mile count falls below 100, reading 99.9, an emotional threshold for me. At less than 100 miles from Cape Town, I think of the many comparisons in life, but I am distracted by the list of things to do before arriving—take down the Bermuda flag, put up a quarantine flag, put away gear, sort out the boat, find clean clothes and wash-up. At dawn, I pull a grey, five-gallon jug of water from below and lay it in the sun. If the sun helps, I'll have warm water for washing up this afternoon. It's an optimistic thought, though not necessarily a realistic one.

I work through the morning chores, sip one of the last juice boxes, and scavenge for chocolate. I enter the date in my log, attempt converting boat time to UTC (Coordinated Universal Time) and then to local time and make a guess at my arrival time. Strangely, I've lost track of time zones and am confused by the difference between local time and the GPS satellites. What

I think is early morning is actually noon. I'll have to recalibrate when I have a chance.

I study notes on the Royal Cape Yacht Club and zoom in on the chart to familiarize myself with the harbor. I'm mindful it's still hours away, though 35 miles, after sailing 7,000 will pass in a relative instant.

In the foggy sun on deck, I strip off my clothes and begin a rag bath—a bucket filled with water, a bar of soap, a naked guy sailing. I can't help but think something must go wrong. I should set up the camera so whoever finds *Bodacious Dream* sailing unattended will know what the skipper was doing in the last moments before slipping on a bar of soap and ending up overboard.

The sun didn't warm the water but the smell of soap, the fresh water rinse, and a dry towel are reminiscent of life at a Four Seasons Hotel. I put on clean, dry clothes, pull on a fresh fleece, and feel super human, basking in the cool sun.

Cape Town is less than 20 miles away. The afternoon sun is mixed with fog, and the winds are fair and favorable, a nice end to the freshman leg of this trip. The fog breaks for a moment, giving me a glimpse of the shore before quickly closing the shutter again.

I think I just saw Table Mountain.

I jump below, check the chart plotter, and see a dozen *AIS* targets. Large ships are everywhere. On deck, I search the fog with bare eyes for anything and see nothing. I jump below, then back on deck, and back below again. I take a deep breath and start clicking on AIS targets, noting their speed and direction of travel. I calculate distances, and begin to make sense of the chessboard. Most of the ships are sitting at anchor, waiting for their turn in the harbor. I plot a path through the anchored ships to the traffic separation lanes, a virtual navigation road in and out of the harbor, and return to the cockpit, this time with my portable iPad so I can follow the navigation on deck while keeping a line of sight open to the chart plotter below and its display of AIS targets.

Opening and closing, the fog continues to break, allowing an occasional glimpse of a ship or the shore of South Africa. The frequency of breaks increases as we close in on the harbor, and soon I've mapped the shoreline, the ships at anchor, the ships moving, and Table Mountain, faithfully standing guard over Cape Town.

Slowly motoring through the separation lanes, we make our way into the harbor. It's confining compared to the wide-open ocean. Five hundred yards seems close and floods my attention with caution. We pass massive ships docked alongside the piers on both sides of the entrance to the Royal Cape Yacht Club basin and stick our nose in the entrance, keeping one eye keenly focused on the depth meter, the other gauging time and distance. The waters are calm and the wind is gone. These are perfect conditions for docking Bo.

My local contacts, Francois and Adrian Kuttel, have alerted the yacht club to my arrival and informed me in emails to take any slip along the first dock where the water is deep enough for *Bodacious Dream*'s 10-foot draft. I nose the bow further into the yacht club basin, my eyes darting around to assess danger and consider dimensions and options. I spot a favorable slip and take note before sliding *Bodacious Dream* into reverse and back out the narrow channel between the docks to the main harbor to prepare fenders and lines.

In the large, open area of the commercial harbor, a tug is pushing a large tanker into position. I stand still until I'm comfortable with their distance and intentions and then drop below to quickly toss the fenders and dock lines into the cockpit; frightened that another commercial ship will bear down on us. It's a foolish nervousness; there is plenty of room in the harbor. But still, a foolishness born during the long time alone in the vast open space of the sea. I push the sails aside to tie on the fenders and lines as *Bo* motors along at two knots, just fast enough for Otto to maintain steerage.

With fenders and lines in place, I return to the helm and point *Bo* for the docks. My heart races with anxiety as we enter the yacht club basin. In the wide area just inside, I circle *Bo* in a three-point turn, back down the long narrow channel and aim for the slip I chose. *Bo* enters the slip with the grace of a fine lady, setting alongside the dock perfectly as I stop her progress with the engine.

I step over the lifelines and with a breast line I make her fast. Another line controls the bow and I inhale a deep breath. Not content to take my eyes off her, I do a quick assessment of the area and continue setting fenders and adjusting lines until I feel she is nestled securely. I look around; no one is anywhere near. We've come a long way, and finished alone.

We've sailed 7,000 miles from Bermuda and landed in Cape Town. Table Mountain looms noticeably over the town and harbor, and the winds are calm. It's fitting no one is around. I shed my harness and tether, and step back on board to dig through the stores for a can of Coke. On deck in the bright sunshine, I pop the top and take a ceremonious sip, now an inadvertent tradition after a long solo passage. Sitting in the cockpit, the sensation of relief starts an intense tingle inside me. For the first time in two months, my worries are limited. I look further around the immediate area, past the masts and along the docks and allow the overload of stimulus to consume me. All sorts of emotions surge forward—elation, relief, sadness, and excitement. Erratic energies begin draining from my body as I stand up and step across the loose gear in the cockpit, and back onto the dock.

I walk back and forth a few yards in each direction, slowly extending my reach into this new world. A couple of dozen boats down the dock I spot a couple and walk their way. "Hello" I offer to the woman talking across the rail with the man on his boat. "I've just sailed in; can you tell me where the yacht club is?"

They seem nonplussed, and point to the blue roof building in the distance, explaining the labyrinth pathway by waving their hands and saying, "Just follow the docks and work to the left. Where did you come from?" The woman asks. "Bermuda," I explain. "42 days." "Very good," her friendly but unemotional reply. "Welcome." They turn back to their conversation and I step away.

I'm confused. It's odd they seem unimpressed. I'll learn in the coming days there is nothing new to sailing into Cape Town from a world away. There's nowhere else to come from but a world away. I'm just another sailor stopping by the Tavern of the Seas.

I work down the labyrinth of docks toward the blue roof to find the customs office and properly enter South Africa. Stepping into the club, I ask a kind man for the woman whose name I had been given by the Kuttels. "She's gone for the day" he responds, leaving me bewildered. "What time is it here?" I ask. "4:00 p.m." he responds. Strange, I think. I thought it was earlier. I explain my situation and the gentleman introduces himself as the club manager. He answers my questions, the first of which is: "Where can I clear customs?"

"Customs? That'll have to wait until tomorrow."

"Can I leave the club and go to a hotel?"

"Of course, no problem." He gives me a quick tour around the club and shows me the locker room and showers. Then points in the direction of the bar and explains: "If you need anything, just ask for me." I thank him and walk slowly back to *Bodacious Dream*, absorbing the colors along the way. My palette has been limited to mostly grey and blue for the past month.

Torn between the excitement of arriving in Cape Town and the fear of land, or maybe it's the absence of the open sea, the change shocks my system. I feel I am in a strange vortex, but like a prevailing wind, I'll flow with it. I pack a bag with scissors, razor, clean clothes, and a camera, and head back to the clubhouse for a much-needed shower and shave.

While searching the docks and pathways, looking for a place to take my picture, I come across three young kids about eight years old playing around the old cast iron cannons at the entrance to the club. I ask if they know how to take a picture and all of them reply eagerly, "Yes." I give them the camera and they work with it, heads and arms bobbing up and reaching over, explaining to each other how to do it. They take pictures of me, of themselves, and one or two with me. They're all over the place. Their laughter is fun and contagious. In a little more than an hour, I've made new friends and have a picture of me before the great shaving event.

In the locker room, I scrutinize the odd looking image in the mirror and speak softly. " Sheeze . . . you're looking pretty wild there guy." My hair is long, my beard is very long, I'm weathered and tanned, thinner and fit—a stranger even to my own eyes. Soon, I'll be back to normal—showered and shaven.

On the walk back to *Bo*, with the intention to close her up and head for the hotel, I pass another sailor on his boat. He's figured out I'm the skipper of the new boat on the dock and stops me to talk about where I've come from and how. The conversation pauses and I excuse myself so I can head to *Bo* and put a few things away, grab my shore bag and credentials and walk up to the club's bar . . . a cold beer my next waypoint.

Moments later, the kind sailor knocks on the deck of *Bo* and hollers, "Hey Dave! I want to alert you. There will be strong winds here tonight and tomorrow—50 knots likely. Be sure to tie the boat up well. If you have any questions or need some help, come get me." Leaning out the companionway and twisting my head to see him, I acknowledge his advice with a question. "It gets bad here? Even at the docks?" I question. "Yes." His reply is simple. This upends my plan for a quick beer. Gear is everywhere—sails on deck, sails on the boom— stuff left around haphazardly. I hoped to avoid taking care of it now, with the intension of doing it in the morning, but having learned my lesson from the autopilots, I start putting things away, tying down miscellaneous gear, pulling back halyards, and securing *Bo* with additional crisscrossed dock lines.

An hour later, the sun setting behind clouds, I'm satisfied *Bo* is secure, and disembark. A few steps down the dock I turn around and look back at my friends, *Bo*, Otto, and Franklin, with a feeling of forlornness, wishing they could come with me. I want to stay but I need to go. I sigh deeply in the waning light, turn, and head to the club.

With a cold beer in front of me, I ask the bartender if he can arrange a taxi to the hotel. The beer tastes good, the local smiles are warm and calm, and the first leg of my journey is complete. I can honestly say I've sailed solo from Jamestown, Rhode Island to Cape Town, South Africa.

Cape Town Tourist

I sleep fitfully through the second night at the hotel, waking to check the chart plotter, trim the sails, and check the gear. A faint light sneaks in around the curtains, growing to a bright fringe as the morning comes on. The first night was even more disrupted as my body and mind adjust to land.

I shake off the comfort of the bed, walk to the bathroom, and break into uncontrollable laughter; my foul weather gear is draped over every available hook or door. Jackets, pullovers, solopets (a one-piece foul weather suit), hats, gloves and bib overalls—all of them hung to dry after being soaked and rinsed in fresh water. How Mary puts up with my Henri Lloyd decorating and lifestyle, nobody knows.

The first 36 hours in Cape Town passed in a flash. After finishing my beer at the yacht club, with *Bo* hunkered down in her slip ready for the onslaught of winds, I took a taxi to the hotel and met Mary who arrived an hour later, flying in from Chicago. We relaxed over dinner at the hotel and caught up with our lives over the past 40 days.

Knowing little about Cape Town and South Africa, we understand from reading the travel guides to be vigilant about safety when away from the hotel grounds. I spent day one at the Royal Cape Yacht Club, lingering with *Bo*, making lists, checking emails, rinsing and washing gear and looking up local contacts. Mary took this time to explore the area near the hotel and develop a list of things to see and do. Last night, we wandered around the V&A (Victoria & Alfred) waterfront, nosed into storefronts, and perused restaurant menus. The streets, decorated for the coming

Christmas holiday were full of happy, engaging people as we sat down in a small place for a quiet dinner.

I stand tall on the first rung of this stepladder I call my dream. I've always believed I should earn my right to be somewhere, to sail across oceans before flying across them. With the exception of New Zealand and Hawaii, I have succeeded. By sailing to Cape Town, I feel I've earned some right to be here.

As I hone the list of preparations for *Bo*, I set the computer to run nonstop overnight to upload photos and videos to *Dropbox* for archiving. I'm worried that an errant, stupid click from me will wipe out all the videos and photos from the first leg of the journey. To keep my fingers off the keyboard, I head to bed.

Waking, I again pry myself from the comfortable bed and turn on the TV to make sure the world remained in order while we slept. The news came in clear. In the short 60 hours since we arrived, the world has changed. Nelson Mandela passed away. South Africa and perhaps much of the world are no longer supported by this giant man, and now stand alone without him. It feels like South Africa has lost its father.

While I finished a major portion of my dream and walk about proudly, impressed with my accomplishment, it strikes me that I am human and overshadowed, understandably so, by Nelson Mandela's greatness. Memorials to Nelson Mandela spring up like grass powering through cracked concrete. Beyond the entrance of the hotel stands a sculpture of four men known as Nobel Square—Albert Luthuli, Desmond Tutu, F.W. de Klerk, and Nelson Mandela. Flowers cover the base of this stoic sculpture acknowledging these four Nobel Peace Prize winners and their struggle to free South Africa from apartheid. My ignorance overwhelms me; I know so little about these four men.

What little I know about South Africa came years ago from the evening news in America. In my memory—apartheid, Mandela, Tutu, Soweto, riots, slums, and *The Long Walk*—these are keyword links to the angry discourse of the televised, U.S. version of the history of South Africa. My history lesson stopped in 1990 when Nelson Mandela walked free to be elected president of South Africa and the bad news stopped. What I expected to be a learning journey across the oceans of the world will not recess with *Bodacious Dream* secure in a slip and me onshore, it is going to continue, in its own way, beginning today, December 6, 2013.

A strange mix of emotions stirs inside me as I walk through the V&A waterfront. For the past 42 days, I've been alone and making no compromises. Now, I step aside to get out of people's way, or wait for a clear lane to walk across the square. While I do my best to reacquaint myself with people and society, Cape Town does its best to remember Nelson Mandela and celebrate the Christmas Holiday.

In equal contrast to this solo sailor walking through the crowd, a Christmas tree stands tall and celebratory just steps from the eight-foot high, blank, white billboard with a simple message written across the top. *We'll miss you Nelson.* People walking by stop and read the thoughts of others before writing one of their own within reach from ground level. Each day, the billboard becomes more swathed with thoughts, sketches, and prayers for South Africa and the world.

* * *

Tim Eades, the captain for the fully crewed Bodacious Racing boat will come to Cape Town later next week to help me with final preparations for the next leg. In the meantime, he's connected me with a close expatriate friend of his from Chicago. Mark has taken time out of his day to come see *Bodacious Dream* and meet us. He helps by making phone calls to local contacts for equipment and supplies, and then hoists me to the top of *Bo's* mast so I can remove the non-functioning wind wands and take them to the B&G representative for repair. With these preparations and repairs underway, we've freed up time for Mary and me to explore Cape Town.

* * *

It's all wrong south of the equator—the rental car, a stick-shifting compact, has the steering wheel on the wrong side, requiring an increase in conscious effort and patience. After complying with the rental agreement, falsifying our confidence in being able to mix and match muscle memory with the wrong side of the road, I take a deep breath, back out of the parking spot and chirp the tires goodbye as we jump into city traffic intent on locating a Starbucks coffee shop Mary saw the other day. I don't drink coffee, but I think I should as I mash gears, pop the clutch, and try not to turn into oncoming traffic.

An hour later, after an unscripted tour of Cape Town, we park the little bugger of a car in a space high on the viewing level of Table Mountain. We can't ascend any higher today; the cable cars to the top are shut down because of the high winds. Cape Town is spread out in front of us, the view extending across the city and harbor to the open waters of the Atlantic Ocean—deep, blue and lovely to the uninitiated around me. To my eyes, the waters are inviting, desirable, lonesome, and yet even at this distance, I see the white tips of waves and know that sailing in these high winds is sporting at best. I work hard to conceal my concerns on this beautiful afternoon.

An avid trail runner and half marathoner, Mary desires to run an event on every continent as well as a half marathon in every state of the US. By following my wanderings with *Bo*, she's run Europe and New Zealand. For Africa, she's entered a run at a winery later this week, but today, at 5:00 p.m., she plans to run with a group gathering at the base of Table Mountain for a lap along the trails. While Mary looks forward to this, I quietly look forward to a nap, my excuse being, to work out my sleep cycles.

Waiting for the running group to gather, we strike up a conversation with a lone runner and ask if he's part of the group. He's not, but amused by our American accents, he offers advice on places to run, telling Mary the trail along the beach in front of our hotel is a well-marked, good and safe run. The group fails to materialize, forcing us to change plans and substitute driving back to the hotel in rush hour traffic on the wrong side of the road for Mary's adrenalin kick.

At the hotel, we regain our balance walking around the waterfront and watch the tablecloth of clouds flow and drape over the edge of the Mountain. The waxing moon is rising and will grow larger each night in the clear air of the cape, helping this harbor to slowly seduce me. It's understandable why mariners refer to this place as the Tavern of the Seas.

Full from a wonderful meal, I slip under the bed covers and promise myself I'll leave Cape Town, knowing better men than I have sold their boats to remain here.

We are precariously balanced between the western ways of the waterfront hotel and the authentic lifestyles we see traveling between the hotel and the yacht club. The industrial harbor complex, made up of large ships, acres of containers, and shipyards full of metal banging and sandblasting covers most of the land around the yacht club, making it difficult to wander far. Mary and I enjoy authentic places to experience local customs, and while driving to the hardware stores, marine suppliers, and metal working shops, we see there is much about Cape Town that we're missing by limiting our wanderings to the vicinity of the hotel.

An authentic, local restaurant named The Afrikan Café catches our interest. Local opinions are mixed, but we venture out for dinner and experience a wonderful evening. Contrived a bit to accommodate tourists, the authenticity of the customs and food, complete with local Afrikan music, makes our evening memorable.

The plan is to stay in Cape Town for two-and-a-half-weeks and the time is passing quickly. Tim is scheduled to arrive in a few days. The work on *Bo* is going smoothly. I'm undecided whether to haul her out to check the keel joint or not. A prudent seaman would not let such a thing go unchecked after the incident in the Atlantic, but deep inside I'm in denial. I want to believe everything is fine, and I certainly don't want to find out it's not.

While these issues hang in lim*bo*, Mary arranges with a tour guide to spend the day wine tasting around Cape Town. South Africa is known for great wines and John Lawrence from Big Blue Sky Tours will introduce us to them.

I wake early with a sense of purpose. Arriving ahead of Mary by a few minutes, I find John waiting in the hotel turn-around. Every morning, Solley and the other doormen graciously meet us and inquire about our plans for the day. Today, any concerns they have are allayed, they know John and know he'll take good care of us.

Following a short round of introductions, John inquires about my sailing journey and wants to know why someone would sail solo around the world, let alone from the United States to Cape Town. Within moments, we're laughing and the conversation is fun and comfortable.

Our first stop on the wine tour is aptly named, Goats do Roam, a spoof on the famous French winery, Cotes du Rhone. As we walk the paths, goats roam the grounds and greet us. John schooled us on South Africa over the 30-minute drive to the winery; explaining that he taught school during apartheid and he and his wife were active anti-apartheid protesters. After experiencing a series of interrogations and missing friends, John, with his wife and children, fled South Africa for England, certain their lives were in danger. He returned home shortly after Nelson Mandela was freed. His stories are rich and thoughtful, and while I think I'm sailing around the world, the fact is, I'm on a learning journey, regardless of the depth of the water or lack thereof.

After learning more about us, John fulfills our desires to know more about South Africa. Between wineries, he fills us with historical facts and personal experiences, and stops at the entrance of the prison where Nelson Mandela walked free after 27 years, changing the course of South Africa forever. Outside the gates of this prison stands a tall bronze statue of Nelson Mandela, his fist in the air and his feet draped with flowers in his memory. Growing up in the US during the 60s, this fist in the air was a defiant symbol of anger, but the expression captured on Nelson Mandela's face says something different. It's not anger, but more symbolic of perseverance and the promise of unity.

At the Lynx Winery, we greet the owner in a small, intimate room to sample his wines. The wines are as exceptional as the stories he and John share about their friendship during the apartheid years. Later, John explains that the owner was the driving force behind erecting the statue of Nelson Mandela at the entrance to the prison.

With the day's tour finished, we return to the hotel tired, but not satiated. We convince John to take us tomorrow to tour the Cape of Good Hope and share more of his South Africa with us.

Following a good morning from Solley, Mary and I climb into John's van where he tells us he talked by phone with his companion, visiting her family in Switzerland, last night. He told her about our day yesterday and explained it was like being with close friends instead of playing tour guide.

Heading south down the coast to the actual Cape, we stop at several places along the way, each with a special point of interest, most of them having a connection to the sea. John points out an old hotel in a seaside town and notes its historical significance having been the home base for many Antarctic explorations departing from Cape Town. I imagine adventurers packing for self-reliance before heading out across an angry sea to an inhospitable continent, unsure of what drives them and not knowing what they will experience or find.

Farther along, we stop by a commercial fishery where John explains South Africa's unusual fishing regulations. Commercial fishing is not allowed within five miles of the coast. In exchange for not fishing this exclusion zone and helping the government patrol for poachers, the government provides commercial fishermen with information on the location of the fishing stock and its migration. This helps sustain the local fish stock while protecting it and the ocean for future generations.

Another stop provides us the opportunity to visit the African penguin colony that mysteriously appeared a number of years ago. South Africa takes great care to accommodate the penguins in this beachside community, providing artificial nesting boxes to keep them safely confined in the protected beach area. As mysteriously as the penguins appeared, one day half the population left and nobody knows why or where they went. After lunch, we convince John to star in a video about the penguins and their special habitat for our website, http://www.bodaciousdreamexpeditions.com— part of my efforts to share these experiences with people around the world.

Driving the rugged coastline, we watch the landscape change from resort towns and expensive homes to desolate, natural areas before reaching the Cape of Good Hope. Staring out the window at the wild sea, I try to make good conversation. The winds are blowing 40 knots; the ocean is whipped into a frenzy, but the skies look welcoming, a deep blue, punctuated with fluffy clouds. While beautiful to the cellphone cameras around us, they intimidate me. I can't help think internally about beating into this weather to clear the southern tip of Africa a week from now. I'd be a fool to leave Cape Town for this punishment.

I feign nonchalance and a disinterested look at the wind and weather, not wanting Mary to notice my concern, but it's hard. We drive a bit farther, then tuck inland to cross the hills and circle back to Cape Town from behind Table Mountain. With the sea out of sight, it's easier for me to fake my cool. I can't lie when looking face to face with the sea.

A bit more than five years ago, I got the last center seat on a flight home from the east coast. By fate, Mary sat at the window. We didn't talk much, but at the end of the flight, we learned she lived a few doors down from my closest sailing friend. Our earliest dates weren't very smooth as our individual stubborn streaks of independence struggled for prominence and alignment, but we grew comfortable with the strength these traits provided our relationship. As we independently pursue our passions, it's comforting to know we each manage by ourselves and don't carry the desire to constrict each other's pathways. From the beginning, Mary has accepted my sailing and seems unconcerned about my safety. This makes it easier for me, though I still try to hide the anxiety I feel.

We stop at the large, Kirstenbosch Botanical Gardens where John's certification as a tour guide requires him to be able to talk in depth about the natural flora and fauna of South Africa. It's not long before his native expertise shines as he explains the various plants and how they thrive in his homeland. One tree in particular, called the *elephant plant*, earns its name by growing large enough to hide an elephant inside as it grazes on its leaves. The tree is the most carbon gobbling plant on the earth. I think of planting these everywhere and barring elephants from eating them.

At the end of the day, tired and fulfilled, I apologize for my ignorance about South Africa. My education ended when

Nelson Mandela was freed and the bad news stopped coming. I was stuck in 1990. John's stories brought us current, but I know there is still more to learn about this beautiful place.

The next days pass quickly for Mary and me as her time to leave and Tim's time to arrive crosses. We plan to climb Table Mountain, but with our time short, we take the cable car to the top and spend the day hiking the plateau. We leave Table Mountain and ultimately Cape Town with fond memories and a sincere vow to return one day.

* * *

With Mary on her way home, my attention turns to preparing *Bo* and prying us away from this beautiful place. Tim convinces me to haul *Bo* out of the water and check her keel. We find the nuts and bolts in perfect shape and no indication of a problem or any reason to worry. As *Bo* was lifted from the water, I understood my reluctance to haul her—I feared it would reveal a reason to stop the circumnavigation. I can now focus my efforts on escaping the seduction of Cape Town.

The final days pass quickly as Tim and I work to finish preparations. The most annoying and yet amusing, is humping 10 five-gallon containers of diesel fuel out the labyrinth of docks to Bo. If it's not blowing 25 or 30 in Cape Town, it's probably blowing 40 or 50. Every day is windy and problematic. With the winds at full strength, one section of the floating docks heel to a 30° slope, making the traverse carrying the jerry cans of fuel a bit crazy. Without the strength and agility of 20-year-old Marine recruits, Tim and I nearly go overboard with fuel cans in our hands.

Tim's flight leaves tonight, making today the only option for going to the top of the mast to install the repaired wind wand. With the help of another sailor, Tim cranks me up the mast as the winds gusts to 45 knots. Holding my tongue tightly between my teeth and wrapping my legs in a knot around the mast, I gingerly replace the wand—removing and replacing parts and screws while trying to ignore the wind. With the repaired wand in place, a check of the instruments shows that something is still wrong. Somewhere in the process, something is not right with the backup wand. I remove it and bring it back down to the deck.

Steve, the B & G technician, graciously returns to pick up the wand and repair it as Tim prepares to leave on the midnight flight and I continue preparing for departure, constantly reminding myself I have to leave—I have to leave.

The next morning, with the repaired wand in hand, Steve explains the delicate repair necessary at the top of the mast. I prepare to haul him up when he tells me, he doesn't do heights. Confused, I ponder the prudency of me doing this delicate and unfamiliar repair, but Steve assures me it's simple, and patiently talks me through the procedure, tool-by-tool, and step-by-step. The winds have calmed, but it still takes more than an hour to thread the delicate wires and pins into the plug. Completed, a check of the wand shows it works. I swap the tools for my camera and take a video from my perch atop the mast, sweeping in a 360° arc, of Cape Town, Table Mountain and the open ocean, committing my view to the memory of the hard drive before signaling Steve to lower me to the deck. With a deep breath, I plan to leave tomorrow.

* * *

In my room at the hotel, I sort and pack my gear and make a list of food to purchase before heading across the street to the grocery store. On the way, I'm distracted and stop in the bookstore to replenish my reading supplies. A number of titles on the discount table catch my eye, but I promised John Lawrence I'd purchase *A Long Walk to Freedom*. The three-inch-thick volume seems daunting, but given the endurance of the author,

I feel obliged to read it. I tackle the grocery store next, stocking up on dark chocolate, cookies, and a few nutritious items like apples, cheese, dry goods, and Biltong, an African form of jerky. As always, crossing one item off my list—*grocery shopping*, adds another item to it—*Get groceries to boat.*

Each item on the list represents a reason I can't leave and yet each item, when crossed from the list, ratchets my anxiety upward. Now, the night before leaving, I head back to the hotel burdened with groceries and books and needing some quiet time to calm down.

Breaking Free
from Cape Town's Seduction

December 20, 2013

I *walk through the hotel lobby, past the reception desk and toward the dining room just minutes after the sun drops behind Table Mountain. Passing through the doors and onto the patio, I stand behind the host waiting to catch his attention . . . I'm losing the battle. In front of us, beyond the harbor and city, the glow of the evening sun illuminates the diaphanous clouds cascading over the edge of Table Mountain. I wait courteously, respectful of the draw of the mountain when the host finally feels my presence and turns around. Apologizing, he explains that he watches the mountain every day and it's never the same. I too am in awe, and I acknowledge my understanding, indicating that I'm not in a hurry.*

The host motions me to a small table at the side of the patio with a perfect view of the mountain. We talk for a moment, him asking how my preparations are going and I explain: "I plan to depart in the morning for New Zealand. It's fitting I finish my day here, wrapped in the arms of Cape Town under the shoulders of Table Mountain."

Morning comes slowly. The curtains, left open, allow the light to wake me early. I slept in short bits during the night, drifting in and out of anxiety and woke at 3:00 am to make calls home to loved ones half a world away. Soon, I'll leave the hotel, Cape Town, the Royal Cape Yacht Club and harbor, bound for Wellington, New Zealand, a couple of months away, beyond another distant horizon.

My schedule for the day is tight but minimal. I plan to depart as soon as possible allowing for a short meeting at 8:00 a.m. with Steve, the B&G electronics technician who wants a short video for his website.

Packing slowly and checking email, I question my motives and ask myself, *"Why am I leaving now? Why not stay a bit longer? What can it hurt? Isn't the weather a problem?"* I search for a reasonable excuse to delay departure and enjoy more of the relaxed time in Cape Town while robotically forcing myself to continue through the list of preparations and ignore the distracting thoughts as best I can. One last check of the weather forecast confirms that today is the best day to depart with the fewest complications from the heavy, prevailing southeast winds. We'll have to beat for the next four or five days, but the morning should be calm, making it easy to get away from land.

The spring-loaded hotel room door shoves my overstuffed sea bags and me out into the hallway. The elevator dumps us at the front desk. I graciously thank the hotel staff and settle my bill. Nothing stalls me as I proceed by forcing confidence out the doors and asking Solly if he can arrange a cab to the yacht club. Solly grabs my bags, and asks, "Are you leaving—leaving Cape Town?"

"Yes, sailing for New Zealand," I answer. There's a genuine sadness in his words as he wishes me well and states, "Please return some day." Solly's been here every morning of my stay and we've become friends. We look forward to the time we'll cross tacks and exchange stories again.

Insistent, time continues to push, and each move on my part seems synchronized to my watch. Into the cab, to the yacht club, to the boat, load gear and set preparations in place. Subconsciously, I search for reasons to support my reluctance to leave, but nothing reasonable surfaces. I grab the local weather briefing from the yacht club and read it word for word—it's of no help. The report offers the same encouragement as the more advanced, sophisticated models I viewed on the Internet early this morning. There's a short window opening to get out beyond the harbor and away from land before the heavy southeast trades start blowing in the afternoon. I'm anxious to meet this timing, to avoid slow maneuvers around the harbor in heavy winds and to get offshore to deep, safe water before something goes wrong.

Steve arrives, bellowing, "Hello . . . I'll only take a moment," and then mikes me up. Setting his camera to record, we walk to the bow where he begins asking questions and suggesting feelings. "Are you feeling anxious?" I respond like an American politician, "There's always anxiety when I'm leaving; I'm never sure if it's remorse at leaving or the excitement of knowing I'm outward bound." I know I'm lying through my teeth. I know full well it's the remorse of leaving solid, predictable ground for the unknown hardships lying just beyond the first left hand turn outside the harbor. Excitement? I hope it's part of the mix, but right now, I'm pushing myself, struggling to overpower the reluctance to leave. It would be easier if I were pulled out to sea by a rip current of excitement.

The interview is over as quickly as Steve begins. In ten minutes, he's gone, and I'm alone with no other obstacles to delay me. Once again, I've wasted the last human contact I'll have for months to come.

I pull out my harness, set up the tethers and fill the water bottles—one for port and one for starboard. I *hank* on the Solent jib, clip on the *halyard* and tie on the *sheets*. I look over my list and walk around the boat. Everything seems ready; electronics are on; autopilot is on; chart plotter is on. I look at the sky and across at Table Mountain. The wind is calm and a light haze hangs in the distance. I start the motor and listen intently before stepping off to make one last run to the yacht club. I need to be certain no world war or pending doom requires staying put in this beautiful harbor.

I want that strange sense of relief that comes when delayed in a harbor, especially by a reason other than *"I just don't want to leave."* Something beyond my control, like bad weather, stalled equipment or some other unanticipated issue. It's the same feeling I had when I was a kid, waking up to a foot of snow and learning school was closed for the day—a free day. Even better now would be two or three free days.

I enter the head for one last civilized chance . . . nothing comes of it. I return to my game plan and head back toward *Bo* while muttering the reasons for leaving.

With one last look around and everything appearing in order, I begin removing the mooring lines. The same lines that moored my dream to the concrete pier in Bermuda hold us to the wooden docks of Cape Town. In Bermuda I couldn't wait to leave, to get away cleanly from the threatening concrete . . . Today, I take my time, making sure all is well. No one is watching, forcing me to raise bravado to surface from an empty well. No one worries about my future or envies my existence.

In synchronicity with the untying of the last dock line, I push *Bo* off, step on board, and reach for the helm and throttle. We motor forward but can't make the radius necessary to miss the dock in front of us. We stop, back up, and proceed, but again, the narrowness of the fairway hampers us, forbidding the tight turn necessary to clear the pontoon. I poke slowly forward to the boats ahead and then run to the bow to push *Bo* to port before scurrying back to the cockpit to back up again. Cautiously, and with a strange, confident calmness, I back within inches of the boat behind and reach over the rail to add a final touch of human advantage to the turning radius. In this moment, I recognize a strange contrast . . . Two-and-a-half weeks ago, I slipped into the harbor so simply and cleanly, without fanfare, but today, I stumble through my departure. Is it me, or does *Bo* not want to leave either? We continue up the fairway, make the left hand turn to the outer harbor and proceed through the calm waters past the large freighters with the strange ports of call written on their sterns.

Beyond the harbor in the traffic separation lanes, I begin setting *Bo's* sails, preloaded with reefs, expecting within an hour to be pounding into 30-knot winds, hunkered down and wishing we hadn't left. We stay clear of the oncoming ships, but one intimidating call from a captain admonishes me for my course and disregard for protocol in the shipping lanes. Though tempered, I don't respond. We aren't in his way.

An hour later, beyond the shipping traffic, with open water over a 270° horizon, I call upon Otto to drive us away from the harbor and shoreline. I feel as if I've forged a reason to leave a lover behind. What purpose and reason was I serving sailing around the world alone? There's no Global Ocean Race. Was I resolving anything? I remind myself I'm teaching kids and bringing the experience to people at home. Advocating my importance in the world, the skies cloud over and the sea turns gray. I wait intently for the winds to increase.

The afternoon passes, the light dissipates and nighttime arrives. We continue pushing out to sea slowly under reefed sails, expecting the inevitable increase in wind and waves. At midnight, sufficiently offshore, I shake out the reef in the sails, causing two things to rise in direct contrast—speed and anxiety. Morning dawns with no further change in the wind.

I set a waypoint off the southern tip of South Africa, an imaginary point free of the bastardly, insensitive southeast gales. With no sign of the gales, I begin to worry we've slipped out of Cape Town unnoticed by the sea, the winds and the universe. If we continue sneaking for another day, we might not see the strong winds . . . but I know better.

The day passes uneventfully, the skies clear and the sailing improves. Embarrassed by my timid actions of the previous day— the reluctance to leave, the search for excuses and the reefed sails, we sail east and a bit south, heading down to 40°S to meet with the favorable westerly winds. Along with the favored winds come relentless cold fronts and endless miles of monotony, loneliness, freeze-dried meals, wet hands, cold feet and the constant query of self-worth and why.

* * *

I'm below deck when I hear the familiar hum of an engine thumping through the water, vibrating *Bo's* hull like a drum. I jump on deck to see a colorfully painted fishing boat passing a few, safe boat lengths away. Old, wooden, and obviously captained by a proud seaman, his artwork, and choice of bright colors his personal expression on the water. I saw him earlier, and after checking his course and speed determined he was safely out of range. The close crossing surprises me. He must have altered his course to take a closer look at *Bo*.

"Capt'n, Capt'n, Capt'n" I hear over the VHF radio.

"Dis is de fishen' boat."

"Hello fishing boat," I respond. "This is the sailing boat Bodacious Dream." "Ah…" he says in a beautiful, lyrical South African accent … "It's a beauuutiful day to be heade-dout. Where are you headed for?" I realize there must be few, if any, sailing vessels heading east by south these days and this is an unusual site for him.

"I am headed to New Zealand," I respond.

"Ah …very nice," he replies. "I've been fishen up north and now have to move south for better fish. You will have a nice sail. It is summer now; the weather should be no storms." I thank him briefly.

"You will see de beautiful bio-luminescence on your trip. It is so beautiful out here. It flows in de wake of my boat every night … You will enjoy," he returns.

"Have a safe journey my friend," I respond appreciatively. The radio goes silent. The hum of his motor fades away behind me as I watch intently for another fifteen minutes until he's gone. I continue staring in his direction, confirming the reason I sleep in short increments; the visible horizon is only 15-20 minutes away. Maybe I'm relishing human contact, not wanting to let go until I have no choice. Maybe the fisherman altered his course, himself missing human contact. I turn and look forward, check the course, Otto, and the wind. New Zealand—8,000 miles away, six or seven weeks, ten cold fronts, maybe more. I sit down, look aft at the late afternoon sun, and let my mind drift away. It's December 23, 2013 . . . Tomorrow is Christmas Eve.

Eastward to the Southern Ocean

*T*he weather strategy for this leg dictates staying above the lows and below the highs. The lows are the intense systems sending cold fronts north with strong winds and huge waves. The highs send calmer head winds. If we're too far south, the wind and seas will be frighteningly brutal. Too far north and the winds will be light and on the nose.

If I were racing the Global Oceans Race as originally planned, we would adjust the strategy to sail as far south as the *ice gate* rules allow, busting along in the huge waves driven by the strong winds. This southerly route not only has more wind, but it's shorter because of the *great circle route*. However, while the winds often rise to 30–40 knots, providing great boat speeds, if we stretched a string from Cape Town to Wellington, New Zealand, representing the shortest great circle sailing course, we would have to sail across the continent of Antarctica. Finding the right balance between course and danger defines the nickname for these races, *"The Sprint Around Antarctica."*

Vigilant race organizers set waypoints for competitors to honor. These *ice gates* keep aggressive competitors from pushing their luck, sailing south into iceberg-laden seas in search of more wind and a shorter distance to enhance their chance of victory. For us, without the press of the race, we'll stay conservatively between 40 and 45° S and not worry about a shorter distance or the advantages of more wind.

Along with the usual weather in the last forecast from shore were small, intense *cyclones* around Madagascar off the Eastern coast of Africa. Ken schooled me on those very intense weather systems that are similar to a hurricane. Their centers show up in magenta on the color-coded wind charts. The magenta color is indicative of fierce winds in excess of 60 knots. It is no wonder magenta is not one of the favorite colors of sailors clothing.

Ken explains that typically, these cyclones dissipate before moving below 40°S and almost never travel east of 80° longitude. It will be a couple of weeks before I'm clear of these parameters. Ken presses his point for us to sail quickly through this region; worried the longer we take to sail east and clear 80° longitude, the more chance we tempt fate. I understand his apprehension. I have no interest in chancing fate or playing tag with a cyclone in the Southern Ocean where help is not available.

We plot our encounter with the first cold front, still a few days away, as *Bo* works east along 40° S. Tutored by the Atlantic Ocean cold fronts, *Bo*, Otto, Franklin and I are prepared for the assault and find our rhythm quickly with the approaching system. The winds come steady and warm from the Northeast then back to the North as *Bo* reaches along in the sunshine of the Southern Ocean. 45–50°F temperatures are common with the radiant sun providing additional warmth when sheltered from the wind. When the winds back to the NW, I calculate the timing of the frontal passage and prepare for the range of sail changes required as the unsettled weather sneaks up from behind.

The winds will build into the 20s, the skies will become cloudy, and squalls will approach us from behind. The first *reef*, a reduction in the size of the mainsail, becomes necessary at 17 knots of wind, requiring a series of interesting, coordinated movements.

The first task is to uncoil the *hank* of main *halyard* to the predetermined mark for the first reef and ready it to pay out smoothly when it's time to drop the mainsail. Second, is to free up a winch and wrap the line for the first reef's *clew*, (the aft corner of the sail) onto its *drum*. I then clip my tether to the *jackline* (the tubular, nylon safety line running from the bow to the stern along the side deck of the boat,) running along the center of the boat from the *companionway dodger* forward to the mast allowing me to traverse the route safely.

To start the reef, I release the halyard and allow the mainsail to drop to the mark on the halyard. With the wind behind us, the mainsail is pressed against the rigging, and resists falling freely. To secure the new *tack point* at the mast, the mainsail must come down six feet. With the 2:1 mechanical advantage, this equates to 12 feet of halyard plus a bit more for good measure.

To help gravity overcome the pressure of wind and friction on the mainsail, I crank the *clew line* on the winch to pull the sail downward. The hesitant main, unable to maintain the equilibrium keeping it aloft, drops a chunk at a time. Once far enough down, I step up onto the companionway dodger and scramble forward to the mast to undo the *Cunningham*—a small block and tackle used to tension the *leading edge* of the main sail. I lead the Cunningham through the new tack point of the first reef and reset the tension, securing the tack to the *gooseneck* where the boom connects to the mast.

I slide back along the coach roof, hop down into the cockpit, and finish cranking in the clew reef line on the winch. The clew lines for the second and third reef dangle off the end of the boom and need to be straightened before focusing on the mainsail halyard and hoisting the sail to the desired height and tension.

Smoothly done, this may take fifteen minutes. If I forget to release enough halyard, or mess up something else, I double the work and often quadruple the time. In 17-kt winds, the reef has no adverse effect on the speed and significantly increases the stability. Unusual for many sailboats, *Bo's* design is more easily driven with a reef, resulting in a higher average boat speed.

As the winds of this cold front continue to increase to the high 20s, and squalls become imminent, the next reduction of sail area is to reef the *Solent Jib*, the largest jib hanked onto the forestay at the bow of the boat. The French sailors, who developed the Class 40 design rule, call this sail a Solent. In the U.S., we call it a genoa, jenny, or J1.

Reefing the Solent is more physical, wet, and exciting. When completed properly, there are few incidences of foul language, deck pounding, and head banging. However, when I do it right, the experience isn't as edgy and exciting as when I miss something and things go awry.

Full foul weather gear is necessary when reefing the Solent, including a PFD (personal floatation device), PLB (personal location beacon), harness, and tether. A knife in a pocket is smart, preferably reached by my weakest hand first but still available to my dominate hand. The reason for this is my dominate hand may get tangled or be in use and my weakest hand will need to cut the line. At night, a headlamp and a pocket flashlight become jewelry. With those items securely in the pockets of my foul weather gear and tied on with lanyards, I load up with sail ties. It's difficult to stuff sail ties into the extreme ocean gear I wear, so, I tie one around my left thigh, one around my right, one around my waste and loop one around my neck. I leave the one around my neck untied, fearing a snag might choke me. It hangs loose, blowing in the wind and slapping me in the face like an annoying jester. All geared up, I could jump up and down like a special ops agent checking for rattles, but it's not necessary out here in the middle of nowhere. No one is around who would care.

I release the halyard, allowing the Solent to fall the prescribed distance. I then clip my tether onto the jackline, and head to the bow, while fighting the erratic motion from the waves attempting to fling me off *Bo* like a rag doll from a bucking bronco. When I reach the shrouds, midway to the bow, my forward progress is blocked, requiring me to clip my short tether (three feet long) forward of the shrouds and release my long tether (six feet) from behind the shrouds to continue. Hunched down or on my hands and knees, especially when the motion is vicious and violent, I shimmy forward to the point of the bow and move my short tether from the jackline to a solid point, preventing me from being thrown no further than the length of three feet.

I grab the luff (forward edge) of the Solent and pull heartedly until six feet of the sail comes down and I can secure the new tack point to the snap shackle on the bow. It sounds easy, but battling the wind-powered sailcloth is a struggle, especially with worn, tired hands. Once down, I throw my leg and knee over the sail to keep it from voluntarily wiggling up the forestay in the pressing wind and burrow into the folds of stiff sailcloth to unclip the original tack point and clip on the new. While this is happening, Otto drives, and instead of avoiding waves as a human helmsman might, he punches into them, shoveling green water over me. I expect to be doused three or four times before the final clip of the tack is made.

At five horizontal points along the reef, I gather up the baggy sailcloth and secure it with a sail tie. One at a time, from the tack at the bow to the clew at the back of the Solent, I bunch up the sail cloth, pull the tie under and around to a loop on the front of the sail and tie it tight enough to control the bunched sail cloth, but loose enough to allow the cloth to move freely as the sail breaths. Moving along, I count . . . One . . . two . . . three . . . four, and finally five. The count from one to five seems to always coincide with waves washing over the bow.

With the reef points secure, we change the *jib sheets* by first untying the *lazy sheet* (loose, unused one) and tie it to the new clew higher up on the sail. While tying on this lazy sheet, the sail is still controlled by the sheet in use. Once the lazy sheet is tied on, I use it to pull against the power of the wind in the sail to slacken the *controlling sheet* enough to untie it. Once untied, the sail fills to the extent the lazy sheet allows. If I've allowed too much or too little, I have to return to the cockpit, hand-over-hand, tether-over-tether to adjust the sheets to make it work.

Once I've made the trip back and forth to the cockpit a few times to ease the sheet, I mark it and try to remember to do it right the first time. With the tack now clipped in, the five reef points secured and the sheets tied on, I stand along the leeward rail and hook my knees under the life line to lever my torso over the rushing water alongside the boat and reach out to secure the baggy looseness of the old clew. This is as precarious as it sounds. Without firm control over the mental jitters that arrive while hanging out over rushing water, thousands of miles from anywhere in the world, the task is difficult. I must keep my mind quiet to finish. Allowably, after countless reefing exercises, the procedure is second nature to me and I am comfortable watching the water rush along at ten or twelve knots. However, more than once, with the waves blasting over the bow, tucked into the sailcloth and clinging to this bucking bronco, I've had my hydrostatic PFD inflate. The automatic inflator is designed to inflate when the unit is held under water to a certain static pressure. This can only mean I've been under water long and deep enough for the hydrostatic trigger to presume I need assistance.

If all goes well, which it usually does, I end up back in the cockpit, sail ties still tied around my legs and only a damp collar to show for my work. If things go pear shape as the Brits say, which seems to happen most often after dark, I can end up with no sail ties, my knife dangling from a lanyard and my headlamp down across one eye, looking like a pirate leaving The Schooner Wharf Bar at closing time just before dawn.

As the winds continue to increase, gusting over 30, with embedded squalls lashing us, it's necessary to reduce the mainsail to a second and third reef. If it really gets bad, there's one more reef after that I call a *Storm Stub*.

The procedure for reducing the mainsail through these reefs is similar, but the degree of difficulty increases proportionately with the rise in wind speed. Wind pressures do not increase in an even progression but exponentially. A 50-kt wind is three times as powerful as a 30-knot wind. This additional pressure and friction against the mainsail and rigging requires a purchase system to haul the main sail down.

My first attempts at this were rudimentary, and after considering the serious probability of being torn from my death grip on the mast and left dangling overboard, I improved the system. It doesn't eliminate the gymnastics required, but by nature, minimizes the time hanging by burning, numb muscles while the sea pokes fun at me.

The process requires clambering out the cockpit and over the coach roof dodger to the mast and clipping my tether at the base using the 6-foot length—I need the mobility the long tether allows. With a length of one-quarter-inch line clasped in my teeth, I climb a few feet above the deck and wrap a leg around the mast with the skill of an experienced acrobat in the circus. With one set of fingertips resolutely holding on, jammed into the small crevasse between the aluminum track and the carbon mast, I free the other set to take the line from my clenched teeth and weave it through a cringle—a grommet in the mainsail. Threading the end through the opening requires pushing the line against the forces of gravity, wind, and momentum—a synchronized team fighting me. I'm well aware that pushing rope is a futile effort, but it's actually possible when encouraged by the snarling face of an approaching squall.

To get the line to work with me, I lay in wait for a change in the direction of *Bo's* momentum. When the momentum momentarily turns in my favor, I push the line, tricking gravity, and thread it through the opening. With the muscles of my resolute grip burning, I grab at the tip of the line and pull it to my clutching teeth. When I'm done, I climb down from the perch and go about the process of securing the line around the winch on the mast and crank the main down a few feet.

Each reef takes three and sometimes four chunks of effort to bring the tack point down and under control. Fun? Sorta . . . but only as long as I keep my mind from sprinting off, uncontrolled and frightened by the obvious stupidity of this nonsense thousands of miles from land. After one experience giving me an unobstructed view of life on the other side of the edge, I incorporate a carabineer, used like a grappling hook to secure the attachment. This improvement significantly lessens the time and recklessness necessary to succeed.

Holiday Depression

The winds continue to increase, rising through 30 knots as the clouds become dense, dark, and intimidating. Ken at Commanders' gave me the location and speed of the advancing front so I can calculate and prepare for the abrupt change in wind direction from NW to SW. When the cold front passes, the temperature drops, the winds shift, and the sails jibe to the other side of the boat. Jibing throws the boom abruptly from angling toward the starboard stern quarter (corner) to the opposite, port quarter.

When we encountered the first front passing in the southern Atlantic, I noticed the wind speed dropping just moments before the front arrived. I now look for this brief indicator, and when the winds drop below twenty, use it to my advantage by gybing the boat on purpose. Now on the other board, I wait for the abrupt change in wind direction and simply adjust the course.

Once the front passes, the waves grow larger with the increased density and speed of the cold air. We sail, making good speed and direction as the front moves on to the NE. The hours turn into days; the winds stabilize, then gradually decrease and shift forward along the southern points of the compass. SW becomes SSW, becomes S and then SE. As the winds veer around the compass to the forward quarter, the waves follow, the pounding increases, and the sailing is miserable. With the wind and waves on the bow, we hunker down and wait for the front to move far enough to the NE to allow the friendly northern winds to flow in behind it and return us to pleasant sailing conditions.

The gray of the Southern Ocean becomes intoxicating as I stare, searching for the slightest changes in her expressions and archive them in my data bank, hoping I can subconsciously learn to detect her feelings and moods. The days flow by, punctuated only by the passing of daylight and the routine inspections of the boat and myself.

Nights are strangely different. The horizon comes forward as daylight abates. My gaze turns upward to the expansive horizon illuminated by the stars above. I am awed by the immensity of the universe and struggle for a comfortable feeling of ease here. I try to assert myself into the endlessness of heavens above. Actually, all around me—I want to be allowed here. But for me, it's like stepping into a large party of people. I yearn to find a place and be accepted. I struggle, night after night to find comfort, my eyes wandering the universe, wanting to be welcomed, allowed to pass and be respected. But am I? I question endlessly.

Eventually, I turn away, unable to hold my gaze with the stare returned from the heavens, and I turn inward. Looking down toward my feet, I'm fascinated with the glowing bioluminescence passing in the wake of my travel. As plankton sparkles behind *Bo*, the distance from Cape Town in miles and days increases. I've drawn a line south from Madagascar and farther east, down from India, the western tip of Australia, then Tasmania, and ultimately, New Zealand. Time and distance equations tease me and I am grateful for the diversion.

Though fantasizing about landing at these places, I focus intently on 80° W longitude, directly below India and safely beyond the grasp of the cyclones of the western Indian Ocean. This line of demarcation lies 2,000 miles from here, two weeks of sailing, and three or four cold fronts. I figure 1,000 miles a week is a good gauge of progress. I'll do better as we reach the westerlies and cold fronts, but this first week from Cape Town has been less than good. I've made only 700 miles. We continue sailing east and south toward solid westerlies, our fortunes increasing each day.

* * *

I am tired and sluggish, an unusual state given the excitement and anticipation of crossing another wide expanse of the earth's oceans. I should be vibrant with anticipation and energized by the new experience, but depression consumes me.

I find myself searching inside my head and body for some answer. In self-preservation, I sacrifice a book overboard that I bought in Cape Town. I don't recall the name of the book, but its subject was *heroes*. I read intently the story of the amazing man who fended off genocide in Rwanda; the story exacerbated my depression with painful examples of the brutality of humanity. I couldn't read it any longer and had to discard it.

I replace the book with *A Long Walk to Freedom* and begin the epic story of Nelson Mandela's life. I'm amazed holding this 3-inch-thick book, remarking to myself how my life would barely fill a 10-page pamphlet.

I stare at the ocean, searching for the root of the strange feelings stirring inside me. I've come to the sea many times to look for answers and reasons to questions of why. Somewhere, in the ever-flowing water, where winds seldom stop, where fish swim for a lifetime and birds float effortlessly, I find strength and answers. I write my woes in the ship's log and date the page numerically, December 24, 2013. I realize—it's Christmas Eve.

* * *

Years ago, I fostered a need to celebrate Christmas Eve in my own way. Our family, like most American families, celebrated the holidays with gusto. Christmas Eve was almost as exciting as Christmas Day. When our family fractured, Christmas Eve became another day, and Christmas Day came and went with much less fanfare.

I began to spend Christmas Eve with friends, and when the night ended, they would head to church to celebrate Midnight Mass, and I'd leave for home. One year, with a strong need to celebrate in my own way with nature, I went for a walk in the winter woods.

On a winter's night, the woods can be spooky or inviting, full of crisp air, moonbeams, and dancing shadows as the winds sway the empty trees. From that year forward, on Christmas Eve, late at night, I walk out the door and into my own sanctuary of nature, and give reverence to the world.

Though usually alone, on occasion close friends, either visiting or alone themselves, join me to walk the beach, up through the dunes and into the woods, and often, somewhere along the way, we begin humming *Silent Night*. I resolved to walk late at night on Christmas Eve wherever I was.

Last year, I walked the decks of *Bodacious Dream* as she sailed from Portugal across the Atlantic toward the Caribbean islands. Now, having found the reason for my depression, I'm anxious to walk *Bo's* decks here in the Southern Ocean.

* * *

Thinking back to sailing into Cape Town, I recall the excitement of a new destination, the vibrancy of the city, the fresh conversations with home and the energy of people. It's all gone, displaced by a different rhythm and noise—the rhythm of the ocean. I don't think I gave myself enough time to recover in Cape Town. To recover from the mental stress of being alone, the physical stress of sailing the ocean, to fill my reserves and yet, here I am again, alone at sea. In Cape Town, I searched for reasonable excuses not to leave; now I see why. I'm weakened by loneliness and fatigued by the distance from life.

I think of stopping into a harbor for dinner—the feel of solid ground, the noise of people laughing and carrying on, the smells of strange foods wafting on the evening breeze while exploring new streets. My eyes open abruptly and I laugh aloud as my mind slips back onboard . . . There's no stopping, there's no returning, there's 80° W longitude, Australia, Tasmania and New Zealand. When I arrive in Wellington, there will be plenty of cold beer, laughing people and fresh food.

I set a new goal, to read *A Long Walk to Freedom* before New Zealand. I would never set a goal like this on shore; it's too much to read. Out here, I break it into 100-page increments. New Zealand taunts me the same . . . 8,000 miles is too far to sail; I divide it into 1,000-mile increments.

I adjust my boundaries on board, my destinations, my goals, and bring them closer, more easily obtained until I can gain strength and perspective. I set lasagna dinners for Sundays, rice pilaf with canned salmon for lunch tomorrow, beef stroganoff with Worcestershire sauce and fresh ground pepper tonight, and Hershey's Dark Chocolate Kisses. Otto drives, Franklin watches quietly, and *Bo* sails effortlessly. I am the one struggling to carry on, to do my share, and follow these fine spirits.

* * *

Pushing past the waypoint at 1,000 miles from Cape Town, I feel the accomplishment of a goal, and my mood notches upward one point. Days later, I note in my log: "*The holidays have passed. January 3, 2014, Latitude 41° 27' S, Longitude 50° 15' E—day 14 since leaving Cape Town.*" I no longer calculate the distance from Cape Town; more optimistically, I calculate the distance to New Zealand at 5,658 miles. The winds are fair and mixed. I point *Bodacious Dream* towards 42.5° S looking for more pressure in the stronger westerly winds further south. Three cold fronts have passed since departing, only one has been heavy. Two cyclones—Bruce and Amara came and went long before we reached their vicinity. Bijesa is building 500 miles east of us, but quite far to the north. Her path is predicted to be S and SW and not expected to give us trouble. The sailing is uneventful. The winds are manageable, moving about the westerly quadrants of the compass, allowing us to make reasonable progress east.

We continue heading south, below 42° S; staying above 42° S means being swallowed by the light winds of a high-pressure system expanding to our north. The pages of *A Long Walk to Freedom* turn as the miles flow by. In my office, leaning up against the companionway door, I look aft beyond the tillers and raft of fuel cans, beyond the nonfunctional satellite dome, and out to the west. The sky behind us is forever changing. There are days when the sky is so clear that the sun is hot, and others when the clouds are so dense, they bring sadness and chills. Some days the clouds are diaphanous, and on others, they completely block any radiance from the sun. This is a reminder of the constant flow of energy on earth, dynamically sculpting the continents and turning evaporated salt water into life-sustaining fresh water.

Seabirds, like these forces, are a constant. Floating endlessly back and forth, banking left to right and then back again—rising on the wind is bouncing off the grand ocean swells, or converting the centrifugal whip of a tight turn to gain altitude. Persistently, these seabirds drift back and forth, like skilled surgeons sewing up the wound we leave in the ocean as *Bo* passes. I hope our passing isn't wounding the sea. I am careful with my garbage, discarding only biodegradables and the occasional, paperback book.

At dawn, I walk *Bodacious Dream*'s deck to the bow and back, inspecting for damage or wear from another night of solid sailing. On the bow, I come eye-to-eye with an unfortunate flying fish, lying lifeless on the decks. He probably panicked as we passed in the dark night, taking flight in the wrong direction and crossing in front of *Bo*, but misjudging the distance necessary to clear. Sometimes I hear these guys land, their erratic flopping and slapping makes quite a racket on the drum like hull. When the noise ends, I wonder if they've flipped back into the sea. If necessary, I go on deck to set them free; unfortunately, I didn't hear this one.

As part of my routine walk, I look aloft to inspect the rig and notice the mainsail shape is unusual. Examining closer, I see the top two batten cars have pulled from the track on the mast. The sail looks ok, but it's unacceptable. Losing the use of the mainsail would be the equivalent of losing the engine in a car. I study what I can with my bare eyes then grab the binoculars for a closer look. What I see tells me the cars have pulled from the track and the track has been damaged. The sea state makes it difficult to stabilize the binoculars for a clear, close, inspection, so I grab my camera, take a couple of pictures and load them onto the computer. I zoom in for a closer, more stable look. The image is grainy, but I see the problem clearly enough to know I need to resolve this now.

I'll have to drop the mainsail, remove the damaged cars from the top, and replace them with less worn cars near the bottom of the sail. Unfortunately, with the damage to the track, we'll need to be reefed perpetually until New Zealand. While this will be slow in the lighter airs, most of the time, in the Southern Ocean, it will be fine. I'll have to adjust my expectations for sailing in moderate winds and only use the full main in the lightest winds, balancing risk and reward.

Armed with a box wrench and Allen key tucked in my pocket, I lower the mainsail to swap the cars. The bouncing and bumps concern me enough to go slowly with the work. A dropped screw or a wrench flicked overboard will drastically alter my life. With the main down on deck, my inspection reveals the top two cars have lost the inner wear surfaces, making the tolerances too sloppy to keep them on the track in strong winds. I inspect the other cars, find the best two, and swap them with the two damaged ones. In doing this, I create a tavern puzzle— swapping cars up and down and loading them on the track until I've placed the two damaged ones at the bottom of the sail, better ones where I've taken the best ones from, and the best ones on top.

Satisfied, I re-hoist the mainsail. With the sail at the top reef point, the top car aligns with the damaged section of track. Not willing to risk further damage to the track or additional losses, I resign to *double-reefing* in all but the lightest conditions until we reach Wellington. This is not an insurmountable setback, after all, we aren't racing, and the winds are often in the mid-20s where two reefs could be considered prudent. In the lulls between cold fronts, we'll need to sail reefed for a day or more, costing us a knot of speed. I calculate the loss at maybe 25 to 50 miles per week and decide it's insignificant.

I chuckle inside. A week ago, with my mind sad and lonely, I would have found this disheartening. Today, it's not so bad. I must be back at home on the sea and this will keep me here a bit longer. "It is a nice day, isn't it?" I ask aloud looking across the beautiful ocean. "Yes," I reply. "It really is a good day in my life."

* * *

The weather forecast shows another cold front approaching and suggests the same routine. Front approaches, winds build from the NW to 20-30 knots, higher in the squalls. The front passes, abruptly shifting the winds to the SW and we continue on our way. Commanders' forecast points me back north toward 40° S. This time the better winds are to the north. The tropical cyclone named Bijesa, up north near Madagascar, is tracking to the southeast, heading to 75-80° longitude. We are safe, 1,000 miles west at 60°. As we sail, daylight and darkness pass one another, and I amuse myself asking the obvious question: Which one came first?

This part of the journey seems like the middle days of my life; they carry on without distinction, years passing in the blink of an eye. Offshore, weeks go by with nothing more eventful than minor punctuation marks, passing a waypoint, a weather front, a small repair, or page 300 of a book. Nothing seems any more significant than putting one mile in front of the other. I am a seaman, this has become my life, and I've become numb to the uniqueness of the journey. Even the incomprehensible heavens above no longer frighten me. A week, and another 1,000 miles have passed since New Year's.

* * *

Commanders' weather report changes slightly. The high has moved north, a small low has developed south at 43° S latitude. Winds will increase tonight to 25–35 knots. Tomorrow, 35–50. About this time tomorrow, the low will pass and the winds will fade to 20–30 knots for the rest of the day. Another cold front lines up on final approach for the following day.

* * *

The instruments atop the mast, reporting wind information to the navigation instruments below decks have been giving me fits since leaving Cape Town. I override them by calibrating the apparent wind manually depending on which jibe we're on. This provides some semblance of true wind direction until the wind and course change. I back this up with a simple analog system installed on the stern rail, using a small batten, a piece of yarn and some tape. Like the days of yore, I tape the yarn to the tip of the four-foot batten and then tape the batten to the port rail. I watch the yarn flowing in the wind and gauge its relative angle to *Bo's* compass heading. I use this information to reset the manual calibrations and point *Bo* to the proper wind angle with regard to the waves. This replaces the standard *Windex*, which is gone from the top of the mast. Windexes don't like long, offshore journeys, often abandoning ship during the first storm. It's not the best of situations, but it's simple, reliable, and the time spent playing the mental calibration game is a welcome distraction.

As we sail along, I determine the necessary amount of calibration by studying the direction of the yarn on the batten and make an experienced guess at the angle of the apparent wind in relationship to *Bo's* heading. This sometimes involves my hands pointing in different directions, like two fighter pilots talking about a midair dogfight. Using trial and error, I punch in various percentages of either left or right correction until the apparent angle becomes an acceptable, estimated number matching the analog yarn on the batten. I quickly jot down the true wind direction and speed, and cross-reference these numbers with my human senses. By constantly making small mental adjustments, I can track the wind to a certain degree as the angles change and the calibration slips.

When the wind builds into the 30s, the speed and direction of the wind becomes less important, and sailing *Bo* to her best course in sync with the flow of the wind and waves is paramount. With thousands of miles to our destination, being off course 30 or 40 degrees for half a day isn't cause for alarm. We are still sailing toward New Zealand regardless of the deviation from course.

The sails are set and ready for the onslaught of seas pushed ahead of the approaching cold front. A thorough check of the boat and gear is needed, so I walk forward, inspect the bow, and look up at the mast. Okay with the gear on deck and the cars on the mainsail track, I drop below and perform the same ritual throughout the cabin, crawling forward to check the lashings holding gear in place, and for water in the compartments along the way. I crawl aft to check the stern lazarette and stop to listen to Otto's hydraulic drive. It sounds fine, but I decide to switch the rams and test the other pilot to assure we still have redundancy. On the way back, I stop and place my weathered hand on the keel bolts and feel my father's hand on my shoulder. The bolts and marks haven't changed since the Atlantic. With everything to my liking, *Bo* and I prepare to hunker down for the brunt of the storm.

The winds increase throughout the day and the reefs go in systematically. *Bo* sails wonderfully, just as she's designed to do. As each hour passes, I check the boat for signs of wear, water ingress and fatigue, and then cross that hour off the list. The routine is comforting and keeps me alert in what is otherwise an endless expanse of gray skies, whistling winds, flowing seas, swallowing time, and building a complacent depression. When the winds climb beyond 24 knots, the halyards begin to slap the mast—this harmonic metronome is a well-worn formality of storm sailing.

The winds build through the storm and reach out to touch 40 knots. Otto drives, surfing down huge slopes of gray water capped by frothy turbulence. I sit crouching like a lion ready to pounce on its prey—*Bo's* tiller just inches away. Otto surfs and the speedo climbs to 20 knots and beyond. As time goes on, I relax my stance and take these adrenaline-spiked moments in stride.

Waves approach from three directions—directly behind us, off the stern quarter, and on occasion, abruptly broadside. I'm caught off guard, unaware, as one picks us up in an instant—*Bo*, Otto, Franklin, and me— and tosses us to port like ragdolls kicked to the curb. We stop hard on our port beam as heavy green water washes over and through the cockpit. Below, loose gear from the starboard side flies across the cabin, unimpeded, until reaching the port side. After steadying ourselves and checking things on deck, I pull the sharpie pen from its snug holder and make another mark on the cabin top. There are ten marks in a row . . . two groups of four with the fifth slashed diagonally across them. Below this row are two distinctly separate marks. The score so far: ten significant waves, two near knockdowns. Despite the score, we continue closing in on New Zealand, now less than 5,000 miles away. The closest land, maybe India, remains 1,500 miles away, the equivalent of the distance between Denver and New York; a week and a half by sea.

The winds ease and then rebuild. The day and hour are no longer obvious. I keep watch, check the boat, and cross numbers off my list while wind and waves continue their journey, circling the world on the open highway of the Southern Ocean. For short periods they ease, then build again. Now, they seem to be easing.

We're over-reefed for the pressure, but night is coming, fatigue is heavy and I need down time. Here alone, there's no one to play to, no one to impress, and no one to hand the watch. I think it's been three days . . . It's insignificant. Duration is measured by day and night passing, by peak winds, abating winds, by waves, near knockdowns and fatigue. So far, I prove to be the weakest of the entities onboard.

We push past 78° longitude. Only two degrees are left, about 100 miles to the line of demarcation at 80°. Beyond this milestone, I should be safe from the threat of cyclones and nearer the Land of Oz—Australia.

The front continues, passing east and easing, turning the seas into a sloppy mess, unsupported by the wind's pressure. Otto drives, *Bo* dictates sail changes, sailing clumsily under an unbalanced sail plan in the lighter wind and large waves. I'm tired, lazy, and slow to shake out the reefs. We sail along at 8–12 knots as I relax my subconscious focus and try to recover in the calming weather. As things settle down, rest comes easy. I take naps, eat snacks, and lie in wait for the next front.

"A Cyclone is Headed
Right at You"

January 11, my report to Commanders' reads: *Position:
39°45'S, 81°30' E. I am now beyond 80° and in
the safe zone. Winds: 18–35 knots in squalls. Wind Direction 285°
NW, Boat Speed: 8–10 knots.*

Commanders' answer reads: Big Change between 21h and
22h tomorrow, winds will back . . . jibe to starboard—winds
15–20 knots. Head south. Monday, expect front to pass, Winds
25-35 with gusts to 40 knots. Winds from 320–340°. Front passes
early Tuesday and winds will ease to 15–20 knots. Going north is
okay . . . up to 38° S latitude max.

January 12, Ken reports the same weather, but extends the
forecast to Thursday and Friday. He finishes his report over the
satellite phone. "Dave, we have to talk about Thursday and Friday.
A cyclone is coming your way." Another cyclone is northwest and
moving southeast, if it maintains speed and course; it will intercept
you on Thursday night or Friday daylight at about 95° E, 40° S.

"But Ken, you said 80° was safe." I retort sharply, and demand
he change the course of the weather.

"It usually is... but not this time. You must keep your progress
up; we need to get you east of the intercept line. I project this to
be 700-900 miles east of you. You can't slow down or you will be
on the wrong side and swallowed by the cyclone."

In hurricane or cyclone terms, there are navigable and
un-navigable semicircles. In the southern hemisphere, systems
rotate opposite the northern hemisphere and the navigable
semicircle is on the northeastern side of the cyclone. We need
to sail under and past it, the equivalent of darting across six lanes

of traffic to clear ahead of a passing semi-truck. One hesitation or spin of the tires could prove disastrous. A broadside from this cyclone won't be any fun.

From the beginning in Jamestown, my mantra has been safety first; there is no race, nothing to win, and everything to lose. I've become accustomed to this pace of sailing, pressing when safe, easing up when required; much different than racing against equally determined, semi-crazy competitors, pressing 24/7. Now, it has all changed. The race is on—the race to 100° E longitude in five days.

Ken's forecast for the next five days is good for making speed. Plenty of wind and the direction will be fair. Monday's frontal passage will help push us east through Tuesday. Wednesday will be very light behind the front. I'll need to push to keep up the pace. Wednesday night and into Thursday, ahead of the cyclone, the winds will increase as I try to slingshot underneath the cyclone. The cyclone is moving southeast, attracted to a cold front coming up from the South Pole. The two will combine and wreak havoc on an empty ocean—empty except for me.

I'm pissed as I hang up the phone, not pissed at Ken, but pissed at myself for believing in another false summit—a false hope. My sights were set on 80° E and my energy has been spent to get there. Now, drained and fatigued, I have to find the depth of character to push another five days . . . probably six before the seas recover after the cyclone passes. I step outside, slam my ass on the deck, and take *Bo's* hand. I hit Otto's off button with a bit more intensity than usual and drive for an hour, staring at nothing, seeing nothing, just burning off piss and vinegar. Subconsciously, I need to find every bit of energy the sea can provide. I sail, drifting on an internal, subconscious current, a high-level conference going on between those of us here at this moment, *Bo*, Otto, Franklin, the sea and me . . . all in one head—mine.

With my bones weary of sitting, I give the helm back to Otto and swing below to look at the chart, reread my notes and plot out our weekly schedule. I understand there is no timeframe at sea, but I can't deal with that now. Weakened, I have to use some of man's tools to prepare our offense. Eight knots or better is my target boat speed, 200-mile days the minimum. Otto surfs, hitting 12 and 14 knots as the waves build ahead of the precursor cold front.

* * *

The strategy we used to develop the sail plan for *Bodacious Dream* now causes turmoil. I choose to go with *hanked* on jibs instead of roller furling, allowing me to exploit *Bo's* upwind capabilities. *Bo's* sisters, hulls number one and two were already noted for being fast upwind against the Class 40 fleet. Using hanked on sails would allow me to capitalize on this advantage against competitors using less efficient roller furling—the time-honored standard for shorthanded sailing. It would mean more work for me, but I've never shied away from work. Six years ago, at age 50, I was still working the bow on a 47-foot racer in Chicago or finessing massive, wooden beams high on a new home overlooking Lake Michigan's shore.

Now, hanked on sails haunt me. They're faster when needed, but alone, they force me to downsize sooner, and upsize later, expending extra energy reefing, which limits my ability to maximize speed. Roller furling sails would be easier right now. They would allow me to simply roll them up as the wind increases, and in reverse, roll them out. Hanked on sails, like the ones on *Bo*, require a 30-minute exercise while bucking the seas on the bow of the boat. Downsizing ahead of the storm, and subsequently shaking reefs out when certain the storm has passed. Right now, we need to push for every mile and get in front of the cyclone. This means waiting as long as possible before reefing, and then un-reefing just as soon as the wind allows.

An hour is all the time and energy I can waste on being pissed. There is no other option. The guys and I must push east. Our strategy is defined—east is the priority. We can't sacrifice east for north or south—Push—Wednesday's winds will be light. We'll have to charge batteries with the engine in gear and may have to use the engine to keep the speed up. The thought of wallowing at two or three knots with a cyclone breathing down our back is scary.

On Sunday, the projection is for the cyclone to be at 91.5° E, 39° S by Thursday. The accuracy of weather forecasts diminishes beyond 48 hours, leaving us with this educated guess. We need to get to 96° E by Thursday to pass ahead of the brunt of the storm.

While I focus my thoughts out to Thursday and then Friday, we continue sailing east in near 30-kt winds. Sailing has become routine in these elevated conditions. Again, my limits have been stretched and don't retract. As *Bo* surfs at 12 knots, I go about my chores, walking the deck to look for wear or breakage that will derail any hope of making 96° E by Thursday. *Bo* is in great condition. I clamber back to the cockpit and take her hand to steer.

When I'm worried, I am more at ease driving Bo. I can feel her. She speaks to me in a soulful language few would understand. Vibrations, rumbles, and squeaks vocalize a surge of power tugging at my hand from her helm. I can tell which one of us is out of balance in a minute. Often, actually most of the time, it's me. In just a few moments, my soul is calmed and *Bo* has me back in balance. I assure myself that I know how to sail, and I know how to sail Bo. She is sailing fine. We will be fine. I know what I'm doing, and I reassure myself that my experience isn't just my imagination. I tap "On" and Otto takes over. Grabbing my book and a handful of Hershey's dark chocolate kisses, I sit and decompress, reading and drifting off in 15-minute intervals between intense chapters in life.

Tuesday afternoon comes as a surprise. I'm unaware of the actual days passing but keep track of my progress with a sharpie pen on a matrix of numbers and symbols scrawled on the overhead in the cabin. Sunday at dawn, I scrawled out six days across a horizontal line stretching about four feet. Marks break the space between S, M, T, W, T, and F. Numbers from 1 to 24 are below each letter. By Tuesday afternoon, not so aware of days passing, I see each of the numbers under S and M and half of T are scratched off. A tally of miles fills the space between M and T and part of T and W. My mind is linked with the speedometer and compass. Speeds over eight knots ring positive, speeds below eight cause a scan of the sails and trim for deficiencies.

A note in my log reminds me I've crossed the 4,000-mile line to New Zealand. I would celebrate the halfway mark if not for the threat of the cyclone. I notice on the matrix overhead, it stops at Thursday/Friday. There's nothing beyond Friday. I'm curious why this is. Is my mind staying focused on what's important? Or subconsciously, is my soul telling me there is nothing beyond Friday? There will be no Saturday.

Late Tuesday as the winds build to 30 knots with gusts over 40, a strange perspective comes over me. If the cyclone weren't chasing me, this front would be a significant one; instead, compared to the threating cyclone, it's not, and I tend to it with a routine mindset. Tomorrow, Wednesday, the wind is forecast to diminish.

Lying in wait for the decrease, I am fully prepared to shake out the reefs as soon as the wind shows signs of easing. We sail solidly, passing 91° E as my mind endlessly calculates time and distance problems. The numbers revolve like a stubborn loop of music stuck in my memory. By dark, the winds are down to 20. Otto, focused and serious, humors me by playing with the waves, routinely kicking off 12-knot surfs while I boil water to rehydrate dinner.

The hands on my watch sweep past 00:00. It is now Wednesday, and the winds continue to diminish, elevating my frustration. We pass 93° E but the engine runs, burning precious fuel, keeping us on pace to 96° E. Twenty-four hours from now, the weather will be downright miserable, with nothing better beyond it. I take advantage of the calmer conditions to prepare us for the onslaught, lashing and re-lashing everything on board. Containers, gear, loose gear, everything is stuffed, tucked or tied down. I've located chocolate, water, and important things, placing them strategically where I can easily find them. I duct tape a flashlight to the cabin sole (floor), a strange thought, but I plan for the possibility I'll have to reach up to grab it. I double-check the *Epirbs* and life raft, knowing they are of little use, but their optimistic intent rings positive in my mind. I leave nothing to chance. In preparing myself, I've stripped my mind of all superfluous thoughts. Life is simple now; there is nothing in my mind but sailing *Bo* safely and properly—and sunrise on Saturday. With the present winds light and 276 miles to 100° E, we need all of today and most of tomorrow before engaging with the storm.

Wednesday drags on; our pace is slow and it agitates me. The test of patience is menacing. The updated course of the cyclone has changed again, moving more SE than expected. By Friday at 00:00 it's forecasted to be at 38° S, 99.5° E, our level of latitude and somewhere near our goal of longitude. I rationalize that I can't control the location of the cyclone; I can only control how fast we get east. I'm tempted to press the throttle forward, but calculate the exchange of fuel for the increase in speed as unacceptable. I do the math one more time and trust I am playing my hand well. We'll be sailing away from the low as it arrives—I have to commit to believing this.

I continue filling the spaces between W and T with miles and cross off the hours below W. I cross off 24 and move to 1 under the T. 152 becomes the first mileage number between T and F. Then, as if standing outside my body, I watch as my hand adds an S for Saturday beyond the F. Like a Sensei, I have to see through the punch . . . I have to see beyond the cyclone. I have to project us flowing with and through this intense moment.

Still focused, I'm unnerved. I head out on deck to look for anything I have missed. I see nothing. I sit down and reach for *Bo's* hand to settle my spinning mind. The wind builds to 12 knots from 000 degrees—True North, allowing us to sail directly east along latitude 38.5° and make optimal distance in VMCs. We proceed at seven knots, almost reaching my target speed of eight.

Continuously checking off numbers, I now slash the 12 under the T with the sharpie. The wind has built to 30 knots. *Bo's* sails are reefed as we pound across longitude 98° E. The game plan is to take advantage of the last light before dark and reef to the storm stub. The peak winds should arrive in 12 hours—about midnight. A day from now, the worst will be over. We hunker down and sail. Every mile to the east is a victory. Every mile east is one less we have to sail in the worst of the cyclone's tempest.

Pushed ahead of the strong winds, the swells build, rising slowly under us before trundling off to the horizon. They mesmerize me. They roll like gentle farmland, making it hard to look away. Seduced, pulled into their dark, soulful eyes, I close my own, and feel my equilibrium lifted into the heavens by the swells, and I feel as if I am looking down on this event from far above. *Bo* looks so small in the immense expanse of these seas, insignificant and vulnerable in the long furrows of water. I resist the urge to drift away and shake my mind back into focus and build a vision of her sailing in full control, solid and delighted with the opportunity to prove she's worthy of what she was designed to do—to sail Category Zero: *Trans-oceanic racing where yachts must be completely self-sufficient for extended periods of time, capable of withstanding heavy storms and prepared to meet serious emergencies without the expectation of outside assistance.* This is *Bodacious Dream* to a "T," halfway between Cape Town and New Zealand, 1,000 miles south and west of Australia—*beyond the expectation of outside assistance while solidly navigating the wild ocean.*

After crossing off each numbered hour, I give *Bo* a routine check and wait for the worst of the winds, still a few hours away.

The winds continue to gain weight gradually, a knot here, two knots there, lulling me into an easy sense of being. The halyards slap harmonically at the mast, taunting me forward to deal with them and relieve the escalating anxiety. I clip on, climb over the coach roof, fully exposed to the sea and wind, and step forward to the mast. *Bo* rises and falls; the winds press the sails hard against the rigging and shove us down the huge swells. I work foolishly on the halyards until they are quiet and then turn and face forward, my back to the mast, my hands firmly clamped on hand holds. I stare forward across the wind and over the old graybeard seas, truing up my nerve and accepting my fears. I came for this. I came for the chance to stand here. I came to see if I am the man I thought I was. I came to see if I were even remotely worthy of this dream. With the wind and spray taunting me, I stand my ground and take it face first, chin up.

Convinced I belong here, believing I've proven my worth, I nod my respect and turn back to the cockpit. With one more solid, respectful glance over my shoulder, I stand proud of the toughened stance we are making in this sea. I unclip and slide below.

Bo lifts in a sudden jerk, slammed on her starboard side by a wave tossing her hard to port. We are in the way and when we fetch up against our insignificant limits, the wave simply continues on, flowing over, around, and through us, crushing the entire boat with a truckload of water. The wave simply washes by, leaving loose sheets and halyard tails flowing in the contours of life. I think quietly; this is why I wear a tether. I push from my mind any speculation of what would have been, had this happened minutes earlier, my soul standing at the mast—because it didn't.

Bo stands up, shakes off the last drops of the insult, powers up, and continues on her way. We are solidly here. We belong here, as much as anyone belongs here. *Bo* and I have proven we are what we believe we are. The Sharpie adds another mark.

Time seems endless sitting here, moment after moment on the companionway step, my back against the center console, my legs and feet compressed to adjust the distance between my torso and the bunk. A quick look to my left, out the companionway at the yarn beaten to death by the wind, assures me that the wind direction is where I want it. Below, to my right, I see the information from command control; in front of me awaits a zip lock bag of Hershey's Dark Chocolate Kisses and *A Long Walk to Freedom*. I promise to finish the book by the time we are free from this cyclone. It seems selfish to be worried about this one storm in the midst of Mandela's life of challenges.

The dark hours of night are the worst, but the easiest to deal with. The moon's glow barely seeps through the broken clouds, blacking out the sea's frightening turbulence and illuminating only the frothing, white tops of the swells. *Bo* continues to sail, I continue to monitor wind and course, and Otto grunts, regardless, as the night passes. The wind levels off in the high 40s, broaching the mid-50s regularly. Occasionally, the wind drops below 40 knots for a moment, stirring me to search for something gone wrong. A strange sense of balance comes over me in this brouhaha of nature. I trust the insane to happen and distrust the sane. Puddles of water and distrust gather everywhere.

Night passes ever so slowly. I'm tired of waiting and can barely see the horizon in the soft grayness when I finally proclaim it's dawn. Venturing out, I clip on before stepping into the cockpit for a look around. I climb over the coach roof and while hunched, nearly to my hands and knees, I shuttle around the deck looking for signs of impending doom. Everything seems unnervingly secure. The halyards clang, but only in the highest of gusts. The sails are soaked but secure. Everything seems fine. The wind and waves are the only evidence of the storm. Though the winds dropped to the low 40s during the night, the waves loom larger than ever, their tops tumbling over in rushes of white water ten feet high. Any loose water is sucked into the passing wind and shattered into spindrift, set free from gravity for twenty or thirty yards.

We crossed 100° E longitude in the middle of the night, the center of the storm behind us at about 99.5°. We missed each other. The storm carries on to the southeast. From here on, behind the storm, the winds will decrease and the skies will clear. Saturday will come.

By late morning, sunlight begins to break through the remaining clouds, turning the massive gray waves into ginormous blue sapphires. The chill in the air feels fresh, clean, and freeing. As the winds continue to ease, my mood and the barometer rise in harmony. By afternoon, the winds are down to 30 knots, and I hoist more sail. This gentle, 30-knot breeze seems pedestrian now. A relaxation sweeps through my body as tensions wane, sucked away to the southeast with the low. I chuckle at the contrast between the different feel of 30-knot winds. On the leading edge of a storm, as the wind ramps up to 30, they are filled with intensity, anxiety, and an apprehension of the unknown. On the backside of the storm, they are a sedating drug, an indication of more settled times to come.

I choose lasagna, my favorite, for the evening meal. Though it's not Sunday, it seems justified. *A Long Walk to Freedom*, her front cover soaked and torn free, the pages salted and dog-eared, now lies in the bin of read books. The storm has passed. We did it.

* * *

The log shows *Bo* just below 38° S latitude, nearing a line drawn directly south from the western tip of Australia, 500 miles away. 1,500 miles remain to Tasmania. 1,200 miles beyond Tasmania, across the Tasman Sea, lays Wellington, New Zealand. We made great mileage over the past week. The new forecast suggests heading south to 42° and then further down to 45° to sail beneath Tasmania and on to New Zealand.

Though I kept track of days, hours and mileage on the cabin top, I don't recall the week passing. Studying the strange matrix of numbers, it feels like just yesterday when I began marking the ceiling, intent on staying ahead of the storm. The hydrographic history shows more than 900 miles passing. Time was just a mental tool for dissecting, cataloging and working through the storm—a tool I'll put away now.

The next cold front is forecast for the middle of next week, four or five days from now. Grateful for the break, I reduce it to scribble in my logbook and put it aside. I let the rest of the day pass, a reward for sailing beyond the storm to Saturday. Otto drives, *Bo* and Franklin rest, and I nap in the late afternoon sun.

Thin clouds layer the sky, blocking the sun as daylight ends and a serene level of fatigue saturates my body. A fatigue where every joint aches, hunger feels enlightening, and sleep could abide glory. This feeling is my reward, earned by the complete expression of my entity, living wholly in concert with this place and moment in time.

Strange Lights in the Night

*T*he following days pass quickly; each an uneventful sail across the waters of this gently curving earth. Every mile put behind us reveals another mile ahead of us, previously hidden below the horizon. Australia is north, Tasmania, a thousand miles to the east. I switch back and forth between the spinnaker billowing in the lighter winds blowing from behind, and the Solent in the heavier winds ahead as they circle around the compass. New Zealand and the pleasures of the harbor might be a couple of weeks away, less than half the time we've already sailed since leaving Cape Town a month ago.

Two or three more storm fronts from now I'll be nearing another milestone, another landmark in life. Few sailors have sailed solo to Bermuda, even fewer carried on to Cape Town. How many stepped off in Cape Town and never returned? New Zealand is within my sights, within my grasp. Beyond New Zealand looms Cape Horn, but for now, instead of projecting through the punch, I'll allow my thoughts to stop in Wellington. Once there, I'll look over the edge toward the Horn.

The storm fronts are less threatening as we jibe back and forth on the shifting winds they serve us. Sometimes we sail north of east. Most of the time we aim south, slipping below 42° S and then farther to 45° S to pass below Tasmania. In the clear, bright days, the harsh sunlight, unfiltered by ozone, warms the cockpit—at times too much. In the evening, with the absence of clouds, the warmth dissipates almost instantly when the sun falls low in the sky, forcing me to replace the layers of clothing shed earlier.

Nothing seems serious, and little, if anything seems important. Whether or not I change my shirt or socks has no bearing on today's activities. I brush my teeth, wipe my face with warm, fresh water discarded from cooking, and take care of personal hygiene. The sunrise ritual requires resetting the Spot Tracker, a device that transmits my location and allows those back home to know where I was when last seen by a passing satellite. I follow this with an email confirming my existence in words—intimating any mood disorders. This seems unimportant to me, now at one with the sea, but knowing I'm well is hugely significant to my family and close friends back home.

Though I long for the taste of a cold beer, the sound of laughter and the smell of food cooking, I convince myself I'll only need a moment in Wellington before heading on. However, the same mind contemplates the familiar names of Perth and Sydney harbor in Australia, and Hobart in Tasmania. I wake from a short afternoon nap thinking—*I'll stop in for dinner tonight.* Quickly enough, my short-circuiting, sleepy mind catches up to reality and acknowledges—*there will be none of that.* Part of me wants to keep sailing. The other part wants rest ashore—a break from the constant, subconscious attention to the sea.

* * *

Australia slips by quietly and Tasmania grows closer, no longer 1,000 miles away as we continue sailing ahead of the shifting winds from the passing weather systems. The low-pressure to the south sucks in the wind exhaled from the high-pressure systems up north. These enormous pressure systems cover hundreds and thousands of miles and move slowly about the atmosphere like the globs in the glowing lava lamps, as they attempt to remain in balance with their own lives. These systems are invisible to all but those aware of the intimate differences of various cloud formations.

At times, we head south, so much that we are nearly 90° off course, making little if any VMC. We work south for better winds and a course below Tasmania. But my frustration at the shallow progress east inspires me to jibe back for better VMCs.

Back and forth, gybing to quell frustration until reason prevails, and then gybing back. Frustration flows into impulsive action again . . . and again. Winds increase and diminish; sails are reefed and shaken out. Life seems to be no more than a circulation of chores, miles and moments, and of sunrises and sunsets. Days pass completely unaware of me. At 43° S and 137° W, we clear an imaginary line I set 500 miles from Tasmania. As the day ends, the clouds tell me to expect an unsettled night—squalls of driving rain are imminent.

I starve myself through the first half of the night, using the anticipation of a hot midnight meal to carry me through the first half of the darkness. The middle darkness is consumed with boiling water and steeping the freeze-dried meal. After pouring the boiling water into the meal pouch, I occupy my time with a chore or two while it steeps and cools enough to eat. I might walk the deck to be certain everything is in order, or write a blog entry, or crawl forward to mop up water from various corners where it collects after sneaking in through fasteners slightly loosened by the constant movement of the seas.

With a sponge in hand, I ask myself aloud, "This is how things change isn't it?" By the constantly moving waves, the up and down, and in and out of the tides, seldom creating change instantly, but slowly, over eons of time, wearing away at hard, sharp granite and churning it into warm, soft sands.

The seas work *Bo* back and forth, twisting, tweaking, and on occasion, slamming. Without the intervention of maintenance, something would fail and the sum of the whole would break apart. Perhaps I too am affected by this constant touch of the ocean, the raw nature of life. Sea water, wind, sun, rain, wear, tear, emotional stress, and still more sea water; all of it changing me one small particle at a time, wearing down hard edges, eroding them into softer forms of enlightenment.

I hear the first drops of rain hit the coach roof as the teakettle begins to steam. I switch the chart plotter to radar mode and see the telltale signs of a squall. Then, just beyond my port bow, a cluster of white dots with red pinpoints in the center approach from the left. As the water heats, I step outside to look around, peering into the darkness, waiting for my eyes to adjust and allow the subtle differences in the contrast of clouds to become apparent.

Flash! Flash! Lightening crosses the sky, startling me. It's the first lightening I've seen the entire trip. Multi-tasking, I shut off the boiling water and study the radar to see the organization of the storm. My senses flip, from being relaxed and thinking of food to being aware of every nuance of sailing—wind, waves, and heel. I'm back on deck, hunkered down next to the tiller with one eye on the wind, the other over the rail at the storm. It passes uneventfully with a few claps of thunder followed by more flashes of light in the clouds. The rain trails off and the clouds separate, revealing stars in the fissures between the subtleties of the black, night sky.

I thank Otto and stand up. The edge of the hard coach roof lies against my breastbone; my hands and forearms lay flat on its top and I look forward, then left and right. The air has a familiar feel to me—cold, damp, and tingly. The water on my fingertips is fresh rain, feeling softer than the seawater typically tossed up by the teasing sea.

Baffled by the strange sight around me—I spin 360° and see glowing orbs the size of softballs floating on the dark sea all around us. What is this? Where am I? I'm mesmerized; I can't comprehend what I am seeing. They are everywhere. I've witnessed bioluminescence in many forms, and I am accustomed to the glowing contrail from *Bo's* rudders as she sails the world's oceans. But this is different. Each orb is separate and unattached, spread out across the sea over hundreds of meters in all directions. They continue coming towards us at eight knots as we sail along. Each glowing orb radiates the full spectrum of colors—blues, greens, pinks, and white.

I drop below and grab the strong flashlight, hoping they won't disappear in the instant I am gone. The strong light intrudes deeply into the sea, rudely disrupting any peace emanating from it. I shine the light on an orb as it passes by; my eyes struggle and make out a tubular shape, maybe six inches long. I light up another and then another. I feel guilty shining this bright light into their world, but wonder and intrigue overwhelm my sense of respect and civil demeanor. After more attempts to capture a picture in my mind and reference it with data already stored, I am left without a match. I lay the flashlight down and stand in awe.

In reverence, I let my mind relax, my voice go silent, and my senses enjoy the peace as I experience this amazing sight. I am certain I'm the only person living at this moment and begin to ask the question *if*"and then stop, suggesting my mind just drift and absorb this serenity. My eyes relax, their focus becomes blurred, and the orbs transform into streams of light flowing by. I am flowing with them through a warp of time.

At eight knots, a mile passes in less than eight minutes. We pass through this group of earthbound stars having no idea how large an area they cover. I gauge it at a few miles given the time passing. The streaming lights fade away and I wait, forever, not ready for them to be gone and hope they will return. More miles pass before I accept that they are gone and I turn away.

The skies continue with broken clouds and passing squalls, but the glowing magic is missing. I drop below to make dinner and find the water is no longer hot. In the time it takes for boiling water to cool, my world has been changed—again.

I drift back and forth, through dinner, naps, reading pages from a book and listening to *Sao Paulo* on the iPad. This night seems longer than others. When dawn comes on unhurried, Tasmania is less than 350 miles away—less than two days sailing.

* * *

I'm suddenly aware of my hand, as if floating above it and witness it writing 45° 22′ S and 145° W in the log. We are even with the southern tip of Tasmania. I write in larger, more enthusiastic lettering . . . *"Passing under Tasmania!! Done!! New Zealand, the next stop!"*

800 miles of the Tasman Sea separate us from the South Island of New Zealand. Another 400-mile dogleg up the coast to Farwell Spit at the northwestern tip of the South Island takes us to the entrance of the Cook Straights before making Wellington on the southeastern tip of the North Island. I calculate the possibility of next Friday. It's strange to think I have a week to consider the transition to hard pavement.

The thoughts continue to flow like the sea beneath us, each having a perspective and reason for being. In a week, I'll close a loop, a circle around this amazing world.

The Feather

*B*odacious *Dream was launched on December 6, 2011, in Wellington, New Zealand. Two months later, we sailed her to Auckland and put her on the back of a large ship heading to Ft. Lauderdale, Florida. From there, she has sailed more than 30,000 miles beginning with the Atlantic Cup in May of 2012. Afterwards, she continued up the Eastern Seaboard—deep into the St. Lawrence Seaway, to Quebec City to compete in the Quebec—St. Malo Race across the North Atlantic to France. In September, the Normandy Channel Race took Bo along the historic French and English coasts, stopping in the famous ports of Cherbourg, Caen, and Lorient. Then, October found us competing in the Mondial World Championships in La Rochelle. With the summer racing circuit complete, Bo and I set off alone, across the Atlantic for home. Hurricane Sandy forced a diversion to Cascais, Portugal until December when we took our first long sail together, crossing the Atlantic to Antigua, arriving in time to celebrate New Year's, 2013. We carried on to Charleston, South Carolina where again we raced for the Atlantic Cup, and won it in Newport, Rhode Island on Memorial Day weekend.*

Today, I can trace the wake backwards to Newport, where four months ago, we left outward bound around the world. In a week, we'll close the circle around the globe for *Bodacious Dream*, but not for me—I missed the first leg from Auckland to Ft. Lauderdale. For me, there's still the last leg to sail and Cape Horn to be passed to port.

My mind drifting backwards through those memories returned to an eventful day in December 2011. I live in Indiana on the beautiful shores of the southern tip of Lake Michigan.

My flight to Auckland for *Bodacious Dream*'s launch was scheduled to leave from Chicago at 6:30 p.m., giving me a few hours to kill. With my bags packed and waiting by the door, I donned my running shoes and headed down the 100 steps to the beach to run off the excited energy building inside me. After all, in 24 hours I'd be in Auckland, touching *Bodacious Dream* as she readied for launch. Inside, I was excited. Outside, I was reserved, as if something this significant happened every day.

I walked down the first flight of stairs to the small landing at the bluff and stopped to look east and west along the deserted beach under the gray December clouds. Continuing down, I reached the last wooden step, covered by blown sand, where the path begins winding through dune grass to the water's edge. At my feet was a single, white seagull feather—a pure, white, downy feather. Immature gulls are mottled gray until they age. Old gulls are starkly white. No sincerer a sign could have been left for me.

Years ago, my friend Mike, nicknamed *Laughing Gull* by fellow solo sailors on Lake Michigan, was lost at sea in a solo race. I am certain Mike left the white feather on the sand for me as a sign of encouragement. The last step of the stairs transitioned into the beginning of a path leading through wisps of dune grass to the water, and from there—around the world. I put the feather under a rock and ran west along the beach, past the wild dunes of the National Park where my passion for the wild earth and its waters incubated as a kid. At the end of my run, worn and invigorated, I scooped a handful of sand into my pocket and gently lifted the feather, carrying them both up the flight of stairs, where I placed them into a zip lock bag and tucked them into my waiting duffle. I have never been shy to recognize the importance of seeing and understanding signs in life.

24 hours later, a short jump flight from Auckland landed me in Wellington where *Bo* sat, eager to be launched. With a cadre of builders, riggers and workers roaming her decks, I slipped below

and removed the feather from the zip-lock bag and with a small toothpick, stole a dab of epoxy from Mattie, the build foreman, and attached the feather to the ring frame above the nav station. Mattie watched quietly and then inquired, listening respectfully as I told the story and straightened out the quills. His smile indicated he fully understood. As I finished smoothing out the feather, Lapo stepped below looking for me. Seeing my fingers touching the feather, his eyes asked the question and I retold the story. When I finished, Lapo spoke in a quiet, respectfully paced tone, explaining that when his daughter was just an infant, he would hold her in his hands and watch her fine hair move as his breath caressed her forehead. He fondly called her Piuma, Italian for *feather*. This past year, Francesca, now an adult, asked Lapo, an accomplished artist, to draw a feather she could have tattooed on her rib cage. The feather on Francesca's ribs is nearly identical to the one I placed on Bo. There is no doubt the spirit of *Bodacious Dream* connects us.

"Call Mom,
She Needs to Hear Your Voice

A hundred and fifty miles into crossing the Tasman Sea, a bit more than a thousand miles from Wellington, I download a batch of emails. One of the messages is from my sister, Nancy, saying, "Call Mom, she needs to hear your voice." Though somewhat unusual, I think back along the elastic timeline to the last time I talked with Mom, presuming it must have been longer than it should have been. I calculate the difference between Universal Time Corrected and Pacific Standard Time in San Diego, and determine the window to call and reach Mom after dinner.

The past twenty years of phone calls with Mom have been mechanically difficult due to her hearing loss. It's necessary to use patience, articulation, and a steady tempo to allow the electronic sounds from her Cochlear implants to connect and make sense with her brain. Landline to landline, with the help of a texting machine we work through it, the fun complication being the confusion of the uncertain conversation suddenly brought clear by the elucidating text. We often laugh about this, but I recognize, regardless of the content of the conversation, Mom benefits from hearing the tone and feelings in my voice; this helps her determine my state of being.

The Iridium phone elevates the complications by disassembling my voice and discharging the small electronic bits into thin air through an antenna aimed at a satellite over this remote ocean. From there, the signal is volleyed back and forth between satellites and ground stations until reaching California where somehow it's captured, sent along a wire path to Mom's phone, and reincarnated into voice and printed text on her machine. Anticipation and mind reading are important tools for conversing this way, but today they're insincere.

The easily spoken, "hello" and "how are you," are interrupted by "let me try the other phone" and a pause to adjust volume and clarity. The strange delay in the long distance transmission exacerbates the confusion and complicates the conversation, leaving a broken collection of emotions scattered across a sky of satellites. The intense, tearful, conversation is followed by "I love you" . . . and then silence, leaving me alone in the Tasman Sea.

The sea is a lonely place right now. The diagnosis is stage 4 cancer. Mom is dying. I step on deck and do what I always do in troubled times—I take *Bo's* hand and sail. The sea is raw, honest and true to me. We sail up and over waves, press down for speed, and shave slivers from the wind to add power to the sails. I consider many things and the challenge of life taking different directions than planned. How long does it take to grow up? Is there really that much more to learn? I press Otto into service and lay down, curling up with my back inside the protection of the spray shield. Using a hard plastic line clutch for my pillow, I drift away. Fifty-six years old, sailing unassisted around the world, and I am reduced to the insecurities of a young boy, curled up fetal, back against the wall, shielded against fear in the dark of night. I am half way around the world from my family, unable to give them my strength, and instead I'm selfishly syphoning off energy they need for Mom. I'm thankful the weather is pleasant and Wellington is a week away. *Bo* knows what to do. She will sail me there.

* * *

Inside 900 miles to Wellington, I am amused to see *Bo* as the little cursor on the chart plotter between Australia and New Zealand, the scale unable to put Cape Town and Wellington on the screen at the same time. I scroll west, along the line running backwards through time and memories, past Australia, India, Madagascar, Cape Town, and up the Atlantic to Brazil. I hover over Rhode Island where I began, 15,000 miles away. 900 miles seems so insignificant, yet the week ahead will punish my patience, waiting to have a clear conversation with my mom and family.

Wanting more information from home about Mom's cancer and her condition, I set up the electronic wizardry for retrieving emails from the satellite links serving the iridium phone. Wires connect the computer to power. *Wi-pipes* and switches connect the phone, all with blinking lights linking to the telltale green bar of progress on the computer screen. The program times out and I hit send again. It times out again and I try four or five more times. Nothing. I troubleshoot known gremlins living on board: battery power, cable connections, salt, and corrosion. I boot and reboot. I wish life could be so easily restarted. My email access is down.

I shut down the computer and divert my attention. An hour later, the result is the same. I shut down and try again, allowing another hour to pass and remind myself of the definition of crazy—repeatedly doing the same thing but expecting a different result. I accept my email is down and call tech support—there are no white knights on duty. My communications have been reduced to text messages and limited voice over the iridium phone. I text Tim Eades and Jonathon, my IT gurus on shore to let them know the email is down, then go about my chores while *Bo* faithfully continues to sail toward New Zealand making eight to nine knots of steady speed. Though we are pounding against the seas, she is intent on getting us there.

* * *

I take stock of my onboard supplies. The cookies are long gone, and chocolate is scarce. I check my shore bag again, hoping to find a hidden present—although I'm sure I found all of them earlier. Two juice boxes remain, but there's plenty of water for liquids. A year-and-a-half old can of sardines from France, a few cans of tuna, and four or five freeze dried meals—enough to get me there, but nothing resembling over abundance. I'm fine. There's plenty of food.

I check fuel and confirm ten gallons on deck with five in the tank. Fifteen gallons is fifteen hours of motoring. I used more than I expected staying in front of the cyclone and charging batteries when the winds were light or the hydro generator was pulled up to protect it from stormy seas. I allow six gallons for charging to Wellington, leaving nine or ten in the event I need to motor, a conservative range of 50 miles. *Bo* is in fine shape; all sails are working. I'm in good shape, most mental faculties intact and physically okay. 900 miles should be no problem. Wellington is just around the corner. The windy Cook Straights are the only obstacle.

I call Commanders' for weather guidance and find the report uplifting. A couple of steady days for heading east toward the South Island coast, then a cold front will push us up to Farwell Spit, the northwestern tip of the South Island and the entrance to the Cook Straights. A high should fill in afterwards and make the sail down the straights, known for intense wind and strong currents, quite manageable. I'm buoyed by the prospects of a clean sail to Wellington and a quick connection to Mom by phone.

I begin to prepare for arrival in Wellington. It's early, but I'm anxious, and it's fun to make the preparations. I pull out my electric beard trimmer, buzz off the overgrowth under my beard, and shorten the mustache to allow food to pass in a more civilized manner. Not thinking the task through thoroughly, the whiskers remained on deck, blowing about for several days, collecting in windrows in the corners. I laugh at the amount of gray hair my body produces in a month.

I take time to do a body wash with a Paper Shower, a large body wipe for this purpose, and change into a clean shirt and skivvies, giving me the feeling of a civilized man. There's a strange contrast between arriving in a 4-day-old shirt vs. a 45-day-old shirt.

To test redundancy and prevent potential problems in the Cook Straights, I play switcheroo with the autopilot rams. The last time we sailed down the Cook Straights *Bo* hit 50-knot winds and crazy times with a crew of six. No need to remind myself I'm alone this time. I revisit the scene several times and adjust preparations with each replay.

I check the deck, mop up water below, and sail along in mixed conditions. The winds are shifty and the horizon is full of squally rain as the front approaches. Shortened text messages from home mimic the weather. "Things are k," "not worry." "Love ya," "ttys." "B safe." I read each text and between every line, sometimes two, three and four times.

* * *

Signs are everywhere; I just have to make sure I don't miss them. On January 9th, I awoke from a difficult dream during a short nap. In the dream, I'm standing in a security line at the airport when an official comes up to me and says, "Mr. Rearick, you need to call home." I am confused as to why or how the security agent knows my name, and like most dreams, after waking, it makes little sense.

Later that day, I call my sister to see if everything is all right back home. Everything is fine. I call other friends and all of them assure me things are okay and I dismiss the dream as a sleepy interlude. Two weeks later, when I talk with Nancy after the heartfelt conversation with Mom, she explained that Mom wanted to wait to tell me when I got to New Zealand, but Nancy told her I probably already knew. January 9th was the day the doctors told Mom she had terminal cancer. I'm not going to ignore any feelings or signs between now and Wellington, even if I have to read simple texts—over and over.

* * *

Night arrives, and with it the winds ahead of the front. I shift gears, reef the mainsail, and prepare to reef the Solent in anticipation of the winds building further. Throughout the rough and tumble night I anxiously await the telltale decrease in wind, telegraphing the instant shift, and then the subsequent increase as the front passes. I wait, napping intermittently and reading paragraphs one at a time, eyes and senses focused on the rhythm of the gusts, the angle and approach of the waves. Intuitive feelings I have come to recognize as the front takes me into its fold.

I'm still waiting for the front to arrive when daylight comes. The front is late by more than four hours. The winds are fair and steady and *Bo* is sailing well. I wonder if we stayed ahead of the front longer than anticipated or maybe it slowed down.

Daylight opens the sky, extending the horizon and showing nothing more than fog limiting my visibility. The weather doesn't make sense. If this were a front passing, the horizon would be crisp and harsh, defined by squalls and heavy cold air, but the skies are soft, daylight bouncing off the minute particles of fog hanging in midair. The seas are calm and the winds are steady. I struggle to resolve the confusion and check my notes on the weather and timing—even wondering if I've screwed up my days. There are no obvious answers, and without satellite communication, I can't access weather files.

The morning hours pass. The sun, now a diffused disk a few fists above the horizon, indicates the front is nowhere close, and the winds are down to less than 10 knots. I need to shift sailing gears again. At the mast, undoing the reef, I notice strange shapes mixed in with the fog to the east. I grab the mast, steady myself, and stare. The unexpected sight unveils itself as the coast of the South Island of New Zealand.

The rugged coastline is outlined by a faint wisp of dark hair. It becomes clearer the longer I stare, the fog lifting and dissipating in the increasingly warm sun. Over a few minutes, as if watching the special effect of a movie, the fog disappears, revealing the entire panorama of mountains, rugged, sharp, and capped in snows of crystalline blue and white as raw as nature allows. The faint blue sky deepens as the hours burn on.

New Zealand.

My last sight of land was the continent of Africa, 48 days ago.

Not expecting this so soon and not familiar with the details of the coast, I jump below to check my navigation and zoom in on the electronic charts indicating *"Mariners should take caution; lack of information defining coastal areas."*

We're nearly 20 miles off shore and 300 miles south of Farwell Spit. The sun is shining; the weather and winds are calm. *Bo*, sailing along slowly, makes a stable platform for catching up on rest. I make a solemn promise to not sleep on the tack toward shore, not even at 50 miles off. We tack to parallel the shoreline, and between naps, I contemplate the weather and fuel reserves— now just 12 gallons. At this calm pace, Wellington is still a three- or four-day sail away. I can't nap. I need to make progress . . . progress to a phone line.

* * *

Although communications are complicated by the loss of email, I learn the weather has flip-flopped. The pressure systems, in a constant tug of war, have beaten the forecasters at their game. A system over the North Island has overpowered the advancing cold front, stalling it and leaving us in a widening convergence zone, a growing area of balanced pressure, and no wind. There will be little wind for the next three days until we reach Farwell Spit where the winds will return, strong and directly from Wellington—the exact opposite of what I was expecting. If the winds had arrived as forecast, strong from the front behind us, we could have reached up the South Island coast. Then, when we made the turn for the Cook Straights, headed east towards Wellington, we'd have had favorable winds to sail the last 120 miles. Instead, we have light or no wind, and when we reach Farwell, the low will pull wind from the east and southeast directly on our nose from Wellington, and probably at 35-40 knots.

Floating for a few days waiting for wind isn't going to sit well with me. I need fuel.

I send a text to my friend Lapo to see if he's familiar with any of the harbors along this coast where I can stop safely and get fuel. While waiting for an answer, I scan the horizon with binoculars, looking for local boats or fishermen. I spot a small, white boat, quite a way inshore, and try calling on the VHF radio. "Small vessel on the coast, small vessel on the coast, this is the sailing vessel *Bodacious Dream*." There's no reply, the radio signals echo along the deserted coast. I'm sure my vague message landed with no interest.

A radio network surrounds the island nation of New Zealand, covering the many open miles of desolate, sparsely inhabited coastlands. It's not long before my hails are returned by the New Zealand radio net. "Vessel *Bodacious Dream*, this is radio New Zealand, how can we assist?" I explain my situation, letting them know we're a sailing vessel in need of fuel and wonder if any of the harbors are suitable for *Bo* or if there is a commercial enterprise willing to bring fuel to us. The radio operator is accommodating, calling a couple of close harbors to extend my request. He returns with the suggestion to contact Greymouth Harbor.

Following his advice, I hail Greymouth Harbor on the VHF radio. The friendly mates there answer my hail and consider the options. Thirty minutes later they call with bad news, they can't help right now. The fuel operator is already closed for the day. The mates suggest I make for their harbor, spend the night and refuel in the morning. I contemplate the option, but Greymouth is 50 miles behind me and going backwards is too hard to stomach. While contemplating their offer, I receive a text from Lapo. *"No good harbor . . . Get away from coast . . . Bad place when weather comes."* I thank Greymouth and kindly decline their generous offer to help. I'll sail as best I can and face head on, the battles in front of me with wind and patience.

A moment later, the radio kicks up again.

"Bodacious Dream, Bodacious Dream, this is *Ocean Odyssey."* I return the hail, "Go ahead *Ocean Odyssey,* this is Bodacious Dream."

"Bodacious Dream, yes, I think we are just inshore of you. My crew and I are fishing and have about an hour and a half more work. Afterward, we'd be happy to try to help you with fuel."

Stunned, I look across the water. The small vessel I had called earlier must be the *Ocean Odyssey.* "That would be wonderful!" I call back.

"Give us an hour or so and we'll call you to make arrangements."

"Roger *Ocean Odyssey.* Thank you very much!" I tack *Bo* toward shore and slowly work in their direction, awed by the generosity of the ocean and stilled by the magnificent view of shoreline in front of me.

The hour passes easily as I watch the real life National Geographic scenery unfold in front of us.

"Bodacious Dream, Ocean Odyssey here . . . We're done fishing and will head your way. I'm not sure how we'll transfer fuel, but we'll figure something out. Do you have cans?"

"Roger *Ocean Odyssey,* I do have plastic cans. I will motor towards you as well. Thank you again." Thirty minutes later, we are close enough to talk across the thin strip of ocean separating us.

"Captain, did we hear you say you've been at sea forty-some days? Where did you sail from?"

"Yes . . . We're sailing around the world. We left Cape Town before Christmas, about 45 days ago . . . headed to Wellington. Your help is amazing. I can't thank you enough."

"Captain . . . tie your cans together and toss 'em over the rail . . . We'll come by and pick them up. In the meantime, would you like some fresh fish?" One of the crew holds up a beautiful fish. "If you want, you can come aboard, and take a hot shower!"

I'm stunned by their generosity but graciously decline, acknowledging I have no way of cooking fresh fish properly. The offer of a shower is wonderful, but it would trouble me to leave *Bo* floating unattended. I tie the jerry cans together, toss the necklace overboard, and move out of the way. The captain turns his vessel adeptly while a crew reaches out with a long pole, hooking the string of empty pearls and pulls them onboard.

"Give me and my mates a few minutes, not too sure how we'll fill them, but we'll get it done!"

Forty-five minutes pass while I circle slowly, watching the seabirds dependent on the fishing boat for scraps of food. The sun is warm and I'm awed by the generosity of New Zealand, not only for providing me this magnificent view, but also for these amazing fishermen—the only ones in sight for a zillion miles in any direction.

"Captain, the cans are full, if you can toss us a long line, we'll send them over to you." I toss a long line, landing it over their rail, and within a few moments, I pull ten jerry cans full of fuel onboard *Bodacious Dream*. We circle around, now rail-to-rail and I thank them and ask how I can compensate them.

"How much do I owe you sir?"

"If it were up to me, Captain, you owe us nothing! Let me give you the owner's phone number, and when you get to shore, after you talk with your mom . . . give him a call and work it out with him." I had told them about Mom. My body and soul needed to share my grief with someone and who better than fellow mariners who understand the loneliness of the sea when home calls.

We continue to talk for a while and share a few stories over the rail. I give them my email and web information to allow them to follow us and after finishing our goodbyes, as gracefully as birds in flight, we turn back to our respective courses and depart. The *Ocean Odyssey* motors south, steadily toward home; on *Bodacious Dream*, we head north toward Farwell Spit.

While Otto drives, I sort the fuel, dump two cans in the inboard tank, and lash the others to the rails. I coil lines and then splash a bit of soapy water on the decks to rinse away any stray, slippery fuel. I check the text messages and see that Lapo has sent another . . . *"Please get away from the shore."* Lapo follows our track on the computer and I'm sure he is confused because we are so close to shore. I'm certain he's worried I'll try to make a difficult landing in a small harbor. I text back, *"I rec'd ful from fshrman and now hed offshore."* He simply replies, *"Thx. C U in Welly."*

As the last minutes of an entirely unpredictable day unfold, I'm spent and fatigued but elated with relief. And now, as if my pockets aren't already overflowing with the grace and generosity of the fishermen of the *Ocean Odyssey*, the skies are unfurling the most amazing sunset. The coast of New Zealand is shaded in progressively darker layers off our starboard quarter behind us. The sun, laying just below the horizon, illuminates the buttermilk skies extending over me, forcing me into a backwards bend and twist in order to see all the varying shades of pink, orange, red and lavender, the subtle hues of human kindness evolving slowly enough for me to absorb and reflect on their spirited meanings.

I sit on the rail, my arms draped over the lifelines and think of the amazing world I live in. Regardless of the winds, setbacks, struggles, worries, and tears, the generosity of the fishermen assures me that I've traveled with grace and respect. No more significant a gesture than their kindness or this sunset is necessary for me to understand the importance and value of being a good person in this world. This short day is symbolic of the values of being human. I've tried to be kind where I could, fair when it hurt, and helpful when I was able to shoulder additional burdens. This day is either exchange for the past or an extension of my credit into the future. For now, all is well. We'll proceed up the coast, headed to Farwell Spit, two days away, and live as gracefully and full as Otto, *Bo*, Franklin, and I can.

Taking a final moment in the fading light, I stand at the back of the boat and look aft at the colorful skies over *Bo's* wake and extend my arms overhead in a human "V." With gentle reverence, I softly utter the words, "Thank You."

* * *

The winds continue to be evasive. A wisp or two from nowhere in particular surges us forward and then mysteriously disappears, leaving us chugging along under motor while slowly watching the coast of glaciers, snowcapped mountains, and rugged land slide by.

I occupy my time with arguments and fuel calculations; arguing the validity of using the engine while at the same time, revving up and down the tachometer from 2200 RPM to 2500, and 2800 to 3000, looking for the best value for the fuel we're burning. The forecast doesn't promise any wind until I reach Farwell Spit, and then I'll have all the wind I want, 20–30 knots building to 50 knots at the Brothers, the name of an island landmark in the middle of the Cook Straights—all of it on the nose. Not only difficult sailing, but hard on the mind and body.

I calculate the mileage from Cape Farwell to Wellington at 120 miles . . . a pittance . . . almost nothing . . . just a short hop after 7,500 or 8,000 miles. But in this mindset, it may as well be forever. I concentrate mental energy on the weather systems and urge them to make up and go about their own ways, leaving us out of their argument. It humors them to think I feel empowered to arbitrate their differences in pressures. My mind runs wild and loose thinking about the difficult sail up the Cook Straights, while *Bo* and Otto steady as ever, truck along at just six knots in the windless, calm waters.

I can't stop. I'm like a kid with a freshly opened bag of Chips Ahoy cookies. I eat numbers, obsessively calculating time, distance, and fuel consumption. I want three-quarters of a tank of fuel for going up the Cook Straights. With less than half a tank, the violent motion of the boat can allow the *fuel pickup* in the tank to suck air or foam, stalling the engine when most needed. My mind is working through problem avoidance—a precursor to problem solving.

Another day turns into another night—uneventful but for the hourly decrease in miles to Cape Farwell, six an hour, 150 a day. The waters are silky smooth without the wind. I rest when I can, knowing I need to fill my own personal tank of energy.

Late in the day, we reach the clouds moving south from the weather system over the North Island. A light rain begins to fall as daylight extinguishes itself 45 miles from the cape. The evening turns dark early and the wind builds into the high teens. I shut down the engine and sail towards Cape Farwell.

Over the past days I've steeled my mind to the task in front of us. We'll hunker down and make the best of it, putting aside goals and expectations to live each moment alone and by itself. Once experienced, it will be tallied with the others and the combination of the total experience will accomplish the goal. I trim the sails and trim Bo. Water ballast is filled to capacity and gear is stored; the decks are cleared and checked. Each moment or mile we sail I mentally toss into the file, and focus on the next.

Our first goal is the Brothers, a group of islands east of the first large bay we'll cross. I'm concerned about the fuel onboard, now less than 20 gallons, and I wonder if it's prudent seamanship to continue. Should I put into the small harbor at Nelson for more fuel? The voice sitting on my shoulder makes a compelling argument . . . warm breakfast, fuel, a day or two of rest, and the phone call home. Let the wind die, and then sail gloriously down the Cook Straights. My conscience ignores the pointed discussion, retorting. "This is what you came for. If you were racing, there would be no dropping out. It's only 120 miles, a day-and-a-half at the worst. Sail each wave, one wave at a time. I remember when I was a kid shoveling dry sand. It caved back into my hole and wiped out visual progress. "It can't be any worse than that," I tell myself.

There's really no turning away. It's just a mental exercise. If we fetch the Brothers without a tack, we'll carry on. If it comes up worse, we can bail out and head to Nelson.

We clear the eastern tip of Farwell Spit in the middle of the night and point for the Brothers; the wind angle allowing us to fetch them, but barely. We hunker down and sail one mile at a time. Twenty miles pass and the wind angle holds. A call to Commanders' for an update lifts Ken's mood when I tell him I'm holding course to the Brothers . . . "You're able to hold a course to the Brothers? That's great! I've checked around New Zealand. The winds are shifting, but if you can hold this and clear the Brothers before the shift catches you, it will be a huge gain, though still a beat the last 60 miles."

We pound through the rest of the night, riding over an occasional wave but nosing through most of them. Spray and water are constant companions with the howl of the wind in the rigging. My only salvation is the slow accumulation of distance, indicated by small dots of accomplishment on the chart plotter tracking progress toward the Brothers. The occasional glow of bioluminescence in the angry waters around us seems out of place, but I leverage it for encouragement.

The Brothers are off our starboard bow as the skies lighten in the early morning. We've *fetched*. I adjust the course as the wind shifts forward, no longer diverted around the landmass. I'm tired, wet, and hungry from the long night of work, but the advance of dawn invigorates me, keeping my mind set to the hard work of tacking in the 30-kt winds of the Cook Straights.

Our course takes us toward the South Island, as far in toward shore as comfortable before tacking back. On the new course, my intention is to cross the Cook Straights and continue to the coast of the North Island where we should find calmer winds and seas protected from the headlands of the coast. Once there, we'll tack along the shore, under the bump, before heading back to the open waters of the Cook Straights to a point where we'll make our last tack to Wellington. I talk it out in simple terms, but calculate it still at 10 or 12 hours of hard sailing. These are long tacks, four or five hours on the same course.

By mid-afternoon we cross the straights and tuck under the wind shadow of the North Island headlands, sailing along the shore in more civilized conditions. The wind and waves are still significant, but only three-quarters of what they are in the unchallenged vein of wind in the open straights. The bright orange storm jib contrasts sharply against the gray clouds as *Bo* shovels away at the proverbial pile of sand, one mile at a time, never looking back, only looking forward to the moment in front of us.

By late afternoon, we're back out in the unprotected waters of the Cook Straights, lining up for what I convince myself will be the last tack of this leg of the journey. I've lost track of time, but the daylight tells me, sunset isn't far off. The presence of life and the rituals that continue on land, regardless of a tempest at sea, begin to appear; the illumination of civilization speckles the shoreline. The AIS (automatic identification system) now sees the ships at anchor in Wellington Harbor.

We close in on the waypoint and exercise the tack. Before tacking, it's necessary to transfer the water ballast to the low side, leaving *Bo* wallowing, slow and sluggish, with the weight on the wrong side. Otto changes course at the touch of the *tack* button while I flail about with winches and lines, trimming the sails on the new tack. She's lively again, the ballast now high on the proper side.

We settle on the new board, adjust the course, and I realize I've misjudged the target. My arrogance is chagrined for claiming it the last tack of the long journey. We continue to sail toward shore and then tack back out in a seamanlike manner. With the harbor entrance in clear view, a few miles away, I allow my concentration to slip. Images of a cold beer and a hot shower, unworried sleep and the smell of breakfast in the morning invade my mind. I try to rein in these errant thoughts and text my ETA to Lapo. He and a friend plan to borrow the yacht club boat to come out to the harbor mouth and meet us. This will be as close to a race reception as we'll receive on this journey.

With each passing mile, civilization becomes more invasive. A cruise ship stands off the harbor entrance, radio transmissions between ships crackles over the VHF radio and the lights ashore increase as the sun, now at the horizon, sends a lone beam through a fracture in the dark clouds. I allow myself the diversion of a short daydream, Walter Mitty style, imagining the taste of victory, leading the phantom Global Ocean Race fleet into Wellington.

Again, proclaiming this as the last tack, I set up and drop the *water ballast* to the leeward side. Two minutes pass, I close the *transfer valves*, start the engine for insurance should something go wrong, and begin the tack for the harbor. Within seconds of pushing the *tack* button, alarms scream in chaotic competition. I identify one as the AIS, the second confuses me; I don't recognize it—and the third I trace to Otto. I dive below to find the source of number two. My eyes divert to a red light on the engine gauge illuminating the international sign of a thermometer. "*Damn*!!" I started the engine but didn't check to be sure the cooling water was flowing—a problem when the boat is heeled in heavy seas with the engine only idling. I've probably toasted the impeller. I shut down the engine and jump back on deck. *Bo* is in irons and wallowing. Otto has shut down and locked the tiller. I do the best I can to back up with the wind, forcing *Bo* to finish the tack while scanning the horizon for the approaching ship—the AIS alarm indicates a "dangerous crossing." The boom swings limply back and forth, lines dangle, snagging and hooking on things as *Bo* drifts backwards and then falls off, responding to reverse rudder commands. The sails fill and slowly, backwards progress reverses awkwardly into forward motion.

I steady us on course again, now pointing at the headlands while shutting down Otto—hoping the problem is only an errant electronic gremlin waking to the arrival in Wellington. I turn Otto back on and set the course. He holds for a minute and then fails. The alarm screams at me. I scream back in self-defense and shut him off, steadying *Bo* on course.

I dive below, change drive rams and arrive back on deck at the helm in time to save face. I touch the *on* button and Otto takes over . . . He holds course—I hold my breath. An extended moment passes and I unclench my teeth and drop below to investigate the AIS alarm. The Ferry is exiting the harbor; we're close, but clear of her course.

I move to the engine and attempt another start, hoping that by revving the engine, the impeller will grab water and begin cooling. Nothing comes out of the exhaust but white steam. Damn—the impeller is shot. I step out on deck and look around, taking the time to make a thorough assessment of the situation.

We're less than five miles from the harbor, the engine isn't usable, there's a big sea running, and I'm sailing directly toward shore, maybe a mile away—calculated at eight minutes. The ferry is passing close, but clear. The solution is simple; I need to tack away from shore, replace the impeller, and stabilize the situation before making for the harbor.

With the sun just above the horizon, we tack again, only this time I forget to switch the water ballast in the hurried confusion. *Bo* is now on the proper tack, but the water ballast is on the low side; 1,500 pounds of weight contributing to the inefficiency of sailing. "Not smooth Dave," I scold myself. "Settle down. You're tired and anxious. Focus—talk it through." Simple things I learned to do many years ago during my first solo sails.

I open the dump valves and drain the water, adjust Otto's course to clear all problems, and ease the main sheet to balance the boat. With no water on the high side, she heels excessively, then settles under the reduced mainsail load and makes steady progress offshore to safer water. I dive below, throw bags and gear out of the way, and grab the necessary tools and spare impeller to begin the simple but delicate task of replacement.

I begin by loosening the screws securing the access plate. One screw drops into the bilge. The screw insists on playing hide-and-seek, rolling under the engine and then back out with each pitch and roll of a wave. I finally time it right and grab the little sucker. The next six or seven screws come out under closer scrutiny and finesse.

I pull the plate, pull the *impeller*, and examine it carefully; nothing is broken or missing. A broken or missing *fin* could lodge pieces in the cooling system and wreak havoc. I grease up the new impeller and slip it into place, wiping my slippery hands on a cloth dangling behind me. One by one, the screws go back in and I double-check my work. I check the tightness of each screw and check the engine to be sure nothing is left in the way or sitting on top.

I start the engine, rev the throttle, and wait . . . anxiously . . . for water to exit with the exhaust. Water isn't flowing. I'm ready to shut down and scream bloody murder when I see the first aspirated signs. I watch it like a dehydrated rat finding a desert oasis before jumping below to check the temperature gauge and find everything has returned to normal.

I trust the engine, and keep it running. Toss the tools, parts, and miscellaneous junk out of the way and check my navigation. Everything seems in order. I plot a new waypoint to reach before tacking for the harbor, take a deep breath and tell myself to slow down. "Slow down. What's the rush?" I ask.

Back on deck, I take *Bo's* hand and push the *off* button to give Otto a rest. I steady my brain, slow my heart, and savor the moment. I've done well until now, sailing each moment, each mile, one at a time, waiting until the end to tally the total. My jumping ahead to conclusions has again slapped me upside the ear.

We reach the waypoint and I tell the crew to hold . . . "Let's linger in this moment. The sailing isn't bad . . . The sky is pretty . . . This will be over in an hour and tomorrow we'll be longing to be back here—at sea." We continue sailing offshore, over-standing the waypoint (sailing beyond) to extend our last moments at sea. I stare out across the open water to the south and Antarctica, a week of horizons away. Twenty minutes pass and I give in. We tack and comfortably lay the course for the harbor mouth.

Behind us, the cruise ship stands off. In front of us, the red reef light blinks a welcome warning as the seas flatten inside the protection of the headlands. Off the port bow, a half mile away, a red and green light approaches, crosses in front of us, and then passes to our starboard before turning around and paralleling our course. Lapo waves a huge wave.

Wellington! Done!

It's still five miles up the expansive natural harbor to the marina, where *Bo* will rest. Lapo watches as we sail gracefully in the protected waters, yelling out a welcome. I don't hear exactly what he says, but I'm sure he wants to come aboard. I know he wants to sail his baby again, so I wave him over.

Onboard, Lapo hits Otto's *off* button and drives, smiling ear to ear in the deepening, damp evening. Lapo welcomes *Bo* home, as if she were a prodigal son—or daughter may be more appropriate. Beneath the crest of the high headlands, Renata, Lapo's wife watches from their warm home. *Bodacious Dream* has returned. We turn the point and motor into the marina. Slipping between two pilings, we make dock lines fast with the help of others on shore. Though at rest, I feel *Bo* giggling.

Gordy, who carefully crafted *Bo's* rigging two years ago, escorts two customs agents aboard and they make quick work of the formal papers. I chuckle at the simplicity and question, if they need to inspect *Bo* for contraband? With a laugh they respond, "If you're smuggling singlehanded from Cape Town, you need more discipline than we've got." Lapo, Gordy, and another couple venture below decks with a cooler of cold Heineken beer, a sandwich, and a pillow. I chuckle, having never thought about a pillow. We laugh, sip, and talk in quick, fractured sentences while I wonder how they can tolerate the smell of a 52-day, seasoned, solo sailor. Just then, Lapo hands me—at arm's length—a key to the showers and they excuse themselves, allowing me the night to adjust to the nearly instant change in my life.

I take a deep breath as I watch them walk away down the dock; the stillness of the harbor immobilizes me. Below decks, I move slowly, sit for a moment, and stumble through errant thoughts while digging out clean clothes, soap, shampoo, and shaving gear. It's nearly midnight when I turn on the shower, adjust the temperature, and step into the stall fully dressed, foul weather gear and all—for a well-deserved rinse.

* * *

I wake up fidgety. It's dawn in Wellington. I calculate the time in San Diego, California to be noon. I grab my cell phone and walk up the dock out of the marina looking for a spot sheltered from the wind to call Mom. I tuck into the nook of a building, punch the number, and hit the call button.

"Hi Mom!"

"Hello, Dave? Wow! Are you in Wellington?"

"I am! I got in about eight hours ago. How are you?" We volley back and forth, Mom wanting to know how I am, how *Bo* is, how life on land is. When I get my chance between her questions, I volley back with "Tell me how you are Mom." Mom's offensive volley is stronger than mine and I have to settle for the ability to hear her voice and understand her inflections. I'll break through soon enough, but not today.

Her swift intelligence sums it up in one succinct answer and then quickly changes the subject. "It's okay Dave—there's no cure. Is it beautiful there in Wellington?" I allow her this victory and go on answering her questions. With her wisdom more mature than mine, she drives the conversation, preventing it from settling to the lower denominator.

The conversation ends with her extending her love and pride of me, and me, as well, of her. As I walk back, I realize in these few minutes, my life and dream has changed. I'll spend the next days and weeks pondering the completion of my dream, bouncing back and forth between honoring Mom's life and living mine. Weeks will pass before I realize they are one in the same.

Decisions

*M*orning *builds full on and my sponsors Jeff and Gaye call to tell me they are in Wellington and will be here for lunch. I straighten up Bo as if friends were coming for dinner; bagging up smelly clothes and storing them on deck, sorting gear, gathering lines, folding sails and preparing Bo for a thorough wash-down. My watch beeps noon and I look up from my work to scan the marina for Jeff and Gaye. I spot them walking toward the locked gate securing the docks.*

As I step off *Bo* to walk the couple hundred feet to open the gate, a different couple steps forward to open the gate for them. The two couples, each unaware of the identity of the other, walk toward me. Jeff and Gaye reach me first and we embrace. Lapo and Renata are one step behind. I introduce the four. We have been in contact through phones and emails over the past three years, but the four have never met in person. We walk to *Bo*, talking and catching up as they inspect her. "She looks nearly new, Dave," Gaye exclaims, expecting to see more wear and tear from her 30,000 miles. But *Bo* was built by some of the best builders in the world, and she shows it proudly.

It only takes a few minutes for the biting winds to chase us uptown for a warm lunch. We talk about the sail, about home, race cars, and New Zealand. Stimulated by the conversation bouncing back and forth across the pentagon seating arrangement, an hour-and-a-half passes quickly. Lapo and Renata graciously stand up and excuse themselves, leaving Jeff, Gaye, and me to talk.

"What do you want to do Dave?" Jeff asks.

"I don't know yet. I do know I need to go home and see Mom."

Jeff and Gaye kindly offer options. "We can ship *Bo* home, or maybe we can ship her home and then back down next year so you can finish the trip . . . maybe you continue on."

"I don't know," I answer.

I know Mom would be hurt and disappointed if I let her cancer stop me from living. I can continue around the horn, but it's getting late in the season and a trip home pushes the season closer to winter at the Horn. The options surface in half thoughts and broken sentences. *"Yeah buts"* and stuttered syllables fill the air, reminding me of the staccato chop in the Bermuda Harbor that threatened the dream and elevated my anxiety.

The options pass back and forth a few more times, but deep inside, I know what's viable. It's a lot to think about so quickly, but the three of us will only be together face-to-face, today. The conversation ends with their unwavering support as we walk back to their car and collectively say our goodbyes.

The time spent with Jeff and Gaye seems unusually short and would confuse most people, but these good friends have a solid understanding of solo sailors and me. I appreciate their sensitivity. They understand the need for a solo sailor to come back to shore one tack at a time. Unobtrusively, they give me the space to do this, to head home and to choose the proper course.

I wallow through the rest of the afternoon. Not much is happening in Wellington this Sunday. The skies are solid gray, and a stiff, chilly wind blows through the harbor. I stumble aimlessly around *Bo* for a bit longer and then close her up, sling my sea bag over my shoulder, and walk out of the marina and along the harbor promenade, stopping at a sheltered spot where I sit and look across the rasped waters. So many things come to mind—friends, home, calendars. The options lay out in front of me, but one thought is anchored hard in my mind. If I let go of *Bo*, I'll never sail her again. The journey will end; the silver thread will be severed. The many variables will make it hard to come back and finish the trip—whether it's next year, another year, another time, or for that matter, another boat and another time.

Life . . . changes . . . plans . . . good turns and bad ones . . . We plan so much of where we want to go, and trust we control the elusive ending. I don't know where life goes at this point. Here on land, I'm distracted and lost—unable to take *Bo's* hand and sail to figure it out. *Bo* has taught me a lot, but it's time now that I set out on my own, with my own sails and trim them to the vagaries of the changing winds. I drift along the harbor streets, sit down for a beer, and then walk to a hotel nearby that I know.

Wellington. Done . . . or have we arrived here to begin the real journey?

New Zealand Tourist

I peel myself from the warm, soft bed and set my feet on solid ground. Today has a schedule, but a manageable one. At 9:00 a.m., a band of brothers—sailors, riggers, boat builders and technicians will meet Lapo and me at Bodacious Dream. Later, David Minors, the B&G Electronics specialist will arrive from Auckland for two days to work on the electronics. Collectively, these fine mates and I will hammer out a plan for Bo's maintenance while here in Welly. While sailing across the Southern Ocean from Cape Town, I relied on my great friend Lapo Ancillotti to round up guys and manage the work lists once Bo arrived. With rounding Cape Horn the next big challenge, Bo needs to be fully prepared before leaving Welly.

Lapo is a composite and sailboat design savant, the brainchild behind the Kiwi FC 40 and the project manager during the build. His expertise shows—Bo is an excellent boat. She stood up to some of the toughest ocean conditions and shows very little wear for it. But now, with a team of experts from Gordy and Stetchy on the rigging; Mattie G, the build foreman looking into composite repairs and refinements; David tackling electronics; the guys from North looking over the sails; and Lapo overseeing things; I know she'll be in the best condition possible. Their help is quite welcome since Mary is scheduled to arrive in Auckland in a couple of days. After spending time with her, I'll fly home to see Mom.

With the season advancing to late summer in the southern hemisphere, the window for rounding Cape Horn, the most southern tip of South America is shrinking. Cape Horn is a solid three weeks away, maybe more. Then add another week of sailing to get around the horn and up the eastern seaboard, clear of seasonal weather issues. Ken tells me winter is coming early to Cape Horn. As important as it is, I should oversee the maintenance myself, but in my absence, my best friend *Bo* will be in the capable and talented hands of these trusted mates. I can't ask for better.

I stretch my way across the hotel floor and dive into a fresh, warm shower; my mind imagines a sit-down breakfast—a real treat for a solo sailor. However, reality will be a chocolate muffin and a quart of orange juice, sucked down as I walk along the harbor to *Bo*.

With the familiar morning rituals ashore complete and my backpack slung on my bony shoulders, missing their bulk after 52 days at sea, I head out along the wandering waterfront pathway toward Chafer's Marina. Each step kicks up dusty memories from two years ago, the celebratory feelings of launching *Bo*, sailing her first miles, the windy waterfront, the New Zealand life, and the excitement of the unfolding new adventure.

Now, walking along these paths, paths I had become familiar with 30,000 miles ago, I recognize the cracks in the sidewalk, the missing bollard at the end of the pier, the buildings, the weird walk/don't walk alarms, as well as the wind and the sun. I feel alive and grounded, sad, but alive. I've sailed halfway around the world alone, and feel comfortable here in Wellington, but back at home in the states, my mother is very ill.

As I walk past the marina office, the door slides open and Bertie bellows out a "good morning," as normal as if we had last seen each other on Friday after a day of work. We cover two years of news in a few short minutes before I excuse myself and open the gate, clomping down the wooden dock to *Bo*. Everything is as normal as ever—except, I remind myself, I'm in New Zealand, and I sailed here. I feel authentic, not like a tourist stopping to check off another country, but vested. I know these smells, these sounds, these places, because I sailed halfway around the world at eight knots to get here. I was not flash frozen and shuttled off a plane with a colorful brochure and unrealistic expectations in hand; no, I sailed here.

The guys are gathered on *Bo* as I walk out the finger dock. Guys, *mates*, the words effectively mean the same thing, just different spelling depending on the continent—Oceania or North America. They're scoping out *Bo*, assessing their portion of the project and checking out how well their part of the build faired against the sea. We step below and gather around as Lapo talks us through his game plan. Each player nods as the work schedule touches his area of responsibility. I interject a change to the schedule . . . I'm going to head home for a week to see Mom. Instead of the intense two-and-a-half-week turn around we had originally planned, it's now stretched to four. These cool professionals adjust to the change, eliminating the necessity for pulling rabbits out of their hats and reserve that option for when the need arises. Making miracles happen and stretching time are solid traits these crazy, competent mates have. Now they can schedule things with a bit more ease instead of using midnight hours and racking up overtime crane fees.

We talk through the items on the list, many I noted while at sea, and a few they added after inspecting and injecting their experience and prudent seamanship. Mattie, Stetchy, and Gordy have helped many boats get around the world—their insights are invaluable. Together they carve up the list and plan the work. My job is simple; make *Bo* as pleasant a place to work as possible, which means empty the boat of 52 days of body odors and salty sailing gear.

In 48 hours, I'll be on a flight to Auckland to spend a couple of weeks with Mary touring New Zealand. Until then, David Minors and I will battle electronic gremlins by day and catch up, relaxing over a few pints and stories of our lifetimes at night. Welly is genuine in the evening, just as it is during the vibrant light of day.

At first light on Wednesday morning, I pack a traveling bag, check out of the hotel, and walk the harbor promenade briskly to meet Mattie G. at *Bo*. Our plan is to move *Bo* to the haul out slip, then drive to the airport and drop me off to catch an early flight. It's blowing hard, as it always does in Welly, so I hand the helm to Mattie; his experience with the swirling harbor winds is invaluable right now. *Bo* squeezes out against the pressing wind and motors down the fairway to open water before making a tight left turn to enter the well for the crane and haul out. The whole procedure makes us look like nonchalant, world girdling sailors—which, by the way, we are.

With *Bo* secured in the well, Mattie whisks me to the airport, and in a powerful whoosh of jet engine thrust, I'm traveling at an incomprehensible speed to Auckland. At sea, things happen slowly. Weather changes are announced by slow, subtle changes in the sky, sometimes days before they arrive. Swells travel thousands of miles before alerting an intuitive mariner to changes happening half a world away. But on shore, everything moves at an intense speed, abrupt changes precipitously rise and fall. 72 hours ago, I was battling my way up the Cook Straights, listening to the rhythm of the wind as its tempo eased. Today, screeching tires, honking horns, and throngs of eyeless people with seemingly purposeful intentions are overwhelming.

In Auckland, I find my way to the hotel where Mary sits patiently in the lobby waiting for me. We have an optimistic, but relaxed plan for the day, and after dropping my bags in the hotel room, we walk briskly to the waterfront, order a quick lunch, and scurry onto a ferry for Waiheke Island. I had minimal input to the plans for the next two weeks, having been out at sea while Mary scoured the tour guides and pared down the interesting options to fit our two-week schedule. But today, my only desire is to sit on the patio at Cable Bay Winery on Waiheke Island and enjoy the late afternoon sun with a bottle of wine.

Two years ago, after shipping *Bo* to America, Mary and I enjoyed Waiheke Island and the wineries. This time, with only the afternoon to play, we'll hop into a cab for the short ride to the farthest away of three wineries and walk back, tasting along the way before ending up on the patio at Cable Bay.

In the casual Mudbrick winery tasting room, another couple joins us. They mention that they just sailed to Waiheke Island on a charter boat from Auckland. Their conversation bounces off the walls with excitement, exhorting the enjoyable time on their very first sail. I relish this moment and their excitement; it rekindles the memories of my first sail. Mary and I listen and keep quiet about my avocation. We chuckle when the gentleman notices my shirt, imprinted with the Trans-Pac Race logo and inquires if I sail.

After answering and sharing the laugh with them, Mary and I stroll the dirt road down to the Cable Bay Winery and enjoy the comfortable late afternoon overlooking the ocean.

In the late evening, the ferry takes us back across the dark waters of Auckland's harbor with the beautiful skyline twinkling in the distance. Tomorrow, we'll begin a journey down the length of the North Island before heading to famed areas of the South Island—Christchurch, Invercargill, Queenstown—their glaciers and mountains famous for the landscapes in the film trilogy, *Lord of the Rings*.

* * *

We'll take a few days to drive to Wellington, stopping at Lake Taupo in the center of the North Island with the intent of trekking the Tongariro Crossing. The Tongariro Crossing is an eight-hour trek up one side of a semi-dormant volcano, through the crater and past the Emerald Lakes before heading back down the sulfur smoking hills on the other side.

On a sunny day, it's a beautiful hike. Lapo warned us not to hike it on a rainy day, as the wind, weather, and altitude will make the journey miserable. Without the luxury of time, we wake to a solid, cold rain and have no choice. We drive to the finish end of the hike where we park the car and meet a bus driver and three others—a couple from England and a young woman working at the B&B where they are staying. On the ride to the beginning of the trailhead, the bus driver tells us the weather will make the hiking miserable and suggests a more civilized option—hike for an hour to the first turn around and call him, then hike back to where he leaves us and he'll come pick us up. We acknowledge this makes reasonable sense, but struggle with the thought of not making the entire crossing.

As we begin our trek up the trail, a young couple appears from around the bend, cold, dripping wet and miserable. They've done exactly what the driver advised. We cinch up our jackets and continue hiking. An hour later, we reach the sign indicating it's a good place to turn back if you aren't prepared to hike the entire route. We look up the ascending grade and consider our options. Everything the driver said makes perfect sense except for the direction of the wind, which has been at our back. I reason to the others, if we turn back, we'll be walking into the wind and rain for the next hour. If we continue forward, an hour from now, we'll be at the peak and cross over the ridge into sheltered areas. We are mixed about this reasoning, but my credentials; sailing solo from Cape Town, lends weight to my argument and the others follow. A miserable hour later, we crest the ridge and begin our decent into the crater, the rain nearly gone, and the route now sheltered from the wind.

Hiking across this amazingly stark and rugged landscape is beautiful. We clear the ridge and descend to the emerald pools. These beautiful pools of bright, emerald water, starkly contrast with the gray skies and brown lands around us. I can only imagine how beautiful they shine under a clear blue sky.

Across the bottom of the crater and out the far side of the mountain, we hike past fissures in the hillsides still emitting a spooky, sulfur smoke before an endless descending set of steps eventually peters out at the parking area and our car. With the zeal of high school kids, we pile the five of us, with our small packs and soaking wet gear, into the tiny, compact rental car and drive our new friends the last mile back to their car. Jokingly, we plan an evening of medicinal protocol at the wine bar in town.

Our next stop is Wellington, for a two-day stay, giving me a chance to check in on *Bo* and the maintenance projects before flying to Christchurch to begin a tour of the South Island. I make it sound easy and comfortable leaving *Bo* in the hands of these caring men, but after two years and half a world of sailing, it's impossible not to check in on her. This stopover gives me peace of mind and a chance to answer questions, not to mention hang with *Bo* for a couple of days so I can travel at ease to the South Island. *Bo* is doing fine; the mates are well in control and my worries are just a way of imposing my self-important, parental influence.

Wellington drifts away behind us as I look longingly out the plane window; the wind rasped Cook Straights passing under the wings. The broken clouds, the sun, the rugged coast, they all pick at my sensitivities, taunting me back to sea. Only the power of a jet engine can prevail over this feeling and carry us to Christchurch on the southeastern shore of the South Island. Christchurch still suffers from a debilitating earthquake that occurred a couple of years ago. The surprise fault line laid destruction to the central business district and much of the surrounding area.

In Christchurch, we have lunch with my best friend Rob's daughter before driving to Dunedin later in the day. We meet Rowan at a small café and hear about her life as a Fulbright scholar studying bees in New Zealand. Her enthusiastic youthful sense of adventure levels the score versus the worry of her parents. After a fun lunch and warm goodbyes, we head off to the southern end of New Zealand. Later, I report home to her father, "Rowan has the world at her finger tips, beginning with New Zealand."

Reaching Dunedin late in the day, we stop for the night. Dunedin's city planners used the layout of the Scottish town of Edinburg as a template, providing us with unique walking routes as we work our way across the center square for dinner.

After a quiet night and warm breakfast, we make the short drive to Invercargill and stop on our way to Queenstown. Invercargill has one important item of note for Mary—the world's most southern Starbucks coffee shop.

While sipping coffee, Mary patiently waits for a chance to have her picture taken standing next to the plaque on the wall declaring this important fact. We ask the locals sitting in the booth under the sign if they would mind if we take a quick photo. Their laughter indicates they didn't realize there was such a plaque on the wall behind them and kindly offer to help take the photos.

With this distinctively important stop checked off the list, we head across the beautiful South Island toward Queensland. The road winds across the landscape, unfolding panoramic vistas at every turn as we imagine being immersed in *The Lord of the Rings*, the famous movie shot in these remote locations. Outside Queenstown, the road hugs the rim of Wakatipu Lake, occasionally narrowing to one lane as it rounds tight outcroppings of rock, making patience and courtesy pertinent attributes of driving. Rushed Americans like us need to take a deep breath and realign our driving protocol.

Queenstown holds a mesmerizing beauty tucked between the mountains and the lakeshore. Our plan for the two nights allows us time to enjoy the area and trek part of the Routburn Track before continuing on to the Fox Glacier.

The Routburn Track is one of New Zealand's Great Walks. Its entire length is 32 km and can be accessed from either end.

Huts are spaced along the way for stopping and camping. Many day hikers, like us, hike in, turn around, and hike back out the same day. Others, called through hikers, indicative of the Kiwi spirit, arrange *key swaps* along the way; an arrangement where a hiker starting at one end of the long track will swap car keys when they meet another hiker trekking the opposite direction to help facilitate car transportation after the hike.

The trailhead for the Routburn Track is an hour's drive into the hills outside Queenstown. Our plan is to hike part way up the Track to a shelter, have lunch, and hike back. The scenery is spellbinding at every step, and the chance to relax at the shelter allows us a stunning view of the rugged mountains rising up unexpectedly from flat meadow with hardly the sign of a foothill. It would be easy to stay and not return, reminiscent of Cape Town, but an unexpected experience awaits us in the town of Fox Glacier.

The road from Queenstown to Fox Glacier wanders along, around, and through the Southern Alps, a string of mountains running the backbone of the South Island. Eventually, we arrive at the ocean and course along the shore to the town of Fox Glacier, named for the famous ice flow. These beautiful, usually snowcapped mountains actually divert the winds and weather patterns of the Southern Ocean and create weather conflicts like the one that stalled us as we sailed north along this coast. It's an amazing example of the interreacting dynamics of wind, sea and land masses. And like our own lives, we too have to exist and flow around eloquently stubborn issues that ultimately change our path and wear away our sharpness.

We wind our way through one of the most beautiful areas in the world. The mountains and meadows clear out as we reach the coast and drive north across a number of watersheds before reaching the small town of Fox Glacier. After settling into a small room, we stroll the couple of blocks into town to gain our bearings and enjoy dinner.

At the main intersection, the road goes one way to our motel, another way up the island, and another, along a block of small shops, a couple of restaurants, and the outfitter we'll meet in the morning for our excursion to the glacier. We look up at the mountains for the profile of Mt. Cook, the training ground of Sir Edmund Hillary, but as is typical, low clouds shroud the mountain.

At first light, as the morning sunbeams work around the imposing mountaintops, we grab a quick breakfast and check in with the outfitter for our tour of the Fox Glacier. The perfunctory orientation involves sizing boots, instruction on the use of crampons and making sure we have sufficient gear to enjoy the trek.

A couple of weeks earlier, *Bo* and I sailed along this magnificent coast line just a few miles further north where white-capped mountains filled with rivers of ice rise up from the sea. These mighty glaciers continue to sculpt the Southern Alps and the South Island. From that vantage point 30 miles offshore, there was little suggestion of the less than delicate dance of dynamic change from global warming going on along the shore.

Along with Jess, our guide, 15 of us board the bus for the short drive to the base of the glacier. Dismounting one-by-one, we are exposed to the beautiful sheer cliffs, the gravel edge, and the mighty river of glacial melt flowing rapidly out to sea.

As we acquaint ourselves with new surroundings, we take pictures, and adjust our clothing as Jess begins to speak.

"What you are seeing is the sculptured work of the glacier; the sheer, barren walls of granite were the edges of the glacier just a couple of years ago. The gravel sand bars are the crushing's from the pressure of the ice. The river is the melted ice from the glacier."

"Where's the glacier?" someone asked.

"It's receded behind the bend. Just two years ago this area where we stand was under the glacier." Collectively, we begin to walk the quarter-mile around the bend, trying to comprehend the statement Jess just made.

As we round the bend, we get our first sightings of the dirty, live edge of the glacier, still a quarter of a mile away. Using great caution, Jess explains we need to pay attention, walk quickly in single file and meet safely at the staging area ahead of us near the glacier's edge. There is still the risk of falling rock and landslides from the unstable land recently revealed by the melting, receding ice. We put our cameras in our pockets and heed her warnings.

At the staging area, we don our crampons and grab ski poles before heading onto the live face of the glacier. Over the next few hours, my breathing is interrupted by gasps of "Wow!" Heartbeats rev and I vacillate between viewing the amazing beauty and scolding myself for my lack of understanding of these things.

Documentaries have done an injustice; easily sharing the melting ice and making the beautiful sights seem instantly accessible, comprehensible, and gratifying. They are not. In reality, I slip, stumble, and watch ice melt in every conceivable way. Droplets flow into rivulets, small streams into pools, and waterfalls into the mighty, turbulent, scouring, muddy river of glacial silt and crushed granite. I'm experiencing something so special and soul touching I am left speechless. The power and dynamics of this glacier are as inspiring and intimidating as the cyclone in the Indian Ocean—all this power resulting from the confluence of subtle energies—water, wind, sun, and temperature changes.

We hike among ice in colors I'll never be able to describe, some of it beautifully dirty, striated with the history of weather. Some of it as clear as glass; tons of pressure and time suffocating air from it. Aquas, greens, whites and lavenders, gray and black speckled ice, with boulders the size of semi-trucks slowly wandering miles from their birth years ago.

We eat lunch by a walled-in, roofless ice cathedral. As we relax, Jess explores and comes back with an exciting find—a newly formed cave, safe enough for us to explore. She claims we'll be the first to see this cave. She finishes the sentence sadly, explaining it will disappear in a few days—melted and gone.

Climbing into the most beautifully sculpted aqua glass I've ever seen, I step carefully through this chamber of the glacier's heart, tiptoeing while sliding my hand along lobes of green ice, my fingers touching her soul. I'm not aware that the glacier is seducing me . . . seducing me to interpret the slow, cancerous death of this piece of nature's art that is so alive in all its magnificence.

Exiting the cave into clear air, released from the grasp of its intention, I look around and notice bare granite walls rising a hundred feet before vegetation grows on the upper ledge. Jess explains that the vegetation line was the edge of the glacier last year. I gasped in disbelief . . . "In just a year, it receded that far?" She explains further. Less than a year ago, they walked the path high above us, and from it, stepped onto the live face of the glacier. My soul wept as if I were watching my brother die.

We spend the rest of the afternoon on a wandering traverse of the glacier, returning to the parking lot in the dying light of day. I find it hard to keep an eye forward, compelled to look behind me at what has been here for many years and won't be here tomorrow. The impact of humans on the ocean and now the earth are becoming part of me, etched on the emulsion sheet of my mind.

Turning in our equipment, we thank Jess and the outfitters for the amazing experience. With the evening comes a new understanding of the earth and a fear for the future. Mary and I walk under the night sky back to our room and look into the heavens. The universe turns at an excruciatingly slow pace. Each day, like life or the glacier, moves so slowly at the beginning we hardly notice any change, then gains momentum and morphs. Frozen water melts—dripping, trickling, and flowing, before rushing forward to the sea as life retreats.

I can't stop thinking of the long boulder, the size of a semi-truck on the face of the Fox Glacier. Seasoned guides have watched it carefully, daily, for six years as it makes its way toward the sea at a pace only the eons old universe can comprehend. Every face of the boulder has been seen and yet, no one has ever seen it move—now miles from where it first appeared.

There is something so telling about this glacier, its contrast so dynamic, I can hear its unique sound and separate it from the symphony of the earth and the other instruments in the orchestra pit—like the painful sorrow of a fine violin emitting its last, prolonged fading note before the lights go down on stage.

The road back to Christchurch winds across the island through less dramatic but still pleasing country. Each curve and moment is filled with longing. The time is passing quickly and the desire to linger and drag our feet, to stop and sit, competes with our premeditated time schedule. Soon enough, jet engines will hurl us across this island built from immeasurable millennia of patient, slow natural forces, and we, living at the impatient speed of humans, will skip across it on winds of change.

The following days in Welly pass quickly as I reconnect with the reality of unfinished business—*Bo*, my plans, and a flight home to see Mom. Mary and I will leave for North America where I'll stop in California to see Mom, hold her, touch her hand and see into her eyes—see her in person and sense her being. The time will be short, but it will have to last this lifetime. It's not hard to consider that it may be our last time together. I have significant risk in front of me; she has a destiny with the end of her life.

From California, I head to my home in the Midwest for a couple of quick days, to touch memories before returning to Welly and powering forward with the tasks at hand—preparation, the weather at Cape Horn, the thoughts and contemplations of life. The glacier has been here for as long as the earth can remember, and we are merely a passing twinkle of sunshine. Collectively though, we change the world, both for the good and bad.

Pushing off from Welly

*B*o glides out past the customs agents at the end of the last finger pier at Chafer's Wharf in Wellington, New Zealand. The agents are snapping photographs, a governmental obligation upon departing. Not for evidence of departure, but for reference in the event New Zealand is called upon to provide assistance if we come under duress within their territorial waters. While there's no question I need rescue at some level, I hope it won't be from the New Zealand Coast Guard. Heading out to sea will serve well to rescue me—not to mention Bo, Otto, and Franklin who have been quite patient and supportive of my journey as of late.

Moments ago, with *Bo* packed, myself loaded, ready, and the weather settled, I wandered up to Duffy Rigging to borrow a couple of friends to help free *Bo* from the confines of the slip. Gordy and the mates followed me back to the dock. The customs agents made their last notations and a few other folks on neighboring yachts gathered to say goodbye. Leaving is never easy, and this time is no exception; but it is time to get on with it. I need to get back out to sea.

This leg of the trip requires we sail east to within 1,000 miles of the South American coast. As we near this waypoint, we'll look for a break in weather systems to head south for Cape Horn—the most challenging sailing on the planet, known as the sailors Everest, and if there isn't a good weather option, we'll turn left and head north, up the coast in the prevailing currents and winds.

If we turn north, each day will get warmer and calmer. We'll eventually pass Easter Island, long known for the large statues guarding a forgotten history. Then the Galapagos Islands, noted for Darwin's documentation of evolution before turning east to pass through the Panama Canal, then Cuba, Florida, and eventually Northeast to *Bo's* home in Rhode Island.

When we turn south for Cape Horn, the weather will grow increasingly worse. The roaring forties will become the furious fifties and then the screaming sixties. Cape Horn lies at 56° S latitude, just 500 miles north of Livingston Island, Antarctica. Life will be cold, wet, and intense, without letting up for at least a thousand miles beyond rounding The Horn.

* * *

The Island of Cape Horn lies at the end of the world, within reach of a sailor's imagination, yet seemingly forever beyond their physical grasp. The mere task of crossing a line to start a quest to round Cape Horn is enough of a trial to turn back multitudes of seasoned sailors.

I don't know what drives us to carry on and venture beyond known limits for days upon days, pacing the march of relentless storms to harness their frightening winds and live among ireful waves traveling unheeded around the high latitudes of the southern hemisphere. It's an unexplainable character in a human being. A character that is neither good or bad.

For me, long ago, during a dark night at sea, battered beyond personal recognition by incessant winds and angry seas, I thought of these Cape Horn sailors battling a lottery of luck, altered only slightly by the thinnest differences of persistence and skill, to determine who passes Cape Horn and who settles to the bottom of the lonely sea.

Like a bacteria, the thought of rounding Cape Horn entered my life through cracks in my weathered hands and permeated my body, festering in my mind and soul, and leaving me infected with a petition to search out this darkest corner of the oceans. To sail past it, not as a conquering hero, but as a respected inhabitant of the earth, standing in honored tribute to the forces of nature and even greater, those of the universe.

Every unfulfilled minute of the past 40 years, this festering germ has reminded me that it controls my weakness as it taunts the disconnect between my imagination and reality. I try to dismiss it, but it's futile. It drives me beyond reason. Cape Horn looms as the summit of my sailing.

* * *

But there will be no decision to go north or south off the Coast of South America. A week ago, after weeks of restless agitation, and heavy angst, I decided to forgo Cape Horn and head north for home. It would have been easy to base the decision on a rational reason—the season is too late, the weather is bad there. Mom is sick, or home needs me. But I'm no longer easily swayed by reason. I'm a man of the sea, a man of feelings, knowing, and intuition—sensitivities that are difficult to explain.

With fierce obstinacy, I held fast to the notion I could sail to this waypoint off the coast and then decide . . . hoping to shed the responsibility of the decision onto the backs of Ken and his weather routers or input from my family, instead of being the one to stand up and take full responsibility for deciding on this conclusion.

After two weeks of restless nights, waking up soaked in midnight sweat, anxious and unsettled, I awoke one morning—both physically from sleep and mentally from my oppressive stubbornness and softly said, "We aren't going around the Horn." As I said those words in the shelter of the worn out, dusty green hotel room, a sense of completeness came about me—a peace.

The universe had allowed me to wallow in my decision, but the time had come to end this balless game. There are preparations to focus on, adjustments to be made, and courses to plot on charts yet to be bought, and most important—selfishness to be halted.

I know my family, ever supportive of me and my foolish ways, is running low on positive energy. Mom is heading in one direction, and I, selfishly in another. It's time to consolidate my gains and align with my family; focusing together instead of dividing our limited strengths in opposite directions. It is time for *Bo*, Otto, Franklin, and me to head home.

After sleeping peacefully for another hour that morning, I woke with a sense of purpose. All decisions require activation, and it was now necessary for me to broadcast mine. I started with sending an email home, packing my computer into my knapsack, and heading through the pelting rain to the boat, stopping at Duffy Rigging on the way to further validate my decision in person.

The usual good morning came from Gordy and the mates, in return I offered up . . . "I'm going to head north; I'm not going to the Horn." They say fellow sailors will warn you off a bad decision, but they won't stop you from going there. I sense a collective sigh of relief around the shop as my words pierce the damp, yet to be warmed up morning. I hear someone say, "Probably a good decision." To this day, I am not sure if the words I heard came from within the room or were an echo from the universe, afforded me at this safe moment in the company of fellow sailors. Regardless, my decision was activated.

"When are you going to depart?" Gordy asked.

"Not sure yet . . . there's a nasty little cyclone floating around northeast of here . . . I'll wait for it to make up its mind and then go out behind it."

I walk down the wet docks to *Bo* and step over the rail, leaving dirty footprints on the wet deck before dropping below through the companionway. I look at the gull feather held fast to the ring frame, then across at Franklin and over towards Otto and say, "We're going north guys . . . I don't think it's the right time in life for me to see Cape Horn." With each verbalization of my decision, I gain comfort with the way it sounds. I know to some it would sound as if I were *copping out*, but I reason none of them have ever had to make this same decision, and if so—not alone.

By afternoon, my decision will have made the rounds at home, and nothing much should change. I'll inform Lapo as soon as I see him. I am sure he'll be supportive. In fact, I'm sure he'll wonder why it took me so long to come to this decision.

As I sit below in the chilled, damp air of the cluttered cabin, encapsulated in the soul of my dream, I let my eyes drift across the mess of tools spread out for various jobs underway. My mind wanders about the many fortunate circumstances of the past months and years and I think, how true to life this moment is.

"You plan, work, and prepare for a journey; stuff a duffle with expectations, sling it on your back and head off, taking the first few, confident, bounding steps, and when you reach the first fork in the road, you find most of your planning was pretty much wasted. The journey you are on will teach you what you need to learn, not what you plan to learn."

Here I am, on the luckiest run of my life, within reach of bagging the Horn, and this bit of wisdom becomes obvious and clear. For reasons more significant than I'll ever know, victory will not be the accomplishment of the obvious goal, but the accumulation of subtler and less apparent experiences.

It will take time, but I will learn the difference between telling people I sailed around Cape Horn and telling them that I sailed around the world. I will learn the collection of these experiences is far greater than the significance of bagging one specific goal— Cape Horn. Someday, I will earn the right to come back and sail Cape Horn, but for now, there's something far more important in front of me—and I am eager to get going and learn what it is.

* * *

Bo continues forward, slips out of the marina and turns for the open harbor. Hoping to slow time, we extend our arms to wave goodbye, symbolically remaining in touch, and again, I wonder what each of us is thinking.

I wave one last time, then turn and face forward, hoping to look engaged in *Bo*, and not appear indifferent to my friends watching from the dock. It must be strange to watch a friend sail away, his back turned toward you, but I have to look forward now, and so, I begin to hoist the mainsail and head out the harbor the same way I had come in weeks ago. As we turn the point, the marina slips from sight. A few miles ahead and to the left—going east, I'll be in the Southern Ocean, alone, sailing to the most remote spot on earth, sailing home.

* * *

By late evening, I am well away from Wellington, her guiding lights, and protective marks now out of sight. The rugged New Zealand coastline stands as a monument to the constant flow of the Southern Ocean, and yet it provides me with a continuously unfolding vista as we sail beyond each point. The seas are wicked sloppy, yet the winds are kind and easy. This is an awful match. Without enough wind to power through the messy seas, *Bo* wallows and yaws uneasily and I struggle with queasiness.

Additionally, I carry the burden of the emotional baggage I've packed on board; the sadness in my heart for my mother and the longing for my friends. I wonder aloud if I've made the right decision to sail off, and compare it to the thought of how nice it would be to fly home right now and be done with this trip. The emotional struggle is familiar. I fought the same feelings leaving Bermuda and Cape Town, and all the way back to when I was a boy, leaving home for summer camp.

I begged to have someone to stop this nonsense, but nobody stepped up—nor should they have—to take responsibility, nor would I. I still have a tenacious hold on this dream.

It will be a few days before the metronome in my body resets to the rhythm of the sea, but until then, with daylight waning,

I am lonely. It doesn't help to think about the five weeks it will take to cover the 5,500 miles of ocean between me and another human being.

With my friends, *Bo* and Otto, pointing forward and never wavering, we bend away from New Zealand and point toward the Chatham Islands, 500 miles away. Sailors joke about the sea beyond the Chatham Islands. It's so desolate; the nearest human friends are on the space station 250 miles overhead. A thousand miles east of the Chatham Islands is an area they call the most remote spot in the world. We'll sail past this spot and leave it to starboard as we turn north, away from my goal. Each day separates me from people, and strangely enough, each day brings me closer to home.

Passing the Dateline and Passing Time

The winds build to 30 knots during the night but fade to 10 by morning. Inconsistent weather will be my frustration for the next few days, winds coming and going, taunting and tricking me into changing sails. I run fore and aft along the deck to make the changes. Most of the time it's useless busy work, but I welcome the diversion and exercise. It helps my body adjust to being at sea.

The fourth day out, my appetite returns. I marvel at how it's taken my body four days to burn off the junk digested and stored while tethered ashore. I became accustomed to double, dark chocolate muffins for breakfast washed down by a quart of fresh squeezed orange juice. Lunch came when I wanted and dinner after a run along the harbor at the end of the day. I slid backwards into a land-based routine and found, rather easily, the weight I lost at sea lying on the shelves of the grocery store, or at the ice cream stand near the end of my evening run, or in the pint of beer at Molly Malone's while listening to music. Now I am slipping away from land and into my onboard routine. Yin and Yang . . . shore and sea . . . chocolate and . . . well, maybe chocolate is still solidly at the center of the universe.

Passing 180° longitude, I watch the numbers decrease. The reverse happened on the way to Cape Town . . . declining to zero and then ascending. 180° is on the opposite side of the earth from Greenwich, England, where 0° longitude exists and the increments increase in both directions—east and west. Through these longitudes and latitudes, I've become accustomed to the size of the world and the delicate dance I perform between time and distance.

The International Date Line will come up next, three or four days from here. Once we pass the date line, I can slip back into the timeless world gauged by miles sailed and a clock warped by wind, speed, and weather. Until then, I'll keep time to Greenwich England's Universal Time Corrected, and wait for the day when time stands still, the day we cross the International Date Line and live the same day over again by crossing from east longitude to west, by going west to east.

Bo's course is just south of east, our latitude increasing to 43° S and climbing as we take advantage of the stable weather conditions on our course to a waypoint near 46° S, 165° W. Ken's forecast shows no strong cold fronts approaching. A couple of minor ones will push winds to 30 knots while they spin around the compass, but for now, nothing as strong as the fronts of the southern Indian Ocean is forecast.

I take this in stride, thankful for the good sailing weather, but begin a regretful spiral around the decision to skip Cape Horn. "What if everything turns out to be just fine?" I ask quietly. I try to force the regret from my head, grabbing control of my emotions with the sternness of a father guiding his son and damn it down as a decision made. I will not pound into waves of depression with regret hard on the nose; instead, I'll sail with joy, relish the blessing of fair weather, and imagine the wonders of the distant Easter and Galapagos Islands.

The unique skirmish with time on the ocean begins as the International Date Line passes beneath us at 46° S on April 1st. This year, we'll watch April Fools' Day come and go and come again. "Why not?" I ask. "If there is any day worth living twice, it's April's Fools' Day." I could choose any day I want by simply logging it in my logbook twice. This is how intelligent men work it out. If today is good, why not have another round of it? Besides, the navigation and math won't calculate properly if I don't. So, with the simple strike of my pen, I clean up the math and live the first of April over again.

The wind is not into foolish replications, and dies off through the night, leaving us wallowing in the seas of this duplicate day. In the void left behind, I wonder about my statement referring to "intelligent men." Is it foolish of us to attempt to outthink time on earth and in the universe? Did the earth, in its eons of rotations around the sun on this axis, before man stepped in, ever consider a line separating today from today to be important? Does it make any difference? There's no effect until we leave our backyards searching for new limits, sailing forward, around this world and ultimately ending back where we began. I argue back—it still doesn't matter . . . tomorrow will be another day either way, right? The questions run as deep as the desolate ocean, and without the white noise of human energy or Google for answers, I am left alone with only the reverberations from the universe to debate these questions. Nothing is more complicated than quiet and simplicity. Maybe there never was a beginning . . . so . . . maybe there will never be an end?

Continuing south of east for better winds, we stay under the high-pressure systems to our north, and above the strong low to the south in the deep Southern Ocean. As the decent weather continues to favor us, we gain distance east, towards the continent of South America.

The wind blows at our face from just forward of the beam, ramping up and down, unchallenged in this desolate ocean, between 15 and 30 knots. The seas build and subside in concert, making the sailing jumpy in the high winds and more comfortable and relaxed when they drop below 20 knots. The miles add up and New Zealand is soon 600 miles behind us. I feel the umbilical cord stretch to the breaking point and then snap as we cross 700 miles—the approximate range of an extreme rescue. A ship might come to rescue us, but not likely, in the time it would take to perish from hypothermia if left floating in the ocean—alone. I look down at the tether bonding me to *Bo* and with a quick touch to my pocket; confirm the Personal Location

Beacon. Solo sailors often refer to these as LILB (life insurance location beacons), considering them lottery tickets, worthless but for a single chance in a hundred million. Then I think, that's exactly what I am, one chance in a million. I think back through the generations in my family and consider what must have been hundreds of near misses in the lives of past relatives, any one of which would negate my presence today. I keep the tether attached and except for this brief moment of awareness, push these ugly thoughts of demise from my mind and focus on the journey ahead and beyond.

* * *

The ocean is vast out here, south and east of civilization. The sky seems perpetually cloudy, though occasionally opening to reveal a chunk of blue sapphire, elevating my emotions and boosting my optimism. Void of sapphire skies, I find myself staring forward, elbows resting on the cabin top and forty feet of boat, rigging, lines and keel pointing to endless miles of ocean, horizontally around, and vertically below us.

My mind works out this seamless infinity, in its own way, to protect me. The miles aren't endless, they are only six or seven by line of sight in any direction and in my mind's defensive imagination, land lies just beyond this visual limit. I chuckle. This leg of the journey is going to be filled with the philosophical thoughts of a seaman going out of his mind, sailing on a near invisible edge, a thin wisp of a line the scale of a human hair laid across a warm globe sitting motionless in the corner of someone's comfortable living room. Yet, out here, the scale of life is immense.

And *Bo*? She just sails, like walking down the street. She carries me as if I were her duffle slung across her shoulders, baggage needing to get somewhere. I feel at one with *Bo*, Otto, and Franklin. I sense they sail an agenda, put forth to them by some faithful spirit in the universe. They know we need to get home, and they sail as if this were the plan all along. I continue to look to starboard, in the direction of Cape Horn while they continue nudging me to port, in the direction of home and life. It seems I have no effect on them, yet they forever, are changing me.

* * *

Ahead and to port, the water looks peculiar. I stare at it but can't make out what kind of disturbance is causing the different shades of color. Pulling the binoculars from their resting place in the unused galley sink, I twist the rings to focus on the strange, bubbling water. I am witness to the endless action of the uninterrupted cycles of the eons; a feeding frenzy—a column of life in the food chain.

The surface boils with activity while just above a flock of seabirds float, occasionally dipping into the turbulent sea. Below, beyond my sight must be a school of small bait fish and below them, larger fish feeding and chasing them, driving them to the surface—the limit of their survivable environment—the equivalent of having their backs against the wall. Perhaps there are just a few layers, but maybe out here in the open wilderness there are many layers. The largest of huge ocean fish swim slowly in the deep depths below, feeding on very large fish that are feeding on large fish that are feeding on good-sized fish, and on up to the smallest bait fish forced to jump into the air to escape their demise, only to be snatched by seabirds.

I notice the familiar shape of a large tuna jumping through the air, feeding, or maybe fleeing, jumping from a large marlin below, out of my sight. I watch and study this amazing cycle of life as we slowly sail by, wondering if they notice or even care that we're here. Would we too be edible except for the fiberglass packaging? A few miles beyond this boiling turbulence, the sight lingers in my mind.

Over the past 15,000 miles, there have been no whales. Tegan Mortimer, our team scientist explained to me during a whale watching trip, that whale populations have been increasing slowly and now approximate ten percent of what they were before whaling decimated the seas. Ten percent . . . I think . . . so when I see a pod of six whales frolicking off the coast of Cabo San Lucas, does that mean at one time there were sixty, or more? I haven't seen a whale since leaving Bermuda.

I think deeper about the feeding frenzy . . . What if the fish population is only ten percent of those times too? Should the sea be teaming with fish and wildlife? Should birds flock in the skies like clouds? Birds are always flying back and forth across our wake, but seldom are there more than five to eight at a time. At home on the Great Lakes, deer overpopulate the forest. Yet, just steps away, fish under populate the lake. My mind wanders down a crooked path, drifting between visions of an abundant world and my earlier proclamations about intelligent men. Perhaps in the balance of time and eons, the elevation of superficial intelligence is overwhelming that of natural progression.

Then, I think about big tunas trapped in cans. I have a few onboard and millions are in cans on shelves around the world, unable to propagate in open waters, hoarded by people planning to eat them at some time in the distant future. Were they not better conserved alive in the ocean? But then, in the sea, they are only available to those within reach. Maybe this is good, maybe not. I look forward to the Galapagos Islands, still 4,000 miles away. The archipelago promises to be exciting and interesting given my odd lot of perspectives.

* * *

The days pass, filled with all kinds of thoughts. I've consumed a dozen freeze-dried meals since leaving, and put enough miles behind that I no longer keep track of the miles from, but instead track the depreciating sum to the symbolic waypoint, known as Point Nemo, in the middle of nowhere. The weather continues to favor us, leaving me to wonder if we are worthy of this abundance of kindness. Is the sea aware of our presence or merely waiting until the moment is right to strike? Will she turn nasty once she finds us trespassing without her approval? I convince myself to appreciate the kindness and enjoy the sailing. The weather will change, not as an assault on us, but because it will—it must.

* * *

Every motion and sound lodges in a dedicated, subconscious data bank inside me. The slap of a wave against the large panels of *Bo's* bow up forward makes one tone; the waves against the stiffer panel amidships vibrating in brittle wavelengths register a higher note. The slapping of a halyard on the mast alerts me to the increasing wind and then fades as the gust subsides. I've tried many times over the 15,000 miles to stop the slapping halyards, but finally give in, learning to appreciate and understand the reason for the noise. I listen to the engine each time it starts and wonder if the sound is the same or different, trying to project ahead of potential failures.

The hydro-generator hums as the boat speed climbs to 8 or 9 knots when the hydraulic pump kicks in to feather the prop for efficiency. The pump makes three distinct notes as it reaches full pressure—I recognize this melody, sweetly indicating things are proper. When I sense the boat speed increasing without the resulting musical notes, I check the blinking lights and confirm my suspicion. 20,000 miles of learned intuition sends me to the stern with a batten in hand to clear weeds from the prop and return the heartbeat to normal. This entire symphony of sound keeps me subconsciously tuned to the progression of time and space while the conspicuous lack of human energy in this desolate region of earth, like the absence of white noise, has me restraining my breath, tense and poised to discern the quiet language spoken by this natural universe.

* * *

Looking aft over the transom with my timer tucked up into the fiberglass corner to increase the echo when it alarms, I relax and drift off in 15-minute naps. The winds are right and easy as *Bo* slides east between 46 and 47° S latitude. Otto keeps a constant touch on the helm, but I am convinced I hear a skip in his rhythm. I calculate the days spent driving with the port ram and consider a proactive switch to the starboard unit, but give napping a priority. This never works. Once a thought is in my mind, I must tend to its demand. I've grown to trust my intuition over years of sailing. A thought is often a reminder, sometimes from within and sometimes, I believe, from somewhere else.

Stretching from my napping pose on the cockpit floor, I sit on the rail and take *Bo's* hand to sense the waves before performing the pilot ram ritual. The swap happens as smoothly as if I were a practiced, western swing dancer spinning my partner away and then reaching out with a perfectly positioned hand, timed to capture her in sync with the rhythm of the music. I have become one with *Bo* again.

I give the helm back to Otto and write in my log: *"Switched to starboard ram, port sounded funny. Be Prepared."* I stretch out on deck and drift off in the gray afternoon, napping with my lover watching over me as we slip below 47° S, headed east across the deep southern portion of the Pacific Ocean.

* * *

The skies darken at the end of the day as I stumble through chores and boredom distracting activities—mopping up water from the bow and stern, checking emails, weather, sorting freeze-dried foods for the next few days, and writing in my log. I do the proverbial math and calculate the Galapagos Islands to be about 18 to 19 days away. Easter Island, a place I had hoped to get close enough to see will be too far to the west. We'll pass 500 miles southeast of her on Easter Morning—another near miss.

While doing math, I hand calculate the compass deviation. Electronic instruments do this automatically, but the numbers I write in my log are confusing to someone not familiar with the system. Compass courses deviate between true north and magnetic north and change constantly as the magnetic center of the North Pole moves. This move, along with the varying angles and distances from the pole, disrupts the earth's magnetic force fields and creates errors or deviations in the far corners of the world. Here in the Southern Ocean, far from the North Pole, a significant deviation exists. My magnetic compass reads 060° while we sail parallel to the line of latitude at 90°—a 30° difference.

In my head, I constantly synchronize these numbers with wind directions and actual courses derived from great circle routes. It only gets complicated when I pencil it on paper. In my mind, it's easy to keep within a relative range. If we needed to clear a nearby island or shoal, it would be far more important, but out here in the vast open ocean, a few degrees one way or another seldom matters. In the end, a degree or two does add up to a significant distance, but with weather changing daily, we aren't likely to sail the same course for a thousand miles.

I laugh and wonder, if I had these navigation skills as a young man, would I have made better decisions? How much better could my decisions have been? The ones I made as a young man led me here, where I want to be.

With the last of the daylight gone and the ocean dark, I sit in the companionway with the iPad on my lap and look aft as we sail off the face of the earth. The simplicity of this machine is strange out here. I touch icons, and pictures change instantly. Everything else in my offshore world changes slowly, sailing thousands upon thousands of miles at a rate of eight or ten knots an hour. I touch the icon for a song and let the music drift as I play a game of solitaire, seeking a diversion to this all-consuming world of striking, raw nature. Even out here in this amazing world, I need to get away sometimes.

* * *

I've lost track of the days since leaving New Zealand. I pen it as *either day 15 or 16, April 12th*. I calculate 2,800 miles to the Galapagos and nearly as far from New Zealand. We're midway between the two and not far from the most remote place on earth. The weather's good, the sea is friendly, and the time is comfortable.

I write down our coordinates and wind info before calling Ken for a look at the big weather picture. Soon, we'll begin a slow turn to the northeast, easing north from 48° and 49° S latitude while still making progress east toward favorable winds . . . maybe we're making progress away from unfavorable winds?

* * *

The conversations with Ken and the others at Commanders' are addicting, the sound of their human voices link me to civilization. I do call my loved ones back home, but purposefully on an erratic schedule. Before leaving Jamestown, I explained that I can't predict when I'll call, and in an effort to prevent my family from worrying about missing a call, I don't schedule calls at regular times. My calls typically end with "Love ya; I'll call in a few days when the weather is good again." It's a stretch of the truth, but it's necessary. If I set a pattern, the onus for me to call on time and the worry if I don't will burden us both. I purposely pick times to call home when the weather is good, my spirits are high, and I'm comfortable with my emotional strength. I don't want to telegraph distress—perceived or otherwise. Close family and friends can always tell.

With Ken and the friends at Commanders', it's business, and a schedule is expected. They've become my human lifeline and pseudo psychologists.

After a round of small talk, Ken briefs me on the coming weather pattern and how best to deal with it. A low sits to the northwest and a high to the southeast. In the southern hemisphere, a low-pressure system circulates clockwise and a high-pressure system in the opposite direction—counterclockwise. I draw these systems out in my logbook where it takes on the look of a baseball-pitching machine—two wheels spinning in opposite directions spitting balls at speeds simulating those of a pitcher. Unfortunately, we again need to go against the currents of life and sail between these systems. Ken and I laugh about the predicament: not too close to the low and not too far away and into the light wind of the high.

It's not a simple route or plan for the coming days. It involves sailing east and north, back and forth depending on the shifts in the winds. When we sail north, we'll sail slow and comfortable, waiting for the wind shift to allow us to tack back favorably to the east. With the winds between 20 and 40 knots, and the seas to 15 feet, it will be a rough stomp to the northeast.

* * *

At the conception of *Bo* Dream, this was to be the Global Ocean Race—a group of adrenalin junkies pushing each other around the world over wild, open oceans. Today, I'm thankful it's not. In the race, I would prevail just fine, and always have, but the lack of the race changes the parameters and allows me to use tools I wouldn't consider for a race (e.g., sacrificing a half-knot of boat speed for more comfortable control). When racing, we can't afford to lose five or six miles over twelve hours unless it's necessary to balance risk and reward or fatigue and endurance—sometimes both.

I work out the plan for the next few days and note when to be ready to reef, when to expect winds to increase and decrease, when tacks might happen and what indicators make good parameters for decision-making. It's a matrix of information I use to manage making choices when I'm fatigued, separating the unimportant chafe from the kernels of predetermined points of action. This allows me to preserve energy for unexpected options, which according to Murphy's Law, always present themselves at inopportune moments, and to minimize wasting energy on things unlikely to happen.

This matches a nugget of wisdom given me by an old salt while preparing *Bodacious Dream* in Rhode Island. I noticed him standing on the hard, looking up at *Bo* and studying her lines. I asked if I could help him, which began a long conversation. We talked about sailing *Bo* and crossing oceans and when he left, he left me with this simply stated wisdom, "Remember one thing. If they say it's going to blow 30, it's probably going to blow 30. Don't spend unnecessary energy worrying it might blow 50, because it likely won't." Unfortunately, ingrained in me are years of experiences on the Great Lakes, keeping me wary of the vagaries of storms. Great Lake's storms and squalls are unpredictable at best; storms on the ocean are more predictable, as the old salt enlightened.

* * *

With the coming rough weather, I prepare *Bo* for storm sailing in the Southern Ocean. Set for reefing, there are sail ties on the Solent and a few more, like a pair of slip-on shoes at the back door, tied on the lifelines around the boat—just in case.

Button by button, my worn, arthritic fingers hank the storm jib to the inner forestay and then bundle and secure it to the deck. I check the mainsail reef lines, now showing signs of wear like old gloves and secure loose equipment both above and below decks.

I pause for a moment in the middle of my work to look across the water and remind myself how beautiful it is out here right now—how great the sailing is. I consciously work to keep my worries of the future from tainting the beautiful sailing of today. It's all perfunctory, nothing special or unusual. This day is one in a hundred. Today may have problems and it may not. It doesn't matter; I'll handle what comes when it comes. An unexpected problem just becomes an interesting challenge, requiring a new use of old tools. Everything we need is here; we just have to configure it to prevail. Like the iPad, every part of it has been on this earth since the beginning of time; only now the materials are configured in an order to do today's job.

* * *

The wind builds on starboard tack as we move north up the western side of the high-pressure system, waiting for a shift to the west of north to force us to tack back to the east. The sailing is systematic, but the wave action is not. With each set of waves, *Bo* lifts over the first and falls into the trough behind it, slamming belly first and exhaling a puff of wind from below as the hull flexes. If our speed is up, she leaps from the wave, and surges clear of the water with the power in her sails, only to give way to gravity and then slam, belly first into the trough ahead of her. She regains her composure, surges to the next lifting wave and continues on, subsequently falling.

I've become accustomed to the first burst of speed and the resulting rhythm of slams that come after it. I imagine being a running back in football, taking a few steps to gain momentum before a tackler abruptly slows forward progression and the next tackler slams me to the ground. Like the running back, we get up slowly and return to the action. Every once in a while, we break a tackle and slide between a few waves, making fast miles until caught. On some occasions, we break completely free and make for open water, getting a good long run in before the waves set up and stop us.

The pounding wrenches *Bo* from the corners of her hull to the tip of her spar. Every part of her shivers in a strange connected synchronicity through endless waves, endless miles, endless setbacks, and endless comebacks. The days flow by and the winds switch back and forth as we work up the alley between the pressure systems. The winds haven't dropped below 20 knots in seven days—mostly logged at 30 and above with gusts topping 40. I'm used to the pounding and stopped worrying about *Bo's* integrity long ago. But in the lonely hours of the night, I beg it to stop, writing in my log:

"This sucks! The waves are endless, pounding my persistence to a pulp, looking for any weakness I have hidden deeply away. The wind won't quit, and neither will I. I pray for a mutual understanding soon."

* * *

The past seven days of relentless weather have taken us far from the roaring forties and the Southern Ocean. We are above 30°S latitude, on a starboard tack sailing a course of 357°, the bearing to the Galapagos Islands, 1,700 miles north. I log the position at 29° 26' S.

The wind and waves are losing their energy and *Bo* sails as if she and the weather have given up fighting and shaken hands in respect. As the evening sky clears to a silky, black canopy of stars, I have some personal business to take care of before leaving the Southern Ocean completely behind. I drop below and grab three *Bodacious Dream* ball caps and what's left of the bottomless, half pint of Irish whiskey Joe Harris gave me before leaving Jamestown last October.

In the night wind, I step out on deck and bare my soul to the sea. We've had a good rout the past week, reducing all of us to equal levels of respect. I twist open the bottle and take a touch of whiskey on my tongue and then raise the flask in toast to the sea and pour a dram overboard. Lifting it again, I pour a splash on deck for *Bo*, Otto, and Franklin. There are no words for this moment, just rivulets of salt water running along the deck and down my cheeks.

I take one of the hats in my hand, caress the bill, and thank Mikey (Laughing Gull) for watching over me before I gently hand it over the starboard rail into the sea. With the second hat,

I pause, speaking a few personal words to my father and thank him in my own way for being the man he was and making me the man I am and let it go over the port rail. It's taken me years to understand how a man can be more influential in absentia than in person. The third hat I've set aside for Neptune, and give it to the bioluminescent wake flowing out behind us.

My unfulfilled goal of Cape Horn, 2,500 miles away to the southeast leaves me longing, but in the spirit of these giant men, this boat and the sea, I feel I have earned a place here.

Galapagos in Sight

Each mile north brings more stable winds and warmer temperatures as I set a mark for the next waypoint, 1,000 miles from the Galapagos. Each day we reach on a fair wind until night when the winds turn fickle and shifty before the first hint of dawn when they rebuild and stabilize. The sun burns hot through the day while I enjoy a game of tag with the squalls sneaking up on us. It reminds me of the Power Hat game I played with my god kids when they were small—tickling, running and staying ahead of them until a point when I feigned weakness and allowed them to catch me, taking the hat off my head and leaving me limp and powerless until it was restored. In the same way, Bo and I try to stay ahead of the squalls until we allow them to catch us, cleansing the decks and rejuvenating my soul with the fresh water rain. As we pass the waypoint, I calculate six more days to the Galapagos Islands.

With 800 miles to go, the weather falls apart and the wind builds into the night. Twenty builds to twenty-five and waves of rain pass through the darkness. *Bo* is out of balance and Otto struggles to correct given input from the electronic wind sensors atop the mast. I suit up in foul weather gear and clip my tether to a padeye on the cockpit sole, excited to take *Bo's* hand and steer. I ease the rudder back and forth, matching the groove in the wind and waves with the one in my centered self, and then settle into tantric sex, sailing briskly through the dark, rainy night. The horizon is closed in with nothing to define it. A light from a distant ship or lighthouse would help, but there's no humanity near here—we are alone.

As the rain ends, the occluded skies break open and I align the tip of the windward spreader with a star in the heavens and guide *Bo* down an ancient course. Miles pass, indifferent to anything. I drift off, instinctively guiding *Bo*, listening to the sea, and contemplating the depth of my experience. If I didn't get what I came for, what brought me here? I flip through the stack of flash cards in my memory—sunsets, turtles, storms, starry nights, glowing fish, and dolphins looking up at me, hinting of something important. The star moves slowly across the sky as a universal hand rotates the earth, making it necessary to pick a new star as a guide to keep us on course while miles flow out behind us in a hiss of bioluminescent water.

The feel of the ocean reverberating through *Bo's* helm and the stroke of soft wind on my cheek instinctively convey there is something to this—something the ocean and dolphins want me to know.

There is no recollection of time passing other than the horizon revealing itself slowly as dawn lightens the sky. It seems like just moments ago I took *Bo's* helm to steer through the rain squall. I hit the button allowing Otto to drive, stand up, and bend backwards in a stretch before dropping below to find some marker to define the lost hours.

A cold meal of freeze-dried chicken and rice sits in its pouch, resting in the sink. My log entry indicates half the night has passed. I'm not tired, hungry or thirsty, but supremely relaxed. I wonder if I allowed myself to travel beyond, finding the place where time, distance and space mean nothing—where being alive is being. I step back into the cockpit, lean on the cabin top and look forward into the morning sky. This is no longer a place to question or wonder about, but a time to accept my part in it.

* * *

The Galapagos Islands are less than fifty miles ahead of us. The sun is setting, and arriving during the night is unnecessary. I slow *Bo's* pace and relax. In the morning, I'll approach the harbor at Santa Cruz and find my way into a town that I learned is populated by 20,000 people. I thought the Galapagos Islands were uninhabited, except for a cadre of scientists and explorers. How distorted my vision of the world is proving to be.

Sailing slowly through dawn toward Santa Cruz, a whale breaches off my starboard rail—I am elated by her welcome. She's the first leviathan I've seen since leaving Bermuda seven months ago. At 0800 hours we nose into the anchorage and call my contact, Mike, on the VHF radio for instructions. A water taxi—an open skiff of a boat with a driver tending the outboard, approaches with a second man waving, pointing me in the direction of a large, yellow mooring buoy. In a smooth and quick procedure, we tie to the mooring and place an anchor behind us to stay aligned with two, much larger, steel research vessels on either side. *Bo* feels secure and Mike invites me to grab my gear and passport and come ashore with him. The step down into the water taxi begins another seamless transition from sailing alone at sea to walking a populated, energetic, shore side environment.

We walk a block to Mike's truck and drive up the road to his business—a restaurant, office, marina, and hotel, all in various stages of construction. Workers, consumed with various tasks, look me over with amusement as Mike motions me to drop my bags in his office.

While Mike invents a shower, I grab my soap and towel and watch with piqued interest. He speaks fluently with the workers as they hurriedly move things about to clear a dark area beneath a roughed-out flight of concrete stairs. They shove a hose through the opening of a riser, allowing it to hang in the space just above head height. A young man drags a sawhorse into the cavern and slaps it, motioning in universal language, "There you go." Mike turns the water on and speaking in the local language, he tells the workers to leave me alone. I'm filled with thoughts of concentration camps and POW facilities, but the cool, clear water washes away 35 days of life at sea and transforms me into a being more suitable for shore in a foreign country.

While still offshore, I had emailed Mike, humorously requesting breakfast, a cold beer, and a shower. Mike finishes fulfilling my request with Huevos Rancheros and a Cerveza before taking me on a tour of Santa Cruz. Mike is certain the customs office is closed for the holiday, but assures me not to worry; he let the navy know I was coming and we can take care of that business tomorrow.

We stop to check in on woodworkers building tables and furniture for his new restaurant in an open, makeshift woodshop down a rutted road away from the town of mostly incomplete, poured concrete structures. I snap pictures of odd plants and cactus along the road and tell Mike I'm looking forward to seeing the large tortoises; they've always fascinated me.

He makes a quick turn off the main road and heads to an area where he knows the tortoises congregate. Just around a curve, we catch up with two large ones in the middle of the road. These are wild tortoises he tells me, "It's good to see the ones in captivity up at the Park National, but these are wild." In 24 hours I have come from being deeply alone at sea, escorted by a whale and cleansed in a makeshift shower, to exploring a natural land of large, wild tortoises. Culture shock barely explains my frame of mind.

Driving back to the harbor, Mike explains the water taxies system—50 cents per ride either way. "Meet them here on shore or call them on the radio from the boat." I ride a taxi back out to *Bo* to slow down the transformation. Onboard, I grab a Coke and sit down on deck, sipping and breathing slowly. I watch the comings and goings of the harbor and ponder the homes of the unusual cruising boats at anchor around us. Within minutes, we drift asleep—my mind, body, and *Bodacious Dream* all relaxing at anchor.

Touring the Galapagos

*T*he *Galapagos Islands straddle the equator. Santa Cruz, where Bo is anchored, is one degree to the south; the northern most islands are just above. The irony of this isn't lost on me; my journey now straddles the long offshore passages of 42, 52, and 35 days, and the short ones of 7 days to Panama, Florida and home. Too, the Galapagos straddle an expanse of time—a time when evolution progressed at its own pace over the eons and that of modern day, where scientists, experts, and philosophers explain the mysteries of our existence in an instant with the technology and intelligence of our modern world.*

For now, this is enough deep thinking. I'm on shore in Santa Cruz adjusting to the life of a busy community in a place I thought would be nearly deserted. A walk to the center of town to look for dinner and conversation— being starved of both for the last 35 days—produces a great find, a small place with music tumbling down from the balcony of the bar next door. Always a sucker for lively times, I find two local musicians entertaining a small group of friends. I lean back in a corner with a Corona Beer, soak up the music, and recharge my body with the abundance of human energy.

I'm limiting my stay here to a week. Day one comes and goes, and as day two quickly passes, I am certain I've made a mistake. There are boat tours to the other islands, diving and snorkeling trips and eco tours lasting one to four and five days. The Galapagos Islands are off limits to visitors without a trained, licensed guide. This eliminates the option of cruising to other islands on my own with *Bodacious Dream*. In my mind, I juggle the work list, the tours, and the need to regenerate my body before sailing off again. Like most of my life, regeneration slips from the juggling and falls to the ground. It's only 1,000 miles to Panama—I can rest there.

The work list is important, but topping the list is finishing legal entry into Ecuador, the governing nation of the Galapagos Islands. Add to this, grocery shopping for cookies and chocolate and then regular maintenance for *Bo* and the day slips into late afternoon. I force myself back to shore, intent on walking to the Park National to see the large turtles and iguanas they nurture in an effort to keep the various species from extinction. I'm fascinated by the huge turtles and find myself trailing a tour guide, eaves dropping on his explanations. The walk is comfortable, the weather warm, and as the day ends, I find myself watching the split tail birds floating high above me. "They're Frigate birds" I'm told by a local walking alongside me.

I wander down the road to the first block of town near the harbor docks and find a seat at the small bar next to the Internet Café, a popular spot for obvious reasons—cold beer and a strong Internet signal. The bulk of patrons are scientists, naturalists, and cruising sailors from around the world, all wanting to check in with home via the Internet. Seating is scattered around a few tables. As the chairs fill up at the end of the day, subconsciously everyone seems to push back from the table in front of them to create a more inviting, informal circle of accents, languages, stories, and tales.

Closest to me is a young man and his girlfriend from Alaska, beyond them a couple from Africa, and farther around the loosely defined circle are two young scientists on a mysterious mission for National Geographic. They ask me for a story about the most unusual thing I encountered on the open ocean and I reply, as I often do, about the bioluminescent orbs in the deep Southern Ocean and how mystified I was and chose to accept them without further explanation.

The two scientists enlighten us, explaining the phenomena are bioluminescent squid, and laughingly tell the gathering about their first encounter with them. There is one breed of gull; a nocturnal feeder, which swoops down to grab the glowing squid from the ocean and fly off into the pitch, black night. Their first encounter was of the globes floating through the night sky in the talons of a bird hidden by the darkness. For the rest of the week, these gatherings at the Internet Café are the highlight of the day.

Inquiring with travelers and locals about the best things to see with my limited time, narrows the options. One person suggests a specific guide named George and any trip he does. In a tour operator's office, I explain my time limit and with a knowing glint in her eye, she seems to know just what I need. After making a few calls, I am booked on a tour to North Seymour Island. The only problem being, it requires a day's delay in my departure. Given the previous advice and the hint of acknowledgement from the tour operator, I accept my luck and agree. My schedule is now defined: a day to work on *Bo*, a day for the tour, one more for prep, and then depart the following day. I dig into my boat chores with earnest to earn my day off for the tour.

The bus stops to pick me up at the designated corner at 8:00 a.m. and then continues through the streets of Santa Cruz, making two more stops for additional tour members before heading across the island to meet our guide and his boat. The small charter bus slows to a stop on the side of the road across from a small, disheveled but neat home. The energetic assistant runs across the road and picks up a cooler and a couple of bags from the front porch. Back on board, he explains he picked up fresh fish and supplies for our lunch.

We arrive at the north end of Santa Cruz where a number of groups are gathered around the immigration dock and outpost. Two dogs with uniformed masters on leashes are ambling through the gathering. I mention to a young man standing next to me, this seems like an unusual place to be inspecting for drugs. He explains they are looking for endangered species hidden for export— sea cucumbers, fish, iguanas. He further explains the program is run and arranged by his organization, The Sea Shepherd, for the local Galapagos government. The young man is on our tour, affording us the opportunity to talk more about The Sea Shepherd's work as stewards of the sea.

Two trips in a small inflatable skiff fill the larger powerboat with 12 of us for the tour. We haul up the anchor and embark on the 45-minute boat ride—out beyond a point of land, and around the corner to North Seymour Island. It's refreshing to let the water pass by under the command of another captain. This time, without responsibilities, I can relax and observe the passing of colorful waters, islands, birds, and wildlife.

The boat slows and anchors off North Seymour Island. The small inflatable shuttles us to the low-lying island of volcanic rock and stunted, gnarly trees, few of which appear to be more than six-feet high. I'm part of the first group ashore and we are instructed to wait in a particular area until the rest of the group arrives. A small sea lion pup stands guard, barking orders to stay put and remain patient. We learn from George that these pups are left ashore by their parents who travel offshore in search of food. With no predators on the island to harm them, the pups are left safely alone. After learning this, I suspect the barked orders are more likely playful offers of companionship.

With George guiding, we stay on the well-worn path through the gnarly brush and spot frigate birds nesting, mating, and starting families. Inflating their bright orange chests, the male birds attempt to attract female mates. Upon acceptance, the females are presented a small stick, the beginning of a nest and their future. The rules of nature define the best males attract the best females and many of these couples have already begun their families. Those remaining are the less attractive, less acceptable (solo sailors most likely), and yet, in nature there appears to be a mate for everyone.

In the shade of a scrubby bush, we spot a relaxing iguana. These prehistoric looking creatures are symbolic of the

Galapagos Islands, their armored skin, an amazing array of various sized scales and overlapping shields, judiciously colored, and perfectly shaped to match the varying contours of their bodies. I find myself studying nature's amazing mosaic, completely unaware it is glaring back at me with a hissing, flicking tongue.

We walk across the highest point on the island, no more than six feet above sea level, to the windward side, obviously blown clear of vegetation by the brunt persistence of prevailing winds. Here, the landscape is more rock and sand, with few trees.

This side is the nesting ground of the famous Blue-Footed Booby. Through the amazing course of evolution, these two different avian species inhabit the same island; frigates live in the trees on the leeward side, and blue-footed boobies nest on the ground on the windward side.

I take a moment to photograph the blue feet of a nesting booby covering two eggs laid in a small indentation in the sand. When I review the photograph, I see I've captured the piercing eyes of the bird. These greenish/yellow eyes are a stark contrast to the comical blue feet. I wonder if nature's balance is in play here. The Booby's eyes send a *don't mess with me* attitude, adding enforcement to *"Don't step on my blue suede shoes."*

We hike around the island along the wave-washed beach of beautiful white sand before returning to the boat where George offers us snorkeling gear and suggests a swim before lunch. Everyone takes the offer and jumps into the warm water. I haven't snorkeled casually in many years and enjoy floating easily in the buoyant salt water, idling on the surface before picking a path of exploration.

Swimming toward shore in shallower waters, I drift with the current, observing a multitude of small, colorful fish, and begin diving and surfacing, acting like a graceful dolphin . . . at least that's what I think. Perhaps a Sea Lion is a more realistic representation. As I twist and turn, I notice a rock moving mysteriously and watch it morph into an Eagle Ray taking off in underwater flight.

This beautifully spotted ray's outer fringes begin to ripple like chiffon fabric tickled by the wind. The gentle movement provides propulsion and the ray takes off, skimming across the bottom, lifting over large rocks and perfecting a turn to the left. I'm mesmerized but have to return to the surface for more air, reminding myself of the boundaries we straddle and the precious need for respect. I watch from the surface until the ray is out of sight and then return to the boat.

Back in Santa Cruz, at the end of the day, I stop at the bar beside the Internet Café with a few members from the tour. The conversation is lively and filled with engaging, mindful people. At past stopovers, I was unaware of the void of human interaction waiting for me at sea and quickly dismissed the last bits of conversation before departure. Now, more aware, I savor every nuance and enjoy the moment with this caring circle of humanity.

I work intently throughout this last day on the island. It's necessary to depart tomorrow to stay on schedule for Panama. A light rain persists, making the completion of tasks more challenging. But these days, I'm more a part of nature than an outsider dealing with it. As the afternoon wears on, I'm heavy with thoughts and return to shore, intent on walking to a beach people have talked about all week.

The path to Turtle Beach begins at a trailhead a few winding blocks through town. I walk the streets, past odd buildings and the occasional, returning hiker who affirms I'm on the right course. At the trailhead, a small station and sign insists the beach closes at "Six O'clock PM." The hardened path is cut through a valley of trees, cactus, and strangely shaped plants, and then crests on a small dune where the canopy opens up to the expansive beach and ocean. White, gently sloping sands extend in both directions. To the left a quarter-mile, a rocky point separates the busy harbor from this protected area. To the right, the beach seems endless, pocked by volcanic rock outcroppings and crashing waves before bending around the corner beyond my imagination. The sky is not the bright, tropical blue of a travel brochure, but a gray, misty mix of clouds, rain, and reality.

I sit in the sand and slow my mind and thoughts. Crabs scramble across the packed sand at the water's edge while birds float on the currents of wind. A few walkers pass as a surfer plays in the waves. There is peace here, my back sheltered by the fore dune and my eyes gazing out across the endless sea. I am tucked in, taken under nature's wing, straddling the shifting border between sea and shore, between dreams and reality, between being away and being home.

Tomorrow, I'll be back at sea.

* * *

I wake early to meet Mike and Diego at their office. Diego, Mike's young assistant has arranged a water taxi to meet us at their shop to load my fuel and water containers and transport us to the boat. The water taxi arrives, uncompromised by the morning rain, and follows suit, transporting Diego and me to Bo. As the taxi leaves, disappearing into the harbor rush hour traffic, I arrange the fuel containers in the back of the cockpit, weaving a series of lines and sail ties through their handles to secure them in place.

I take advantage of Diego's presence and explain a repair I need done up the mast, successfully convincing him to help. I'd go up myself, but Diego's unfamiliar with the winches and clutches, essential gear for ascending the mast safely and preventing an unexpected fall. I convince him it's safer to teach him the repair than explain the clutches that would hold me aloft. I'm not sure how reluctant he is, but Diego agrees and I gear him up, tying the halyard to the harness and wrapping it around a winch. Aloft, his white knuckles indicate he's not very comfortable, but he eases into the job and makes the repairs with instructions spoken calmly from the deck.

With Diego still up the mast, I grab my camera and snap a few pictures for his Facebook page; his wide smile tells me he's okay up there. I am sure only a few young men in the Galapagos have a picture of themselves hanging high in the rigging of a sailboat mast. Back down on deck with tools and gear put away, Diego reaches into his pocket and pulls out a small, wrapped gift for me. I'm astonished, and thank him. It's a small tortoise, carved from local stone. I chuckle, and sincerely thank him, finding a secure place for this little guy down below for the rest of the trip home.

With *Bo* and I prepared and eager to be on our way, we have one task left—to clear out of Ecuador's customs. Diego is calling for the water taxi when his words become confusing. "Dave, are we moving?" he asks. I look up with what I am sure is a confused face, thinking, "of course not, we're tied to the mooring." I'm looking at the large, yellow mooring with our bowline securely tied to it and respond as quickly as I'm thinking, "No."

"But weren't those boats up there a minute ago?"

I take a more judicious look and concur the situation has changed. It takes a minute to realize we're drifting free. The other boats are still moored in place and strangely, we are still tied to the mooring ball, a large, metal can about four feet in diameter fit for a commercial ship like the two 100-foot research vessels, which moments ago were on either side of us. The mooring has broken free from its anchor with *Bo* still tied to it. We are drifting backwards, over the stern anchor rode making use of the engine unwise. Crashing surf is just 75 yards behind us and we're moving quickly towards it on the incoming tide. Diego reacts quickly, calling for help over the radio. Water taxis come and the crew from the research vessel jumps into their rib (rigid, inflatable boat). In a flurry of activity, they corral the rogue mooring and tie our bowline to another while I recover the anchor line. A half-hour later, confident that we are secure, Diego and I climb into a water taxi and make a quick trip to the customs office to finish my business. Obviously, *Bo* is anxious to get going and I'm worried she won't wait for me.

Cleared from customs and back onboard, I untie *Bo* from the mooring and motor out of the harbor to the safety of open water. The last four hours of the day become a water tour meandering through the surrounding Galapagos Islands. We sail slowly up the eastern shore of Isla Isabela, shaped like a sea horse, past Pinxon and North Seymour, past a large rock, and about midnight, back into open water—destination Panama.

Sailing for Panama

*T*he greater part of the Galapagos lies at one-degree south latitude,
a degree below the equator. Sailing northeast from Santa
Cruz, we soon cross the equator into our home waters of the northern
hemisphere. Abiding tradition, we make a ceremony of it and share our
bounty with Neptune asking for a safe passage in return. Panama is less
than a thousand miles away, but with the light winds of the conversion
zone, I expect it to take six days. Six days seems like nothing. It feels like
I've exited the long freeway onto the local streets of my neighborhood and
have only a few turns remaining before home—Panama, the western
Caribbean, Cuba, Florida and then onto Jamestown—all easy, simple
sails.

Transiting the Panama Canal requires a more scheduled,
logistical effort than the past 20,000 miles of sailing. We engage
an agent, Francis, to handle the paperwork and schedule a passage
slot requiring *Bo* to be in Panama in six days. An additional five
crew are required—four line handlers and a local pilot. Being
lackadaisical with my sailing and arrival will cause all kinds of
problems.

For now, the winds are fair and we're making good time
toward the scheduled arrival on May 14th. The sailing is easy but
squalls fill the skies in all directions and we enjoy their cool, wet
paths. With them come fresh water and more wind, mostly from
behind. Otto drives while I lounge in the cockpit. Miles and days
pass; the sun burns hot during the day and forces me to sleep
on deck in the soft, warm winds at night. The hardest time has
become the middle of the day when I slip below to hide from the
harsh environment. Franklin seems to enjoy the weather, looking
a bit healthier, plumping up from the expanding warmth.

Commercial ship traffic is everywhere as we cross the conveyor of products circling the world. Items from China head to Europe, European wares head to the west coast or South Pacific and Indonesia. Ships are passing regularly during the day. At night, even more ships are visible; their distant lights burning through the haze generated by the hot sun and evaporated sea that cloaks them during the day.

Plastic waste floats in the water everywhere, a simple sign we're encroaching on civilization. No sooner do I pass a floating, plastic bucket than I see another piece of plastic ahead. It's sad and endless. The sea is sick; I hear its cry. In the Southern Ocean, wild and free, the sea seemed okay, but here, I see it's not. And if it's not okay here, it's not okay in the Southern Ocean. Like our human bodies, we may seem fine, but an abscessed organ or joint sickens our entire being.

I pass another frenzy of boiling water, fish, and birds living out life's endless pattern of feeding. My hope for the sea is revived, to an extent, it's still alive, but I can't help wonder if a commercial ship would steer clear and avoid destroying this frenzy. Would they dodge it like an automobile dodges a squirrel on the road?

Years ago, when the ocean was teeming with fish, would it have been like dodging bugs on a windshield? So many fish, it was unavoidable? In this present day frenzy, I think about fish mistaking pieces of plastic for food. As we sail by, I watch and wonder.

As Panama comes closer, the winds lighten and diesel power helps keep us on schedule. It's a strange, new dynamic to need to push to meet a manmade time schedule. At sea, time seems unimportant, conjured up by us for comfort; closing in on land, it becomes an essential part of human life.

A day from Panama, sailing along in the hot midday sun, I calculate the navigation to determine if we'll arrive before sunset or need to wait offshore until daybreak to make sense of the unfamiliar harbor. Sailing along the northern coast, we come into an adverse current, slowing our progress and changing the ETA calculations. We'll have to wait offshore tonight.

We press to get within radio range and acknowledge our presence with harbor control before sailing back offshore to wait for daylight. It's well after dark when we make the western buoy and call harbor radio to alert them of our presence. I take down the Solent and coast up and down the shore under mainsail alone; ten miles one way, then back, timing the night to arrive at the western buoy at dawn. We need to be at our assigned dock by 8:00 a.m. to meet the officials for the required inspections to qualify for our scheduled slot to transit the canal.

Ships pass throughout the night in groups of three and four like an endless conveyor. To keep clear of these huge giants, I call the lead ship as they approach to confirm our location and intentions. Some of the Captains acknowledge seeing us, and others don't until alerted by our call. There's no reason for them to expect a blip on their radar to be a small sailing vessel out here in the commercial shipping lanes in the dark hours between midnight and dawn. It's more likely they presume our blip to be a wave top or electronic clutter. Cautious, I plan my naps carefully between the clusters of ships released from the canal.

While below deck, boiling water for freeze-dried food and keeping one eye on the radar, my attention is averted in the middle of this simple task by sharp pins of adrenalin shooting through my veins. A cracking, hard crash on deck registers in my brain—my instincts know something large has fallen from the mast.

Leaping into the cockpit, I expect to see something obvious; hoping it's the wind wand and not a more vital piece, but there's nothing. I look aloft and everything is in place. I look around and all seems normal. The nearest ship is a mile away. I grab my brightest flashlight and search the mast, spreaders, and sails to find what broke. My nerves are on edge; I am certain something important has failed—everything aloft looks ok. I shine the light on the deck and find nothing unusual. Then, in a corner, I see a strange sight—an empty, disposable plastic lighter. I'm puzzled. How? Why? I look around, the sea is calm; a gentle 12-knot wind blows. There are small wakes from passing ships, but nothing wavy enough to toss this up onto the deck. I'm certain this is the reason for the alarm. In an instinctive instant, I hear the voice of the ocean crying for help. "This doesn't belong here. Please, help me." I grab my camera and document the errant piece of disgust before picking it up and salting it away below decks. I know the sound of a cry for help; this one comes from the sea.

A few hours later, we're motoring our way into the harbor among the giants of the sea, commercial ships they call Panamax—the maximum size for transiting the Panama Canal. The stench of fuel oil, exhaust, the rumble of huge engines, the filth of the water, floating trash everywhere . . . and I wonder, was the lighter cast overboard by a non-caring seaman? Can someone who lives on the sea be so heartless? Could someone who has spent months or years at sea, not be in love, seduced by her serenity like me? Or did some non-caring person inland discard it as trash, allowing it to eventually find its way to a river and then the sea. I know the answer, but am truly afraid to ask.

In the marina, I turn *Bo* around and back into the assigned slip; the morning sun already hot, the air thick and steamy. Sport fishermen on the dock put their tasks aside to grab a line and help tie *Bo* in her temporary home. This is a simple, respected tradition within communities—helping when necessary, and seamen are no different. We exist together, passionate about our simple lives, caring enough to help when needed, and autonomous enough to live and let live—alone. As soon as *Bo* is secured, the fishermen slip back to their respective tasks.

I step below, grab a small can of Coke, now warm in the near equatorial weather, and quench my thirst.

Panama—Done.

Transiting the Canal

Within minutes of arriving in Panama, Bo is inundated with Canal Zone officials organized by Francis, our agent, to inspect and approve Bo and meet our scheduled slot for transiting the Canal. Each vessel passing through the Canal has to meet a list of requirements, and Bo, being sleek, simple, and of racing pedigree with no cleats on her bow and stern, stymies the officials.

"How are you going to cleat off the docking lines in the Chambers?" (The sections of the canal that fill with water to lift or drop a vessel). My explanation of how we'll use the winches receives a headshake indicating an unacceptable answer. More officials arrive, along with additional experienced personnel, and eventually, I convince them I know how to handle the boat. The fact I sailed *Bo* around the world alone isn't nearly as convincing as my promise to take a tour of the Locks and witness the turbulence of the water in person.

I'm thrust into this shore-side system ahead of my mind, but our agent, Francis, is very knowledgeable and moderates the conversation. Accommodating the official's request, he schedules a driver to take me to the chambers after lunch and a much needed shower.

Watching a private vessel buffeted by the swirling waters filling the chamber, I understand why the officials are concerned, but *Bo* is a special boat, built to handle the wide-open ocean and I assure them there will be no issues. They accept my confidence and in return, schedule our transit slot two days from now. The rest of my afternoon is spent catching up inside my head with the sudden change of lifestyle.

I'm on the Pacific shore of Panama, and this evening, four friends from the U.S. will arrive to fill out the required crew of five— a helmsman and four line handlers. The Canal Authority will assign us a pilot the morning of our transit. Additionally, Francis arranges for Tito, a local friend of his and an experienced transit crew to join us. I'm a bit overwhelmed with the count of seven crewmembers, but they will all prove to be vital, and Tito, especially so, smoothing the broken English/Latin conversations with the pilot.

Pierce and Rob bound onboard with a cold six-pack of beer, and a few hours later, Joe and Bruce arrive. We share a late dinner together and make plans to prepare *Bo* in the morning with extra lines, tires for side bumpers, an awning to protect us from the all-day sun, fuel, food, drink, and a few other miscellaneous necessities required by the Canal Authority.

Recognizing the importance of having viewed the ships in the canal, I arrange for the five of us to take another tour of the facilities where we witness an unusual contraption. As it settles in the chamber below our viewing platform, we finally recognize it as a submarine, decommissioned and now on her way home to the Pacific.

Before returning to finish our preparations, we wander through the visitor's center, and learn about the amazing work and inventive equipment required to create the Panama Canal 100 years ago. The opening of the canal secured a much safer route for ships and yachts between the two oceans, ending the need for ships to endure the risks of rounding Cape Horn. Today, only ships too large to fit through the canal and the occasional adventuring sailor or research vessel sail around Cape Horn.

With *Bo* prepared and settled, Francis shows us to a lively dinner spot before retiring to prepare for an early morning and hopefully a long day. Tomorrow morning, we'll leave the docks at 6:00 a.m. to motor out to the rendezvous point and meet our pilot at 7:00 a.m.

At 6:00 a.m., we arrive at *Bo* to find Tito sleeping on the decks. I am concerned, but he assures me he does this all the time. The bus from his hometown runs in the middle of the night, so he just catches a few winks before the owners arrive. I chuckle, realizing he'll fit in well with us on *Bo*, now transformed from a sleek, world girdling, racing sailboat to a floating junkyard, complete with tires, a flogging blue tarp and hawsers large enough to secure a 100-foot vessel. And me, transformed from a purposeful, solo sailor deeply in touch with the sea, to a team leader with a crew of five, soon to be six. It's good that the additional crewmembers are friends who are aware that their skipper is slightly deranged from 20,000 miles of being alone.

Forty-five minutes later we float aimlessly, waiting in the general vicinity for meeting a pilot. At precisely 7:00 a.m., as prescribed, a pilot boat approaches and Raphael steps from the ladder onto *Bodacious Dream*. We make our introductions and with little ceremony, Raphael directs me to put *Bodacious Dream* in line behind the enormous freighter ahead of us and to keep pace with her. To Raphael, it's just another day of work moving boats. For us, it's the experience of a lifetime.

We enter the first chamber behind the Panamax ship with her escort tug followed by an excursion boat that allows us to tie alongside, making the use of the tires and hawser unnecessary. Raphael is amused at our system of docking *Bo* and has yet to understand how she maneuvers. Nonetheless, I work on him, and soon he trusts me to place *Bo* where he wants her as we carry on smoothly through the subsequent chambers.

As the lock doors close, swirling waters fill the chamber and gently lift us from the Pacific Ocean—*Bo's* home for the past few months—to begin our terraced ascent to Lake Gatun, in the Panamanian interior.

Stepping up through three chambers in the first lock and two chambers in the second we eventually exit onto Lake Gatun. Tito explains that Lake Gatun was a small lake in the interior of

Panama before being dammed to increase its size and allow ships to traverse a route through the interior of Panama.

The next twenty some miles are under full power, against a wind, trying to keep pace with the schedule and not lose our slot which would force us to anchor overnight on the lake and finish transiting the following day.

The blue tarp is a godsend on this sunny day, blocking the sun, as we sit on deck and keep a constant lookout for floating logs. Tito, tired from his night of travel, naps under the tarp while the rest of us laugh and share stories with Franklin and Raphael.

Instantly, Tito sits up and alerts us to a floating log just in time to dodge it, and then just as quickly lies back down to nap. We wonder about his magical senses and are grateful he's with us.

With the weight of seven people onboard, *Bo* falls behind the pace of the other vessels in our group and after a flurry of communications with the canal authorities, Raphael allows us to cut the corners of the route to make up time. I sense this is not an acceptable practice for a pilot, but Raphael allows it and accepts the maneuver as a necessity. Approaching the last locks, we pass the large ship and tug waiting for us, and enter the chamber first. Following in behind us, the ship maneuvers within inches on either side of the chamber, the doors close, and the water recedes, leaving us in a deep steel and concrete canyon until the door, stories high in front of us, opens, allowing us to progress into the next chamber and secure *Bo* again.

Sitting on *Bo* in the last chamber, I realize I am looking over the last door. Thirty feet below me lay the waters of the Atlantic Ocean.

The chamber empties, the enormous doors open, and we slowly motor free of the Panama Canal into the contained waters of the Atlantic Ocean. Minutes later, a Pilot boat comes alongside to unceremoniously pick up Raphael. We bid him farewell and thank him for his company and guidance transiting the canal.

As evening approaches, Tito guides us north along a sparsely marked channel to a marina where *Bo* will rest for a few days. We make fast work of converting *Bo* back to the elegant lady she is, removing the blue tarp, tires, hawsers and rinsing her with fresh water while waiting for Francis to pick us up. Other boaters in the marina, waiting for their chance to transit westward, congregate around *Bo* and engage us in conversations about our transit and my journey.

Tired, we settle around a table at the Balboa Yacht Club for a few beers and burgers, aware we have just experienced one of the amazing engineering feats of mankind.

The next few days are spent relaxing around Panama. Rob, a fearless adventurer, leads us astray in the old part of Panama, a world UNESCO heritage site. Francis instructed us to stay within the perimeter of the gentrified downtown area, but Rob, having lived and worked in many third world countries and a climber of Mt. Everest, leads us out of bounds. Our reward for the act of defiance is a vendor at the local market offering a dozen options of ceviche, any one of which, in a quart container with four beers is just $10.

With the week near its end, Joe departs to explore the San Blas Islands, Bruce and Pierce fly home, and Rob and I spend the evening checking out the lively rooftop bar of our hotel. In a quiet moment, I ask Rob about Everest, understanding he came within 200 yards of the summit before being forced to turn back and descend. I search his story for morsels of wisdom I'll probably need in the coming months to sooth my own mind struggling with my diversion from Cape Horn.

The Last Thousand Miles

Leaving Panama is hard, but in a different way this time. This crossroad of mariners has been intriguing, but I'm ready to get on my way to the next planned stop—the U.S. mainland. Bo and I will leave the harbor tomorrow for the Atlantic Ocean and head up the eastern coast of Central America, through the Yucatan Channel within a couple of miles of the western tip of Cuba before crossing the rippling Gulf Stream to Florida.

My sister Nancy and I have worked out a schedule so Mom can be in Jamestown when I arrive. Contrived to a certain extent, my goal is to arrive in Jamestown on June 14th, three weeks from now. This allows for a stop in Florida to make a few repairs, catch up with dear friends who have supported me, and recover. I'm hoping to spin off some wear and fatigue before the final passage home. This final segment seems more an expanse of emotions than distance.

I call Mom and listen closely to her weary voice. She's reluctant to tell me she's stopped chemotherapy, and uses optimism as her defense. "I can't wait to see you in Jamestown!" I tell her I'm leaving Panama tomorrow, heading toward home, and outline the route. She reminisces about visiting Havana, Cuba when she was young before we close out the short, broken conversation, smoothed out by her transcript machine. It ends with a distinctly enunciated, "I love you—goodnight."

Bo's neighbor in the marina is a young man heading in the opposite direction—to the South Pacific for his solo sojourn. While I have Otto and Franklin, his best friend is a rambunctious dog who's taken, like many, a protective liking to Bo. He comes running up the dock every time I approach; this time I carry two cans of diesel. He declines to shoulder a share of the load, but willingly nudges me along with his nose.

Across the dock, a couple waits their turn to transit the canal, also investing their coming years in a cruise to the South Pacific Islands, paradises *Bo* sailed by, though a few thousand miles to the south. It's intriguing how we interact with each other, exuding wonder and envy about our respective lives and passages. I realize how few places I've seen compared to their itineraries as they ask me questions about my solo adventure. Inside I stumble with my own feelings, wondering if I'll be happy at home or wish I were going with them to the islands.

Every day I seem to cross another bridge on this journey, some new, and others very old. The most trying is interacting with people. Am I starved for them or do I cower, protecting my space, still needing to be alone? Perhaps I'm addicted to these extreme promontories in my spirited soul.

Excusing myself from the friendly interaction on the dock, I continue with my preparations, loading fuel, tying on sheets, and pulling off covers. When I finish, I step into the cockpit and take a deep breath, stalling to consider my readiness.

I decide a trip up the dock to the pub is in order for a sandwich and I grab my wallet. Halfway up the dock I stop walking. I'm not hungry—I'm just stalling. I turn and head back to *Bo* and ask my neighbor if he will help with lines. In a flash, *Bo* is free from confinement and heading out the marina. I look back to make a final wave to the neighbors, their eyes showing the same haunting story—the story of wonders beyond the horizon and prayers for safe passage. I know a day will come soon when I'll be the one on the dock woefully waving goodbye.

Bo slides through the narrow marina entrance and along the sparsely marked channel to the deep water of the huge harbor that exits into the Atlantic. The skies threaten rain with nothing but solid, dark clouds in all directions, drawing a depression to the surface from deep within me as we pass the harbor heads in the wake of two large ships. The ships continue east to the Caribbean islands and ultimately the open Atlantic, likely bound for Europe or the Med. I turn north and begin to set sails, when a line parts high up the mast, dropping to the deck in a snarled coil.

The lazy jack's job is to hold the boom up and contain the heavy mainsail when lowered. It's important, preventing the boom from falling to the deck and crushing me if the main halyard were to part or the sail to rip. It's a simple fix, a reflex, like fixing a broken bootlace. Once complete, we head northeast in the grey mist and light winds.

Leveraging the anticipation of my midnight meal, I coerce my attention to the future. There's trepidation inside me, a resistance to move forward to tomorrow. It's not the fear of calamity, but the opposition to the approaching end of the journey. I know it's three weeks away, but in a heartbeat, the exotic life of extreme foreign oceans will become the blasé boredom of familiar seas.

Nothing is fun; even calculating navigation is unappealing. I don't care how many miles or days until our arrival. I put off mopping water from the corners below and grab for chocolate; then toss it back, uninterested. Depression dominates my psyche. *Bo* sails, Otto drives, and I just ride. Tonight I'm nothing more than crew—rail meat.

With each long passage, the first couple of days don't really count. They're filled with adjustments and quickly pass. In a blink, it's the second night and I begin to find synchronicity with the flow of the passage. The final days don't count either; fueled by the turbocharged energy of anticipation. After several thousand miles—a couple of days or a few hundred miles seem insignificant.

Just seven days long, this leg, like the last, is almost over before it begins. Casting off the day-and-a-half at the beginning and accelerating past the western tip of Cuba to within a hundred miles of the U.S. mainland leaves just a few days in the middle.

Nonetheless, we enjoy the steady winds and gray skies pocked with squalls as I begin to count down the distance toward the Yucatan Passage and Cuba.

I watch freighters come and go, turn pages in a book, and pass through daylight into dark. During the night, I humor myself with Sky Walk, an application for stargazers on the iPad, allowing me to watch and explore the heavens through the clouded skies above. The haunting background music and the clear sky on the retina display afford me the fantasy of a warm night in the wide-open waters of the South Pacific.

I feel confined here with Central America a few hundred miles to the west and the islands of the Caribbean not much further to the east. My senses visualize us sailing up the confines of a small bay, my mental defenses of the vast Southern Ocean having returned.

To the east and from behind, a ship approaches. I check the radar and AIS to find we're traveling parallel paths in the middle of the night. I've heard intimately told stories of ships with watch officers reading a book or playing computer games and not paying attention or looking outward. I make a precautionary call to the ship, asking for an acknowledgment of my presence. The captain, responding in an unfamiliar accent but a pleasant tone, assures me we are not in his way. Through the rest of the night, he passes unusually slowly.

Typically, a ship comes within sight and passes in less than half an hour. This ship passes much slower, leaving me to conclude they're ahead of schedule and in no rush to meet their arrival in some exotic Central American port of call. At daybreak, they're still in sight and cross in front of me. By late morning, they're on the horizon and nearly out of sight. However, in the mid-afternoon they're alongside again. My imagination conjures up possible conspiracies: pirates, drug runners, rogue vessels, or tramp steamers. I consider danger, but reason it is unlikely; after all, I'm just a short distance from civilized North America.

I devise the scheme of heroics I'll perform in the event *smokers* (the jet skis from the *Waterworld* movie) drop from her deck and chase me down. But by late afternoon, the ship is gone and I've returned to the more mundane existence of sailing and putting miles behind us. Sunset and darkness follow, and through the night I write in the log, check email, read, and nap while waiting for dinner, and then later, wait for sunrise.

As daylight opens the horizon, I walk *Bo's* decks in search of excitement, but find nothing unusual or out of place. Below, I plot our course and speed, and calculate that by tomorrow morning we'll be off the western tip of Cuba. While working this out on the chart plotter, another triangle of a ship appears on the AIS. I step on deck and confirm its location off our port quarter. The vessel is about 80 feet long with a red sash painted diagonally down her bow. She's missing the additional, familiar white and blue colors of the U.S. Coast Guard, indicating it must be another nation patrolling these waters. I dismiss any worries and expect they are friendly, competent seamen.

They shadow me for hours, moving from one stern quarter to the other, sometimes easing forward and at other times falling back. As a squall approaches, they disappear in the rain. The vessel moves closer to get back in sight and then, as the storm passes, moves with it, leaving us alone with nothing but our imagination blowing freely in the wind. It's not long before my mind has a screenplay ready for Hollywood.

The plot is thin, but given time, I'll flesh out the characters and create an exciting conflict between a tramp steamer, overreaching authority, and a political fugitive escaping safely offshore onto an unwitting oceangoing adventurer's boat. A desperate fate hinges on the benevolence of the solo sailor, convinced the risk is worth the value of freedom for the cold, wet rogue figure in the frightening dark night, alone at sea.

Hours pass as I plot the story in my mind, and by morning, the ship and story are both gone, replaced by the faint outline of

Cuba rising from the horizon. Cuba! Key West is just 90 miles beyond; we're nearly home in American waters.

Late in the morning, we pass the Cuban coast, no more than five miles away. I'm not worried sailing through these waters; anyone concerned with who I am can find a lengthy trail of my intent on the Internet. We could sail farther away, but it would only lengthen our course, and besides, I've sailed these waters before without problem. I don't anticipate one this time.

Strange shapes in the water approach and I pull the binoculars to my tired eyes for a better look—small whales. I drop the binoculars and grab my camera, taking pictures of the four of them. They are small, black, and swimming in a pod, their course crossing ours. I snap photos and hit the video as I watch them roll up and down slowly in the small swells. They dogleg alongside us before turning back on their original course to their destination. In this instant, I feel the same sense I felt from the dolphins. A sense they have come to engage me, to ask me to speak for them. In my head, I hear their voices . . . *"You've sailed through our ocean and our life, will you please tell people what you saw, what you felt. You are one of us now. Carry on. Enjoy your journey home."* I keep an eye on them long after they pass. Like a close friend, I watch until I am certain they no longer see me, and yet I wonder if they still can.

* * *

Rounding the tip of Cuba at midday, a squall builds and moves over us. Spitting rain and exhaling wind, it proves more than anticipated and forces me to scramble for control of *Bo* and *Otto*. I reef the mainsail and take the helm in the unexpected high winds, wanting to ride the squall across the straits to Florida, but it moves too fast. In less than an hour, I'm shaking out the reef and aiming *Bo* on the best course in the *Gulf Stream* towards the southeastern corner of Florida.

The *Gulf Stream* pushes us along, adding two or three knots to our speed over the ground, accelerating our approach to the coast. I navigate *Bo* to stay in the current along the edges of the *Gulf Stream* because it's not worth the expense in miles to stay in its fast axis many miles offshore.

The gap between Florida and us decreases steadily until I see the islands of the Keys and adjust our course to parallel the high-rise developments lining the shore. Evening comes and the light bloom of southeastern Florida overpowers the darkness, hiding all but the brightest stars. The Big Dipper still powers through the glow of civilization, but many of the stars I've come to know over the past eight months are no longer strong enough to compete with the power of electrically driven humanity. In my back yard at home, the Big Dipper hangs in the northwestern night sky, now she guides me home.

The anticipation of arriving warps time into turbo mode as *Bo* sails with ease, arriving off West Palm Beach at dawn. We spent many of her younger days here at the Rybovich Marina, learning the ways of each other's personality. Entering the familiar *cut* at Palm Beach, we turn south and motor down the Intracoastal Waterway before turning into the Rybovich Marina and tying up quietly by ourselves in the early morning.

It's strange, these legs from New Zealand, the Galapagos Islands, Panama and Florida, each unfolding without much ado. I remind myself what has gone on, but it all seems uneventful and perfunctory. Again, I've arrived quietly and confidently by myself. Sipping a Coke, I walk the dock and nod to the only other person awake, a fellow crewmember from another yacht.

The morning passes easily and quickly. *Bo* moves to a better dock. I shower, tidy up, and arrange a ride to the customs office to clear into the U.S. An hour later, I'm with a customs officer who's uninterested in the tramp steamer, the rogue figure, or my passage around the world. He merely looks up at me, stamps my passport, and unimpressed, without a word, hands it back.

Without the slightest hint of ceremony, we head back to the marina. A Starbucks passes by the van window. I'm back in the U.S.—in full-on culture shock.

The short stay at the Rybovich Marina allows me precious time to connect with old friends in Florida. I share dinner with Tim Kent, a fellow solo sailor and friend over many difficult years. In 2001, Tim and I spent time with his open 50, *Everest Horizontal*, as he pulled together an amazing week of friends to prepare for the starting line of the Around Alone race in 2002.

A formal repair to the lazy jack is followed by lunch with my old friend Jack Harrington and his friend Dave, giving us the chance to share great stories and laughs. Jack and his wife Karen have listened to my quixotic dreaming for twenty-five years.

Dick and Ann Hirst drive cross the state to spend the afternoon. The grandparents of my god kids, Brett and Harry, Dick and Ann are always entertaining. For years, Dick and I sailed his boat to and from its winter storage on Lake Michigan—Dick steering and eating potato chips, me listening to him tell stories of his amazing life.

With the soft reentry and solid repairs behind us, it's time to journey home to Jamestown. With the account settled at the office, *Bo* slips her lines one last time as I look around at the giant yachts towering over us. Little *Bo's* been the pride of the marina this past week, the captains and crew of the other yachts stopping by to say hi and congratulate us on our journey.

* * *

The last time we left Rybovich was a season ago after sailing alone across the Atlantic from Portugal. I was proud and confident when things turned bad quickly. Those awful memories flood my mind as *Bo* motors slowly out the narrow Intracoastal Waterway, staying between the markers for shallow water on our port and the expensive homes holding gently to the fragile, barrier island on our right.

It was a beautiful day a year ago; our destination was Charleston, SC. The wind was fresh and the tide was flowing out. In a couple of days, I'd be having a beer in my favorite pub in Charleston after a long season of racing in Europe. The weather forecast was good for easy sailing. As we came to the same cut leading out to the open water of the Atlantic Ocean, the wind against the tide pushed up a steep wave pattern.

In my home harbor of Michigan City, Indiana, these conditions are common, and 30 years of experience gave me no reason to worry. A moment later, the Solent, which I had failed to secure down to the deck, volunteered to set itself and wiggled up the forestay in the fresh winds. This is not an unusual occurrence; it is often considered a humorous animation of the boat's desire to go sailing.

I locked Otto on, clipped in, and ran forward along *Bo's* bucking deck to secure the Solent. I pulled it down but couldn't find a sail tie or spare line to secure it and had to let it go to run back to the cockpit and grab a tie. Back at the bow, as I pulled the sail down again, two waves stood up, one in front of the other, prouder than the rest and with nothing but empty, deep troughs behind them. In a one-two punch, *Bo* dropped six feet below me, I followed her down, but at the bottom, she rose up with the next wave, the bow pulpit smashing me across my face and left eye, crushing my glasses and splitting my forehead. With the momentum now upward, we rode the wave up only to fall into the hollow trough behind it, again my face smashing the pulpit as my knees caught up to the deck and slammed down hard. I hung on with instinct and continued my task of tying down the jib—but as I looked up, *Bo* was on a collision course with the rock wall on the side of the channel. My task unfinished, I hurriedly returned to the cockpit to correct Otto and avert an even more severe incident.

In the cockpit, I reached up to touch my forehead and my hand came back covered with blood. I checked myself for more serious issues and reasoned my only choice was to continue out through the waves to deep, safe water to further assess my situation.

Quickly back on the bow to finish my work, I looked up to see Otto had over corrected and steered directly at the large steel red marker on the other side of the channel. Back in the cockpit, I grabbed the helm and sat still for 30 minutes until we cleared the furthest mark out, the Safe Water Mark. *Bo* was safe. Now I had to figure out how I was. I considered two options: to carry on or turn back and seek medical attention.

With anxious nerves, I reviewed the past few moments and realized how close I had come to being a news story. I shivered thinking how hard the feelings would have been for my good friend Tom to hear of my death, a mere 30 minutes after he had cast off my lines. I began to tremble and then turned my eyes outward to sea, steering *Bo* away from the angry harbor. I knew that if I returned, the incidents surrounding the situation might preclude me ever sailing *Bo* again. I steadfastly focused my course on Charleston while asking myself if I was all right, and only allowing stubbornly, affirmative answers.

Today, the tidal rip of that memory floods my mind as we move up the Intracoastal Waterway to the same harbor cut, more experienced and more determined than ever to avoid simple issues, yet acutely aware that even without issues, like those waves, the keel coming loose, or Mom having cancer, this will be my last solo voyage with Bo. The weather is beautiful, the sea state manageable, and soon enough, the ghosts of a year ago are gone—*Bo*, Franklin, Otto and I are safely beyond the safe water buoy and headed for home.

The afternoon passes into an easy sunset over the Florida coast as the Gulf Stream, flowing beneath us, rushes us home at two, sometimes three knots faster than our sailing. I plan lasagna for midnight, now a tradition for my first night at sea.

The days pass smoothly up the swift Gulf Stream. Memories of Charleston pass inshore along with many other adventures along this coast. With each day and mile, I slowly reconsider life ashore. It's all so close now, just a few hundred miles away.

Approaching famed Cape Hatteras, I think of the times I've been here before, the struggle Tim Kent and I had aboard *Everest Horizontal*, and the Atlantic Cup in 2013 when *Bo*, Matt and I lead our competitors around the Cape finishing first in New York City.

Below decks, hiding from the midday sun, the familiar sound of a fighter jet whines. I rush on deck to catch a glimpse of the plane, remembering fondly the amazing displays these competent, testosterone jockos put on. This guy is alone, diving and then turning away quickly. It's a rush seeing the talent and precision, and today, in its pure element, it's even better. With the satellite dome now working in northern waters, I email the event to John Hoskins, Bodacious Racing's navigator. His brother is a former fighter pilot. John quickly replies, "He's probably using you as target practice." I chuckle . . . lucky guy. If he were really shooting at me, I'd have to drop him in his tracks. The laugh's on me, my only offensive weapon is a parachute flare.

* * *

The forecast for the last of the passage to Jamestown is light and miserable—little wind, mixed clouds, fog, haze, and sun except for one line of thunderstorms arriving soon. To the west, I see the familiar outline of thunderheads mixed with hazy, flat gray skies. The radar highlights the outline of a serious storm with a deep red center. In high gear, I prepare *Bo* for battle and settle in to manage the brunt of the storm. Lightening approaches slowly, teasing and tormenting us enough for me to rig a makeshift electrical ground of old wire cable wrapped around the shrouds and tossed over the side to drag in the water. There's little reason such an invention would work, but if nothing else, it grounds my nerves.

The storm hits with hard rain and intense lightning, and an expectation the winds may reach triple digits. The lightning is some of the most concentrated I've ever witnessed, but fortunately, the winds level off at 30 knots. I think of the irony one final storm could wreak on my dream. Then I take *Bo's* helm to steady my nerves and focus on getting to the other side of the red blob on the radar.

The storm persists hour after hour. I check my watch, presuming it must have stopped. It might only be an hour, but the storm is lasting far longer than necessary. I set Otto to driving and drop below to study the radar where the truth becomes quickly apparent. *Bo* and the storm are crossing at acute angles prolonging wedlock and keeping us in lock step for some time to come. I adjust *Bo's* course to open the crossing angle and shorten the duration of exploding lighting and pounding thunder.

An hour later, we're separated. The storm has moved on to the east and us somewhat to the west. Thunder continues rolling in from the east for another hour, but the rain has stopped and we are free to head home. We've not been hit by lightning, and all electronics are working. I'm not sure why we're so fortunate, but I'm certain, our generosity with Neptune when crossing the equator has played a part in our good fortune.

I turn my focus to the next couple of days. As the time winds down, I'm excited to finish, and yet, scared to end this journey. Will it mean anything? Will anything ever come of it, or will it be just a personal folly? Am I ready to be finished? I can't answer the questions.

The last day and night I continually think about my family and friends, 150 miles away in Jamestown, planning to be there for the ending. I think about my frail mother, her body nearly spent, but her mind and spirit as bright as ever, standing on the pier as I come alongside.

I think of all the times I dared to allow myself to dream this dream. About the promises I made, the friends who had come and are now gone, and the naysayers who proclaimed I'd never go. I think of those who couldn't dream with me, and the days spent searching for reason and direction when the only landmark available was the light shining from this dream.

I think of Mary, who acknowledged my departure with a letter tucked away in my sea bag to be read once I was gone, and of her brave release of me as I slipped lines eight-and-a-half months ago. She took a tally of our relationship up until then and logged it in black ink and not red. Now she waits to greet me back at home.

I mumble aloud, "Thank God this is over. Now I can focus on living a life instead of pursuing this all-consuming, friggin' dream." I don't know what this means, but it feels good to say it and think that for now, there will be no more storms while alone at sea.

Midnight comes with no wind and a pea soup fog. Less than 40 miles remain to Narragansett Bay and the guiding lights of Beavertail Point and Bretton Reef. Targets pass on the radar, though we never see them. Visibility is less than a quarter mile.

I douse the damp, limp Solent, and hoist the bright orange storm jib to make us more visible in the fog, and begin motoring slowly. As we inch our way toward morning, my eyes stare forward at the non-existent horizon on the inside of a Ping-Pong ball while an intuitive nerve keeps watch on the radar. We plan to arrive twelve hours from now at about noon. I should be confident my mother and friends will be there, they're following me on the Spot Tracker, but my insecurity sends an email to redundantly remind them.

At dawn, the fog gives no more insight to my small world than night did. With only ten miles to go, I spot a sport fishing boat and alter course to avoid colliding. I intensify my concentration and strain harder, my eyes looking for the coast of Point Judith off my port bow. Near the end of an eternity, the fog lifts slightly and the coastline comes into view. Beavertail light shines brightly beyond the tone of her foghorn.

We're here. I'm here. We're really here. I can't explain how normal everything seems. Somehow, I expected the world to have changed. Instead, I find it just as it was, the same harbor, the same lighthouse, and the same navigational marks.

A boat peaks out from the fog and approaches. Onboard are my close friends Jeff and Gaye, along with other friends shouting congratulations and offering a cold beer. I beg off the cold beer, wanting the moment to linger as long as possible.

As we travel the familiar route into Narragansett Bay, Billy Black arrives to photograph us, and Franklin comes on deck to witness the festivities. I think quietly how grateful I am Billy is here to photograph the end and that I'm not one of the sailors he was only able to photograph leaving. I see Billy raise his camera and touch the shutter; his photo now documenting the end of the journey.

Moments pass slowly while my emotions run at lightning speed. I navigate the mooring field where I choked at the start. Bruce jumps onboard to help with lines and docking. We make a final turn to lay *Bo* alongside the pier and toss lines to the many outstretched and welcoming hands. A couple dozen close friends are gathered with all the accoutrements—smiles, cheers, tears, beer, a bottle of Champagne, and plenty of hugs, handshakes and photographs. Pam, the young girl who had taken me sailing my first time, forty some years ago, was there with her family and a known quantity of joy—four double chocolate muffins, fresh from the bakery.

I step from *Bo* onto the dock, bridging the incomprehensible expanse between who I was and who I've become and embrace my mom. By God, she made it! We made it! My sister Nancy and Rick made it, parleying mom's enthusiasm to get her here.

We gather in a loose semi-circle and Billy, with the touch of an artist, memorializes the moment with a photograph of these friends, while *Bo* rests, securely at home alongside the dock.

All gatherings end and people wander on to their respective lives and duties. I have no desire to let go, so I stretch the afternoon into dinner with a contracting group of friends. We make plans for tomorrow—to sail *Bo* up Narragansett Bay to the Hinckley yard—everyone included. I allow time and emotions to flow through me, absorbing what I can, knowing the following days and nights will be a mixture of strange feelings, some difficult, some incomprehensible, hopefully—most will be joyous.

At noon the following day, we meet at the dock to sail *Bo* up Narragansett Bay to the Hinckley yard. Nancy, Rick, and Mom—she wouldn't dare miss the chance to sail *Bo*, along with Mary, Jean, Tim Eades, and others. As I slip her lines for the last time, *Bo* heads out through the moorings to open water. This will be my last sail on Bo.

We set *Bo's* huge mainsail and Solent and ride the fresh, clear wind up the bay. Mom's blue eyes are as bright as the waters, and her smile, a simple expression of joy. I feel *Bo* and know she wants to take Mom's hand and show her what I felt two-and-a-half years ago when we first sailed together. I give Mom the tiller and she giggles, now allowed to have her own special moment with Bo.

As we come around the island just outside the Hinckley's entrance, a strange thought crosses me. I look at the smiles onboard, the people who believed in me and my dream and I think of the days and moments I spent on this foolishness. The hours put aside, the days sailing to gain experience, the times the dream seemed impossible and the inspired moments. I think of the teachers and guides who scoffed at such dreams and of others who dismissed it without further thought. I think of the many mentions of wasted time and it occurs to me, this moment validates all of it. This moment is one block in the spreadsheet of life, and with this moment, this block now filled in; the Excel spreadsheet goes into motion. Each moment of life spent on this dream is now being tallied, the clicking and ticking adding up to a final sum in today's value. This final moment, validates every moment—wasted or not—devoted to this dream over the past 40 years.

Epilogue

The sea haunts me as I sit quietly in the evening light watching the endless roll of waves, trying to understand what has happened to me and what I have learned. Why the sight of a rolling swell consumes my being, why the last light of a pink cloud in the western sky sooths me, why the pinhole of a planet shines directly down on me. I'm not alone here, there are people all around me on Beavertail, the same point of land which led me away from and then graciously welcomed me home—they too seem drawn to the sea for quiet reasoning.

Reading history, I realize *unknowns* scare us, compelling us to conquer them. We talk of taming the West, of conquering space, conquering our fears and we attempt to conquer the unknown sea. We sail off to far-away lands to implant our will on their soils, harness tidal rapids to turn wheels of power to dominate economies, build ships large enough to be titled, *"unsinkable"* and fish with technology capable of scooping entire balls of life from the sea, rendering endless miles of open water virtually lifeless. Did we set out to conquer the ocean, to control this frightening unknown as if we were kids yelling at the boogieman under our beds on a dark, windy night? Or, have we merely attempted to plunder the sea, our victim slowly recoiling and waiting for our false celebrations of hubris to render us vulnerable before returning a simple, unexpected, terminal blow.

As a reader, I hope you are touched by some part of this book like the sea has touched me. Maybe you'll relate to the challenging tempest while being jostled on a commuter train, or allow yourself to drift with the beautiful bioluminescence as streetlights pass outside the rain covered windows. You might swallow hard at the claustrophobic lazarette where the heart of Otto needed tending as you ride an elevator driven by an unknown electronic brain, or maybe you'll lie awake at night wondering if you can touch the depths of fatigue necessary to reach the elevation of peace found in the dying wind of a blown out storm.

In every encounter along the way, someone asks me to tell the tale of the most frightening moment, or the deepest emotional ravine, and I can't because these aren't individual parts of the journey. I didn't go to sea to beat it or fear it. I went to sea to live it. To exist in a symbiotic way with the wind and the sea, with my sails and my worries, with the strength of the build of *Bo* and the power of significant waves, with the dark night and the comprehension of sailing the oceans of a star in the middle of the universe, to sync the laughter of a dolphin with the skipping beat of my heart—none of them equal, but all of them balanced.

I journeyed to learn more about what I am and where I live than to experience the fear of a single unknown. And so, in the raw breath of this evening wind, stranded on this comfortable shore, I ask myself—*What did we get from all this?* The answer isn't easy, nor is how it came to be, but to get it, I bared my soul to the sea, I reduced myself to heart, mind, blood, fatigue, torn tissue and tears, to a vulnerability wide open enough to hear the cry of the sea and the whimper of the dolphin. From their tales I learned we don't need to conquer the sea; we need to live it. We don't need to have more than enough, but enough for now. We don't need to reduce the sea to a level we understand, we need to understand the sea at the level it is and grow ourselves with the accumulation of this knowledge.

This isn't easy to comprehend, and in fact, it's taken me 45 years to confidently declare myself a novice—but that I am. I have been tired and open, forlorn and hungry, and in being vulnerable, the sea spoke to me. It asked me to see the vast endless miles without a single whale, to watch humanity flow seaward from a small town, to pick plastic from its shoulders as if picking lint from a navy sweater. And, when I wasn't listening closely enough, it threw a cigarette lighter onto my deck, shouting at me to look around, pay attention and realize that the simplest part of the solution is us.

The sea asked me to speak for it. It asks us to consider our lives—to stop ravaging the blood of our earth and heal the gaping wounds. I am optimistic that something in this book touched you and opened your vulnerability like the sea opened mine. I hope you felt the same tingle, the same urge, and the same inspiration that I did. The inspiration to be better, to not feel the need to *play along* with bad manners, to not need another disposable bottle of water or the accumulation of unnecessary things. I am optimistic we've been inspired to understand this is our only life, and our only chance to be responsible to our land, to our hearts, to our ways, inspired to be aligned with our world as an ally of the ocean, the earth and even beyond—an ally of this immense, unfathomable universe.

Bodacious Dream
Deck Layout Drawing

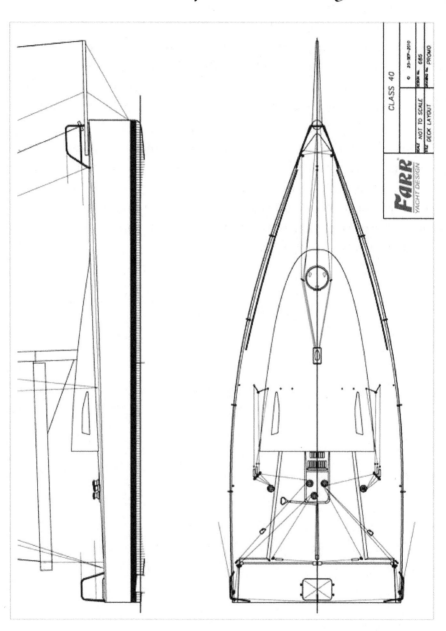

Bodacious Dream
Interior Line Drawing

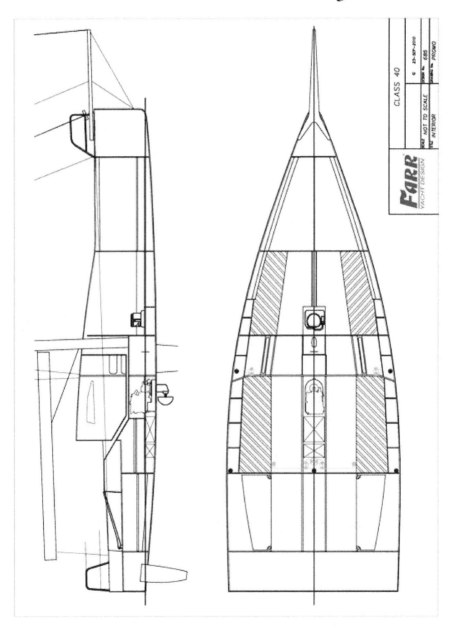

Bodacious Dream
Sail Plan Line Drawing

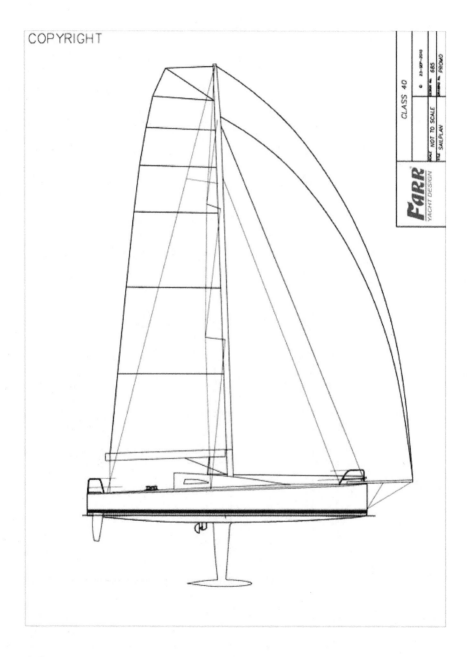

About the Author

*D*ave has been sailing for more than 45 years, racing both crewed and singlehanded on the Great Lakes and across the oceans of the world. In 2003, he was presented the Mike Silverthorne award by the Great Lakes Singlehanded Society and in 2018, inducted into the Lake Michigan Sailing Hall of Fame. Dave manages the Kids Education Program for The Atlantic Cup and serves as an ambassador for 11th Hour Racing, a program of the prestigious Schmidt Family Foundation. He has spoken to many organizations, universities, and corporations about his sailing adventures.

Dave still claims his most significant accomplishment in life, other than wearing out hundreds of T-shirts, hats, and sailing shoes is that of sharing sailing and the water with so many kids and adults over the years. He continues to live on the Southern Shore of Lake Michigan, a stone's throw from where he began sailing, and he'll be the first to tell you, with a wink, he never got very far in life.

To request information or inquire about speaking engagements with the author, please connect with our website, www.spiritofadream.com.

The Atlantic Cup Race www.atlanticcup.org
11th Hour Racing www.11thhourracing.org

Made in the USA
Las Vegas, NV
02 May 2022